THE PERSON
REBORN

THE PERSON
REBORN

PAUL TOURNIER

TRANSLATED BY EDWIN HUDSON

HARPER & ROW, PUBLISHERS
SAN FRANCISCO

Cambridge
Hagerstown
Philadelphia
New York

London
Mexico City
São Paulo
Sydney

1817

This book is a translation of *Technique et Foi*, published by Delachaux & Niestlé, Incorporated, Neuchâtel (Switzerland).

The text of this book is printed on 100% recycled paper.

Library of Congress Catalog Card Number: 75-12283
International Standard Book Number: 0-06-068375-9

80 81 82 83   10 9 8 7 6 5 4 3 2 1

Contents

v

IV · FAITH

V · THE SPIRIT OF ADVENTURE

PART I

Technology and Faith

CHAPTER · 1

Technology or Faith?

When I was quite a small boy, I used naïvely to dream of performing some great act.

With my Meccano set I started building a mysterious machine, bristling with springs and gears. One day I was bold enough to tell my sister about my ambition. It was not going to be any ordinary machine, but one that would create life.

Unfortunately my sister asked me to explain how it worked. I did not know what to say, and had to admit that I was depending on prayer: I would pray hard, and God would work a miracle by means of my machine!

"In that case," my sister exclaimed, "what are all the gears for?"

I was utterly abashed. I had no reply. My dream was collapsing about me. Nevertheless I have pursued it in one form or another all my life.

Every one of us has some dominant idea which with remarkable persistence permeates our whole life from childhood onwards, and imparts unity to it. I can see this in the case of all those who tell me the story of their lives. The daydreams of the child, beneath their apparent absurdity, conceal a symbolism which later on will throw light upon the development of his life.

All my pride, my desire to use God for my own personal glory instead of serving him, was in that childish machine of my boyhood. This reversal of roles was to become the occasion of my toughest spiritual battles.

One can also see in it, however, my desire to bring about a synthesis of the widely divergent aspirations that I felt within me. On 'the one hand there was my interest in religion, and on the other my bent toward technique, invention, and biology and science generally. I was unwilling to give up either of these two interests. I wanted to experience the explosive energy of the spiritual life, which human technology and science seem quite incapable of reproducing. But I was at the same time unwilling to turn my back on technology,* in which I was passionately interested, and which I felt must after all have a living purpose to serve.

Since then it has time and again been granted to me to see the breath of the Spirit rekindling the life of the soul even when it seemed quite dead.

"I have found my soul again," a woman patient said to me recently, with touching simplicity. I had done nothing, used no science, no technique. I had merely listened. Many years before, she had had marital troubles, and in her jealousy had cursed her rival. It happened that this rival died in an accident shortly afterwards, and she was overcome by an ineradicable feeling of guilt. The reason why she had come to tell me—without my putting any questions to her—what had been weighing on her mind for so long, bringing psychological disturbances in its train, was that she wanted to confess it to God, who alone could remove the burden from her. Her prayer answered, she said over and over, "I have found my soul again."

My heart sings for joy to hear her say that—there is no purer and deeper joy than to be the witness of such a great spiritual event, when the sunlight bursts through a somber sky. At the technological level, human effort is like an endless labor in which, generation by generation, bit by bit, a monument is built, always precarious and never finished. The solution of each problem raises a thousand new problems. But when the spark of the Spirit lights up the darkness that has gathered around a person's life, it is as if there has come down from heaven, perfect and complete, a quite simple truth that sets at rest all the disquiet of the soul.

But the career of the man who devotes his life to helping people solve their personal problems is not made up only of such luminous experiences. It seems rather that the very vividness of the experience

---

* "Technology" is used here according to the meaning in Webster's International Dictionary, 2d ed. (1959): "Any practical art utilizing scientific knowledge, as . . . medicine."

of grace can dazzle people and so hide from them all the meanness and imperfection that remains within them.

There was one young man who had such an experience while at school. He was a prey to sex troubles which distracted him from his work and isolated him from his comrades. He lived in a torment of worry which was having a serious effect on his studies, and he was incapable of pulling himself together. Then he met certain classmates who had a living faith. This was a revelation to him, and quite changed his life. Freed from the temptations that had haunted him, he was able to work properly once more. Joyfully he bore witness to those around him to the victorious power of Christianity.

Then he went on to the university. There, separated from his friends, he gradually fell back into his fears and obsessions. He changed to different studies, and then spent his time in fantasies instead of attending lectures. He felt himself once more on the slippery slope. He was overcome with shame and worry, and this tended to isolate him more and more and to paralyze his will to put things right.

Nevertheless the memory of his spiritual experience remained like a faint glow within him, and he came to see me a fortnight before his examinations, which he had already failed at the first attempt. He frankly admitted that he had done hardly any work. He unburdened himself still further. He knew quite well that there was a close connection between his failure in his work and a whole series of failures in the sphere of sex. I felt that his humility was sincere, and that his confidence in God had survived all his failures. And so I suggested that he should perform an act of faith: believe that God forgave him and could entirely renew his state of mind, giving him the strength to persevere with his work, inner freedom, confidence, and as a result, success. From the human point of view, this was almost folly, but faith dares to believe. I threw myself wholeheartedly with him into this adventure. We prayed together. We drew up a program of work for every hour of each day left before his examinations. We arranged all sorts of details in his life.

Success! I was as happy as he was. It was as if I had passed the examinations myself. We thanked God, and he made great resolutions for the future.

I saw him again a few months later, just before a new session of examinations. He had collapsed completely. The fact that his prayers had been answered had not taught him any new fidelity to his work. Instead, he had wasted his time in thoughtless self-indulgence. He was back once more in the old impasse and the old anxiety.

This time I felt it would be tempting God to suggest a new act of faith on the young man's part. The examinations must be postponed, and a deeper and more lasting solution found to his private difficulties. Some might have questioned the authenticity of his two spiritual experiences. I was more inclined to think that the reason why those very promising experiences had not borne fruit was that there were hidden forces at work in his unconscious. They had for a moment been held at bay, but they were not yet vanquished. It was necessary to have recourse to technology in order to unmask the hidden enemy, which the Bible calls a devil, and which the psychoanalyst calls the superego: the false moral code, the secret and all-powerful veto which spoils and sabotages all that is best in a person's life, despite the sincerest aspirations of his conscious mind.

In early childhood he had been sent, on the birth of his younger brother, to live for some years with a female relative who had lost her own child, so that she transferred to him the affection which had thus been cut off. Anyone with a knowledge of psychology will easily guess all the complexes that resulted, without my having to go into them in detail. We explored them gradually over a period of several months. There was the depersonalization of the child who is identified with another who has been lost; jealousy of the brother left at home; an ambivalent attitude to the parents; and defensive reactions against the excessive and compensatory sentimentality of which he was the object. Many symptoms bore witness to the profound disturbance caused by all these factors: significant dreams, feelings of inferiority, unsociability, feelings of unworthiness, exorcistical rites, a serious dislocation in his psychosexual development, and uncertainty concerning his vocation.

The result was that a secret force in the depth of his mind was putting on the brakes and blocking the road to success, in matters of sex as well as in his work. When he was shown the forces at work in his unconscious, he found it hard to accept that he was in their hold. "If these unconscious obstacles date from my childhood, how is it," he asked, "that on two occasions, under the power of grace, I have been able to feel myself so completely liberated?"

I replied by means of a parable. A religious experience is like a revolution. A prince has taken over a country by means of a *coup d'état*. Among the crowd that acclaims him, the followers of the fallen monarch, who is now powerless, are for the moment the most zealous partisans of the new ruler. But their change of heart is not sincere, and they are the enemy who will secretly scheme the gradual undermining of the new regime. If the reigning prince wins some triumph, they bow down and pretend to submit, only to raise their heads once again at the first opportunity to undermine his power.

This is what happens in the case of these submerged elements in our mental make-up. They hide themselves away when we are winning spiritual victories. They camouflage themselves and share in the inner unanimity we feel. But they have certainly not capitulated, and they succeed in sabotaging those victories if we do not unmask them. The process of unmasking them is a slow one, and is a matter of medical technique.

But the state police is wasting its time pursuing the conspirators if the monarch does not use the security thus won to accomplish his task nobly. In the same way, technology is not an end in itself. It ought only to prepare the way for a man to respond freely to the call of religious faith.

This is the way in which faith and technology can and ought to work together in the difficult ministry of tending men's minds.

We are much more prone to set them one over against another. I am no exception.

I have had many patients come to me in search of a liberating spiritual experience after having been disappointed in what psychological technique could do for them. I have often been surprised to see them discovering in themselves, in the light of religious faith, unconscious resistances which psychological treatment had failed to bring to light. I could give many more examples of this. Opposing religion to psychology is but a short step from here. It is a step we must not take.

A woman patient once told me of how she had undergone a course of psychoanalytic treatment that lasted sixteen years, with daily sessions for the first few years, and later on at less frequent intervals. It had been unsuccessful. She had become so attached to the psychoanalyst that he had finally been forced to terminate the treatment. She was left wallowing in a sea of introspection. Then one day she met a woman who talked to her about God, and suggested that she should lay her troubles sincerely before him. A quite new light came flooding in. She saw that a certain sin had been warping her whole life, and felt a tremendous sense of liberation.

In mentioning this case, I do so in a spirit quite different from that in which I might have regarded it a few years ago. I see it as striking evidence of the power of the Spirit. But I think also that the long technical effort of psychoanalysis had prepared the ground well for the decisive experience of faith. On the other hand, the reason why the woman came to consult me was partly that in spite of having experienced such complete liberation, she was still conscious that many difficulties remained to be faced. The technique of the psychoanalyst had enabled her to see what they were, and now she was in a position to try to resolve them in an atmosphere of faith.

In the same way, psychiatrists could doubtless point to a long list of patients who have sought in vain for healing through a religious experience, either with me or with other believers. Other patients, after some momentary victory, have had to turn to them because the way forward was blocked by some tenacious complex which could be dealt with only by the technique of the skilled psychiatrist.

Thus, faith is not opposed to technology, nor renders it superfluous. On the other hand, the climate of faith is one in which the fruits of technology can thrive, and without which its success is only partial.

It is only fair to say that the majority of the patients whom I have been able to help through the message of religion, after psychoanalysis has failed, have admitted to me at the time that they had not been completely honest toward the psychoanalyst. Through lack of confidence they had held back certain facts, or else they had invented them in order to make themselves appear in a better light. I have before me the story of a young woman whose life was in fact straightened out later on, but who had invented dreams and fabricated a romantic life story for herself. She was annoyed with herself for having sabotaged her treatment, particularly since she appreciated and liked the psychoanalyst concerned, but she was the prisoner of the attitude she had adopted. In fact, one can see in her paradoxical behavior the unmistakable sign of the unconscious negative forces which were thus cutting the life line that might rescue her. Possibly her doctor was not so taken in as she imagined. In any case, it was not the technique that was at fault here, but the moral climate in which it was being exercised. This same moral climate is also to blame, and not technique, in the admittedly numerous cases in which a course of psychological treatment ends in disaster. As, for instance, when the doctor, with the laudable intention of liberating the patient from an attitude of hollow conventionalism, advises him to have sexual "experiences" which are really against his conscience and throw him into complete confusion—advice which in any case has nothing to do with psychoanalytic technique. The same is true when treatment is prolonged endlessly, and the doctor, in order to cover up his failure, insists that there must have been some serious emotional shock during childhood, which is now so deeply repressed that it is impossible to bring it back to consciousness. Such a gratuitous hypothesis suggests to the patient that he can never be cured, since this supposedly all-important memory cannot be recovered. In fact, the doctor's assumption of its existence and its importance is based on an entirely theoretical generalization, and not on scientific certainty.

On the other hand, I have seen a large number of patients who, because they are Christian believers, insisted exclusively and obsessively on relying on religion for the cure of their psychic troubles. They come to me, saying that only a Christian doctor can help them, since they have no confidence in psychologists who do not share their faith. They want me to pray with them, and expect that by waving a magic wand I can produce an exciting cure. They are often in conflict with their parents, whose advice that they should undergo technical treatment they have rejected. The success they look for at my hands they hope will enable them to crow over their parents and demonstrate that they were right to refuse. They are the victims of serious complexes, and it is manifest that it is their psychic "censorship" that is preventing them from realizing the fact, and which therefore makes them refuse psychological treatment.

Or else they are undisciplined, and dominated by false suggestions. In this case they stand in need of real re-education, but are attempting unconsciously to avoid it by taking refuge in religious discussions.

In such cases all spiritual action is not only vain, but dangerous, because it makes light of the disease. Never succeeding, because of the wholly disordered state of their psychic functions, in achieving the decisive religious experience they long for, they merely come to doubt both God and themselves, and to believe that God does not love them—that he accords to others favors which he withholds from them. All they get from the Gospel—the good news of salvation—is despair at being sinners.

When this happens my one aim is to bring to an end the religious discussions they hanker for, in order to submit them to the discipline of a course of technical treatment. What they need is a methodical course of mental re-education, such as that provided by the remarkable exercises invented by Vittoz;[1] the patient straightening-out of all the wrong ideas harbored as the result of harmful suggestions received in the past, practiced by Dubois; a systematic course of psychic hygiene such as that of Rohrbach; a course of treatment using autosuggestion;[2] the "waking dream" treatment used by Desoille; or else such a course of psychoanalysis as I may advise.

After that, with healthy minds, with normal psychic functions, with new self-knowledge, they will be able to enter into the harmonious spiritual life that at present they seek in vain.

Sometimes what happens is that a patient's relatives refuse, for religious reasons, to entrust him to technical medical care, claiming that if he is converted he will be healed without such treatment. It can only harm a patient to realize that instead of being properly treated, his sufferings are being made use of as a means of bringing him forcibly to accept the doctrines that someone wishes to impose upon him. Nothing is more surely calculated to turn him away from faith. He is, of course, sent to me with the idea that I will become the instrument through which this moral pressure is exerted. This is enough to take away from me all desire to talk religion to him, and I institute a strictly traditional course of treatment.

We have something better to do than to enter into controversies between the partisans of religion and those of science. To do so is to perpetuate the awful habit of thinking of faith as being opposed to technology. People are suffering. Medicine is a very difficult art. There are not too many of us persons of good will to work together to heal the sick.

I believe in the value of a real marriage of technology and faith. Lucien Bovet, in a lecture on anxiety, was most enlightening on the subject. Anxiety, he said, finds its sustenance in the painful events of

[1] Roger Vittoz, *The Treatment of Neurasthenia by the Teaching of Brain Control*, translated by H. B. Brooke.
[2] C. Baudouin, *Suggestion and Autosuggestion*, translated by E. and C. Paul.

the past, its occasion in some physical weakness in the present, and its specificity in fear of the unknown future. It is the job of psychological technique to explore and liquidate the past, that of physical technique to rectify the present, and lastly, that of faith to illuminate the future with the assurance of God's love.

Instead of criticizing each other's methods, boasting of our own successes and denouncing the failures of others, let us try to discover what we can learn from each other. Our controversies may bring disaster to men's souls.

A devout woman patient had been carefully tended by a Christian psychoanalyst. He himself advised her to go and see a certain man who practiced faith healing. But the faith healer upset her completely by declaring roundly that psychoanalysts were the instruments of Satan.

The discoveries of psychoanalysis are of inestimable value in the light they throw on the Christian ministry of soul-healing. The works of the Rev. Leslie Weatherhead,[3] and of others, are an eloquent testimony of this, and my own experience confirms it. Conversely, even the most expert technicians can learn something from the Christian religion, which through revelation has penetrated more deeply than any science into the central drama of human life—namely, the inevitable question of whether to say "Yes" or "No" to God.

Enlightened psychoanalysts, even if agnostic, recognize this to be so. I once treated a man to whom a psychoanalyst had said: "I can do nothing more for you; you need a religion." In this case I have to admit that I was no more successful than he had been. Another of my patients, with whom I had more success, was a woman who had undergone lengthy treatment by a psychoanalyst who did not mince his words with believers. He had once said to her: "You have faith; you ought to find in God all the help you need in liquidating the problems we have been analyzing." The trouble is that in order to help a person to win the victories of faith, one must have found faith oneself.

Why is it, then, that the work of the psychoanalysts has been received in a spirit of general hostility in religious circles? It is probably owing in part to the peculiar doctrinal heresies which psychoanalysts have often thought fit to formulate as a result of their experiences. But it must be admitted that this is also the result of a

[3] L. D. Weatherhead, *Psychology, Religion and Healing.*

certain resentment against the fact that psychiatry had begun to compete with religion in the field of the cure of souls.

I have before me the records of several cases in which psychoanalysts have been completely successful. In each case it is clear that one of the factors in this success has been the real spirit of honesty, love, humility, and purity in which the treatment has been given. This spirit is precisely that of Christianity. Take, for instance, the case of a young man to whom psychoanalysis had made it clear that the origin of his difficulties lay in mistakes made in regard to him by his mother when he was a child. It is well known how revelations of this nature can set up violent reactions in a son. A terrible conflict can take place, in which the son blames the mother, who cannot understand why he should do so, and seeks to justify herself. The usual result is an irremediable break between them. This young man, however, talked the matter over affectionately with his mother, who was a sincere Christian. She honestly examined herself before God, and recognized the mistakes she had made. For her this was a profound experience which enriched her faith as well as her relationship with her son.

I have also before me the notes on a number of patients who came to me after having undergone courses of psychoanalytical treatment for considerable periods, which had not succeeded in liberating them completely. Later on they had come by various roads to a spiritual experience which had been much more fruitful. But in each of these cases it is clear that the psychological treatment created a self-knowledge and a habit of honesty about themselves which prepared the ground for the liberating religious event. Psychoanalysis brought out into the open unsuspected inner resistances which could then be broken down when the spiritual crisis took place. It is certain that patients who have been psychoanalyzed are able rapidly to achieve a most fruitful insight and sincerity in meditation when they find faith. I am well aware myself of how much a knowledge of analytical psychology has enriched my own spiritual life, how the analysis of a dream reveals to me unconscious guilty propensities which can then be humbly confessed and by God's grace forgiven.

On the other hand, while meditation, as I have shown, enlarges the field of consciousness, and reveals the hidden undercurrents of the mind in a way that is very similar to the operation of psychoanalysis, it is also true that unconscious complexes can present an obstacle to meditation, disturb its course, and distort the spiritual life through the spiritual blindness to which they give rise.

A patient who is dominated by an unconscious complex is blinded in his consciousness by it. He is unable to see his wrong behavior in those areas that are ruled by his complex. He displays unbridled aggressiveness, for instance, and yet has no conviction of sin on account of it. He is unable to see that it contradicts the brotherly love he believes in.

This is where the analogy between the religious cure of souls and psychoanalysis lies. The patient may be cured by either the one or the other: a spiritual experience may suddenly open his eyes, bring him to a conviction of sin concerning his aggressiveness, and so lead him to recognize the complex which is its cause. In this case the cure of souls has worked as a technique. On the other hand, psychological treatment may make him aware of his complex, and from there he may come to a realization of the aggressiveness that flows from it, and to see that this aggressiveness is a sin which he can bring to God and give up. Here technique has brought about a result that is spiritual.

CHAPTER · 2

Ⓦ

Psychoanalysis and Soul-healing

Imagine a puppet theater, in which the movements of the actors are governed by hidden strings manipulated from behind the scenes. These secret strings represent the psychic mechanisms by which the mind is attached to its unconscious complexes, behind the screen of psychological censorship.

Analytical technique proceeds by probing behind the screen until it is lucky enough to cut through the string so that liberty of movement is restored to the person.

Spiritual power, on the other hand, is capable of pulling so hard on the person that the string breaks.

Probing as it does, analytical technique does violence to the mind and causes it pain. It breaks through the "censorship" of the mind, tears apart the screen, and allows light to shine into the dark corners. The experience of grace also causes pain when it breaks the string; it too tears open the screen and, like psychoanalysis, throws light upon the dark places of the unconscious.

Christians take pleasure in quoting cases where the string has broken, resulting in a cure similar to that obtained through psychoanalysis, without any need to resort to psychoanalysis. Analysts, on the other hand, take pleasure in quoting cases where the string has been too strong, where religion has failed because the person remained tied, and recourse to psychoanalytical technique has been necessary in order to cut the string. I consider that, as always in medicine, this is not a matter of fundamental doctrine, but of which kind of treatment is more appropriate. When the string seems to be tough, when the complexes are massive and quite unconscious, the patient must be sent to the psychoanalyst. But when the patient pretends that thin threads are thick ropes, when he pretends he is suffering from complexes in order to excuse his moral disobedience, endlessly analyzing himself instead of taking stock of himself and repenting, then he must be brought into the presence of Jesus Christ, the source of all spiritual growth.

I hope I have helped the reader to see what is, in my view, the much discussed relationship between soul-healing and psychoanalysis. As in every other branch of our art, the doctor's first task is to make a sound diagnosis, so that he can see what sort of case he is dealing with and so know what is the appropriate treatment for it, whether it needs spiritual or technical action.

I feel it is my duty, as a believer, to show the extent to which technical ignorance can spoil soul-healing. Here is a simple example. It is a well-known fact that the child's first idea of God is largely determined by the mental picture he has of his own earthly father. The term "heavenly Father" used by Jesus in speaking of God has contributed to this mental association. But it also has a quite concrete sense. To the child, his father is at first a god—omnipotent, omniscient, and perfect. The child eventually abandons this illusion when he discovers that his father is not exempt from weakness, faults, and ignorance. He then projects these attributes upon the Heavenly Father about whom he has been taught, otherwise he would sink into despair. With them, however, he also projects upon God his mental picture of his earthly father.

This would seem to be the cause of the crises of doubt to which every believer is subject. Having in the past been let down by his first god, he is in constant fear of being let down in turn by this heavenly God.

One further important result of this is that those who have suffered in infancy from brutality, hostility, or authoritarianism on the part of their father find it extremely difficult to believe in the love, providence, and forgiveness of the Heavenly Father. They cannot pray confidently to him, and to suggest that they should do so, without at the same time using the technique of psychoanalysis to unravel the complexes formed in infancy, is to lead them into an impasse from which they cannot escape. They consider themselves to be great sinners because they cannot bring themselves to pray. They think they are rejected by God and damned. If anyone tries to help them by offering spiritual aid, the only result is that the blockage in their spiritual life is made worse. I once observed a similar result in the case of a young woman who had lost her father in her childhood. The rebellion aroused by this shock in that young child's mind prevented her in the same way, despite her real piety, from believing in God's fatherly goodness.

"Basically, I am afraid of God," a young woman writes to me; "I do not really believe that he loves me, me in particular. My difficulty in believing firmly in God the *Father* comes from the fact that I do not know what a real father is like. In my childhood the only idea I had of a father was that of an ogre. When I was quite small I was terrified of being carried off by my 'real' father. Later on, what terrified me was my stepfather's riding whip, and being locked in my room on a diet of bread and water. Later still, when I would not fall in with my mother's whims, they used to frighten me by threatening to send me back to my 'real' father, who would pack me off without delay to a convent."

"God must have deserted me, because I am filled with anxiety," another girl said to me. To say this was to fail to recognize the psychological origin of the anxiety, and to give it a false religious interpretation. It is unnecessary to say that this error in interpretation, by creating an artificial religious problem in the mind of a fervent believer, only made the anxiety more acute and more difficult to get rid of. It disappeared when psychoanalytical investigation uncovered its origin.

There is another way in which a lack of knowledge of psychology can harm the religious life. It is well known that the law of the association of ideas is such that any thought, however outrageous or shocking, may at any moment cross our minds, as a result of an association with some quite ordinary idea. These associations form as it were a kaleidoscopic film ceaselessly running through the back of our minds. We scarcely notice them, so swiftly do they chase one another across our consciousness, unless we pay particular attention to them or take particular pleasure in them. There is no question of moral responsibility being involved in this automatic process of association of ideas. A sincere believer, however, lacking proper instruction in the matter and clinging to the ideal of moral perfection, is shocked to find an improper and vulgar thought coming into his mind. The effect of this is to concentrate his attention upon the intruding thought—"stopping the film at that point." And so the whole religious life of the patient is thereafter concentrated upon an unreal problem arising from a confusion between free association and temptation, as well as between temptation and sin. The more lacking in true moral content the problem is, the greater is the tendency for it to become obsessive.

St. Francis de Sales wrote about this problem in a way that accords remarkably closely with modern psychology. Take, for instance, these words addressed to St. Chantal when she was assailed by doubts about her faith:

Those temptations about your faith have returned. . . . You have not answered them back: that is well, my daughter; but you think about them too much, fear them too much, they can do you no harm otherwise. . . . No, no, my daughter, let the wind blow. . . . Recently I was near some beehives, and some of the bees alighted on my face. A countryman said to me: "Don't be frightened, and don't touch them. There's no chance of them stinging you—unless you touch them; then they will." So, believe me, you must not fear these temptations. Do not touch them, and they will surely not offend you. Pass them by, and spend no time on them.

On the other hand, psychoanalysis without faith often leads to a sort of mental vertigo. There was a young woman who had undergone a course of psychoanalysis, and who shortly afterwards had experienced a sudden religious conversion. For several years her psychic life followed an even course. Psychoanalysis, however, had given her a habit of constant self-examination, and when she had to face certain new difficulties this habit took an even stronger hold upon her. She was soon obsessed by the idea of all the dark forces which she felt moving like powerful monsters deep within her, and which she tried in vain to chase away. Her failure to do so was the more painful to her in that since her conversion she had learned to bring all her problems of conscience to God to be freed from them.

"Christ is the Lord of our unconscious as well," I said to her. "He knows all about it, and will protect us from it if we hand it over into his keeping!" My remark was unpremeditated, made without any estimate of its importance, but it put an abrupt end to the young woman's anxiety, and restored her peace of mind at once.

I remember another of my patients who, when analysis began to show her herself more clearly, stubbornly insisted: "But that is not me, that is not what I am really like. I've never had wicked thoughts."

One can imagine the dismay with which people who have no faith may receive this discovery of the hidden power of the unconscious functions of the mind. Psychoanalysis can never reveal more than a small part of them. Most of them must inevitably remain unrecognized, hidden tyrants.

"None is righteous, no, not one," says the Bible (Rom. 3:10). Nothing is better calculated than psychoanalysis to disabuse those who find this difficult to accept, and who believe themselves to be honorable people. It shows them in the depths of their minds the dishonest, selfish, impure, violent, and cowardly tendencies which education and training seek to cover over with a fine mantle of virtues.

In the face of this discovery there are two differing reactions, which are, I believe, a matter of temperament. For example, let us suppose that analysis shows a man the extent to which repressed hostility toward his father has interfered with his psychological development. If he is of an active, positive, superficial nature, he will concentrate his attention on the faults in his father which provoked his aggressive reactions, and will then feel free to give expression to his aggressiveness on the conscious level. This causes people to denounce the treatment as having a perverse moral effect—wrongly, in my view. First of all, the aggressiveness was already there, and to have it exteriorized rather than camouflaged in compensatory sentimentality is at any rate more honest, and consequently more Christian. Further, it is not really analytical technique that is in question, but rather the manner of resolving the psychological problem which it has brought to light.

If, however, our subject is of a passive and depressive temperament, he will be aghast at all the sin he has discovered in his heart. Whereas the aggressive dynamism of the first man brought him, if not moral liberation, at least psychological healing, this man achieves neither the one nor the other. Only Christianity can give him the solution he needs, namely, the assurance of God's forgiveness for him, which will in turn lead him to forgive his father.

Here is another example. Analysis often shows that troubles are due to the persistence of an infantile psychological dependence on the mother. In order for the personality to develop and strengthen, it must be freed from this dependence. The umbilical cord must be cut, to use an expressive image. This was the conclusion to which we came in the case of a young woman, after long psychoanalytical exploration. One day while meditating she saw that she must have a long heart-to-heart talk with her mother, that she must go over many details from her childhood about which she had never before dared to talk to her, and that she must make clear her personal convictions on certain subjects she had always avoided for fear of provoking an argument in which she would be defeated. It seemed an almost impossible thing for her to do, but she found in her faith the courage and assurance she needed, and the interview was in fact an extremely happy one. "I remember," she wrote to me afterwards, "that one of my acquaintances, in the course of her psychoanalytical treatment, used to beat her mother, on the pretext of 'cutting the umbilical cord' which attached her to her. It was only the other day, after talking to my mother, that I realized that my umbilical cord had been cut. But I am grateful to you for having helped me to get rid of it like that."

Psychological technique, then, is morally neutral. It is neither good nor bad in itself. Everything depends on the spirit in which it is used and in which one tries to solve the problems it reveals. "Psychoanalysis," writes Perceval Frutiger, in *Tribune de Genève,* "a mere tool with which one can do good as well as evil, is a valuable aid in religious soul-healing when used by a believer." Analytical technique can serve religion, and together they can achieve results of which they would be incapable separately. I have written elsewhere[1] of a case which illustrates the point clearly, one in which each of the three stages can be easily followed. It concerns a young man who had obtained some relief through psychoanalysis, which nevertheless had not cured him, but rather left him with an unhealthy habit of introspection. Then came a conversion which brought meaning and joy into his life, but which also failed to cure him, because there was an unconscious blockage which still impeded the free flow of his spiritual life. Finally came the quite technical intervention of a psychiatrist who put his finger on the hidden obstacle—repressed aggressiveness toward his father. Then, thanks to the faith which he had meanwhile found, this patient was able to experience a more complete liberation, marked by his forgiving his father.

Here is another example. This was a young woman who, without being aware of my religious outlook, had placed herself squarely in

[1] *Nouvelles,* Berne, May, 1944.

the field of moral responsibility by making a courageous confession to me of certain wrong acts which she could not think of without remorse. This was the beginning of a long and interesting series of experiences in the course of which her faith was fortified, her social attitude was transformed, and her physical health improved. Spiritual meditation was frequently the occasion of her bringing back to consciousness long-repressed memories, so that I was tempted to use her case as an argument against the psychoanalysts, in favor of soul-healing as compared with their own techniques. What I ought to have seen, however, was that these discoveries she made, together with the scientific insight which I owed to my knowledge of the techniques of analysis, imparted to our interviews the character of a course of psychoanalysis, though freed of all rigidity of method.

I felt that our interviews followed an oscillating, pendulum-like rhythm. Sometimes they took on the character of a technical psychological exploration and explanation, which threw new light upon the determinisms at work within the patient. Then we would tend to get lost in this labyrinth, which, though it satisfied her intellectual curiosity, did nothing to help her to live. At other times, however, impelled by the Spirit, she would come back to confession and spiritual self-denial. She felt her own moral responsibility for acts and attitudes which, from the technical point of view, seemed to be determined by factors beyond her control. Nevertheless this brought a real living sense of liberation and a new spiritual impulse. Whereas in the technical analytical phase everything tended to become more and more complicated, in this spiritual phase everything became more simplified, even too simplified, so that fresh failures revealed the persistence of an unconscious resistance to the specific acts of obedience for which she had begun to see the need. We had then to turn once more to analytical technique in order to bring this resistance to the surface, and then to consider it in the light of her faith, so that it could be resolved through prayer.

So we proceeded, oscillating between the technical and the spiritual aspect of her difficulties.

It is the common experience of all, that humanity moves between these two poles of simplicity and complexity. People who have the sort of mind that sees only one side to every question tend toward vigorous action. They succeed in everything they do because they do not stop to split hairs and have abounding confidence in their own abilities. Your successful journalist, for instance, is inclined to simplify every problem and condense it into an arresting phrase. On the other hand, those with subtle and cultivated minds tend to get lost in a maze of fine distinctions. They always see how complicated things really are, so that their powers of persuasion are nil. That is why the world is led by those who are least suited to raising its cultural and moral standards. It is only very few who manage to combine both tendencies, and in my view a lively Christian faith is the best precondition for the accomplishment of this miracle, because it gives both profound understanding and simplicity of heart.

But there was more to the case of that young woman than this. Despite all the progress we made, and the development of her inner life, there subsisted a serious functional disorder which caused her acute suffering and was irritating to us both because the fact of its persistence was a sign that the cure remained incomplete. It was a thorny problem because it caused a tension between us, and this not only made it harder for us to deal with it, but aggravated the disorder itself. In spite of her gratitude toward me for all the spiritual and psychological help I had given her, the patient harbored an unexpressed feeling of resentment against me for my failure to cure her completely. For my part, I defended myself by silently blaming her because her religious faith, despite all its fervor, had never inspired her with sufficient confidence in a successful cure for the functional disorder to disappear.

It was only after reading the works of Dubois that I was able to return calmly to a consideration of the scientific laws of suggestion and their ineluctable determinism in the genesis of functional disorders, and at last we won through to victory. Even after that there were relapses and oscillations which made it more and more necessary for us to exercise this complete conjunction of technology and faith.

CHAPTER · 3

The Two Aspects of Man

Thus it seems to me that man can always be looked at from two points of view: from the technical and scientific on the one hand, and from the spiritual and moral on the other. I think that each of these two points of view gives a true but incomplete picture of man. As in a pair of stereoscopic photographs, both pictures are true, but neither of them separately gives the lifelike view of the subject that is obtained by looking at them together in the stereoscope. Nevertheless, the fusion of the two images into a lifelike picture demands a difficult effort of visual adjustment. Similarly, it would seem that our minds are too circumscribed to see man at the same time in his mechanistic as well as his spiritual aspect, and to fuse these two partial views into a single living synthesis.

In the oscillating movement I was referring to just now, we consider man alternately as an objective reality, susceptible of scientific study and analysis in his elements and determinisms, and as a spiritual being, an entity whose destiny the believer perceives. The first is the domain of quantity, complexity, and necessity: the triumph of science is the reduction of everything to numbers and laws. The second is the domain of quality, simplicity, and liberty: here what matters in the infinite diversity of life is always the same choice between Yes and No, between obedience and disobedience, between being and nonbeing; and in this choice the whole person is committed. There is no possibility of a logical reconciliation of the two alternatives, because our minds are too small to see both sides at once. But our intuition assures us that both are true. That is to say, they each present a different aspect of the same reality, and any attempt to use the one to refute the other is vain.

I once saw in an Italian railway station a poster advertising some product or other under the name "Cervino." The picture on the poster represented the Matterhorn, which, as a French-speaking Swiss, I had known as Mont Cervin. The picture had attracted my attention, however, because there was something odd about it. I soon realized what it was: it was the Matterhorn seen from the Italian side, with its peak pointing to the right. As a Swiss I was always used to seeing it with the point toward the left. I remember thinking that here was a sort of parable of the irreconcilable double aspect that I am describing here: two images, both true, but incapable of being seen both at the same time. You cannot view the Matterhorn from the Italian side and from the Swiss side at the same time. Nevertheless it is still the same mountain.

But just as it is possible with the stereoscope, using an optical device and visual effort, to fuse the two images into a more lifelike one, so we can use intuition in an attempt to form a synthesized concept of man, in which his two aspects are fused into one.

I studied physics at the University of Geneva under C. E. Guye, whose work on the evolution of modern physics has had such a far-reaching effect on our conception of the world.[1] He affirmed that "it is the scale of observation which creates the phenomenon," a maxim whose scientific and philosophical importance Lecomte du Noüy has underlined. Science studies phenomena, but it does so within a certain frame of reference, and the laws it deduces are valid only within that frame. At the beginning of this century, scientists had a quite rigid conception of the laws of nature. Determinism, attested at every point within the frame of reference, was made a dogma. Extrapolated into fields outside the range of scientific investigation, it seemed to exclude all liberty and all spiritual values. With the rise of molecular, atomic, and intra-atomic physics, which have presented us with a concept of the discontinuity of matter, and with the adoption of the principle of relativity, physics has been completely transformed, and has overturned established concepts of the world. Hitherto, only biological, sociological, and psychological laws have been looked upon as statistical, because of the inevitable heterogeneity of the experimental data.

[1] C. E. Guye, *Physico-Chemical Evolution*, translated by G. H. Green.

They were contrasted with the rigid laws of the exact sciences. Now these laws too—or at any rate the majority of them—seem to be merely statistical. Their apparent fixity arises from the fact that on our scale of observation we see only the general trend, which neutralizes the fluctuations of the individual elements. Had we been able to observe the same phenomena on a different scale, we should have seen these fluctuations as indeterminate.

The whole concept of scientific determinism has been shaken, so that science is today bringing us back to a spiritual concept of the world.

It is my conviction that psychology will undergo a similar transformation, resulting in the reconciliation of its technical and spiritual aspects. Each constitutes an autonomous system which is true within its own frame of reference. The two propositions of determinism and liberty, while seemingly contradictory on one level, are seen to be true on another.

As I write these lines I am reminded of a remarkable essay by the Genevan psychoanalyst, Henri Flournoy,[2] which goes far to suggest a possible reconciliation. He recalls the work of his father, Theodore Flournoy, who extended to psychology the two fundamental principles of science, namely, "the exclusion of transcendence, and biological interpretation." The son, however, adds: "But it should be pointed out (and it cannot be too strongly emphasized) that *exclusion* is not the same as *denial*."

The fact is that in order to evolve, science had to adopt a certain point of view and to refuse to depart from it. This involved the conventional *a priori* assumption of the exclusion of transcendence. Science had to set transcendence aside because all scientific curiosity disappears as soon as the cause of any phenomenon is attributed to God. In order to proceed scientifically, psychology must do the same. I do not wish to deny that Theodore Flournoy's principle is indispensable to the rigorous method of scientific psychology; but in setting aside transcendence it ought not, as his son says, to deny it. Scientific psychology moves within a frame of reference which limits its outlook strictly to the point of view it has adopted. But on a higher scale there is a synthesized psychology which steps outside this convention, and puts together the two pictures seen respectively by

[2] In *Archives des sciences physiques et naturelles*, May–June, 1944, p. 67.

scientific and by spiritual psychology, each observing from its own individual viewpoint.

On the level on which absolute psychological determinism and moral liberty are usually considered, they appear to be irreconcilable, and science and religion are at war. At the level of our habitual modes of reasoning, there is nothing but contradiction—an irreducible antithesis—between the technical and the moral aspect of things. I do not intend to attempt in this book to give a logical demonstration of their possible synthesis, since by definition it must be a philosophical synthesis that goes beyond the limits of logic. But by means of reflections of various kinds drawn from my own work, in which I seek to understand man both scientifically and spiritually, I shall try to convey the intuitive feeling that at a different level the apparent contradiction between them may disappear.

To this end I should like to refer here to what may be termed "double causality." From a scientific, technical and objective standpoint, man appears to be ineluctably determined in his physical and psychical constitution and evolution by an immediate and absolute causality. It seems that if one could assemble together at any given moment all the physical, chemical, and psychological components of his being, one could thereby determine what must necessarily result from them a moment later. But first it is necessary to distinguish, as Dalbiez has shown,[3] between physiological and psychological determinism. From the technological point of view the second is as rigorous as the first. That is to say that by means of analysis we can understand the origin of any idea or feeling by going back to the ideas and feelings that are its cause. This understanding, however, is always only a matter of hindsight. In the psychical life there are too many influences that may intervene (among them may well be direct intervention by the Holy Spirit), for us to be able to foresee with certainty the psychological reactions that will supervene upon any given psychic state. Foresight of this kind is specific to physical determinism.

But further, even in the case of physiological determinism, it is clear that one cannot expect to find it as rigorous as physical determinism (itself, as we have seen, already called in question), since the nature of life is still a mystery that eludes us. "Vital determinism," writes Georges Regard, "must be distinguished from

[3] Roland Dalbiez, *Psychoanalytical Method and the Doctrine of Freud,* translated by T. F. Lindsay.

physicochemical determinism. Whereas the latter is absolute, the former is relative."

By means of scientific analysis the scientist reduces life to a collection of physicochemical reactions which have nothing specifically vital about them, so that life cannot be subjected to any technical definition. Life might just be defined, in accordance with Helmholtz's hypothesis, as contradicting the second law of thermodynamics—but even so this would be tantamount to saying that it is not subject to determinism.

But as Lecomte du Noüy has shown with incomparable clarity, although life is not susceptible of definition at the level of the physicochemical phenomenon, it can nevertheless be defined at a different level—that of the "evolvent" relationship of those phenomena. Characteristic of the living thing, he says, is its organization, that is to say the reciprocal concordance of a set of concomitant phenomena, such that we are compelled to accept that they are coordinated by a superior will, that they are meant to be in a state of concordance, that in this concordance the purpose of the organism—the life for which it is organized—is fulfilled.

Similarly, although science seeks—and even here, only with difficulty—to penetrate the links of immediate cause and effect which have governed every change in the evolution of living things, it is unable to explain the process of evolution itself, and why it moves in a set direction, in obedience to a plan, manifestly fulfilling the destiny of the world—the life of the world, a life which is lived on a level different from that of each individual organism.

There is, then, alongside immediate scientific causality, and independent of it because it is on a different scale, a transcendental causality. That is to say, there is an over-all plan governing the relationship of individual phenomena, and imparting to each of them a significance within the evolutionary process, so that they all move together toward the fulfillment of the destiny of the world. To say "destiny" and "over-all plan" is to say "Spirit," the reality that transcends and governs visible reality.

Science studies each physical phenomenon, and the laws of immediate cause and effect relating to it, in isolation, each on its own level. But consideration of the whole process, of the phenomenon of phenomena itself, is beyond the scope of science. At that level intuition alone tells us that there must be a cause that transcends the whole, since it obeys an ordered plan. Science gives answers to the immediate questions: Why does the earth revolve around the sun? Because the sun exerts an attraction upon it. But to the overriding question of why there is a universal law of gravitation, science has no answer. Faith alone replies that it is because Someone has given the universe all its laws in order to fulfill His purpose thereby.

The universal process is, one might say, like a chain attached at one end to the ship and at the other to the quayside. If you ask why a particular link is where it is, analytical science will study its relationship with the links to right and left of it. That this immediate relationship determines its position is an objective mathematical fact. But if, on a different scale, the chain is viewed as a whole, that link is seen to be an integral part of a series of links having a direction and a purpose which are in accord with the will of the sailor who placed the chain there in order to attach the ship to the quay. This too is a fact, a mediate fact, imparting a transcendent purpose to the immediate relationships of the individual links.

We can now see how this fact of the two kinds of causality applies to the actual lives of the men and women whom we observe. From the point of view of technical, scientific causality, each of their reactions seems to be determined by an immediate and objective cause, and so appears to be inevitable. For instance, I should never think as I do on a given subject if I had not read a certain book, heard a certain person speak, received a certain suggestion or undergone a certain physiological action on my brain. And since one can comprehend the Spirit only through ideas, it would seem that even all my religious convictions must have been determined by the influences I have undergone and the experiences I have had. From the point of view of transcendental causality, however, the linking together of these physical and psychic phenomena is seen to be the working-out of a person's spiritual destiny. The whole succession of the events which have influenced him is like a chain whose purpose has been to bring him, in obedience to a higher will, to where he now is.

When I am the witness of a spiritual event, in which I see a man humbly coming back to God to dedicate himself to Him, I am well aware that this is the result of an inner crisis determined by the influences to which he is subject, but I know also—and he feels it to be so—that God has brought him on purpose to this point, using the whole process of the events through which He has led him. Similarly, in the life of a nation it may seem to the observer who looks at history on the level of immediate cause and effect, that a certain event is the necessary consequence of the action of a certain man, and that it is itself the cause of another event which necessarily results from it. But if this process is viewed as a whole, there becomes apparent a line of evolution and a more general causality. A certain man or a certain event must play a part at a certain moment in history, in order that the destiny of that nation should be fulfilled. Such a destiny will be perceived by a vaster intuition.

On the vaster scale all the events which go to make up the life of a nation, like those in the life of an individual, become significant— even the misfortunes that have befallen a man, even the sins he has committed, even the injustices he has suffered at the hands of others. All these things have contributed to the tracing out of the road along which he had to travel in order to reach this moment in which he hears God's call and that of his own destiny. His child has been killed in an accident? Scientifically the cause lay in the group of facts which caused the accident. But now, as he looks at his life as a whole he sees that the accident set in motion a whole evolving process, without which he would never have known this present fertile moment.

From now on, while still being able to make a technical study of the immediate material and psychological cause of an event, he will no longer be content with such a study by itself. He will also try to find its meaning—what God is trying to say to him through it, where God wishes to lead him. He will reintegrate God into life. That is, instead of thinking of God as being outside events, like a mere hypothesis or a spiritual consolation, he will look for Him in the events over which He rules. Then everything, even technology, even the natural laws studied by science, even the mental functions which psychology analyzes, takes on a transcendental meaning.

Charles Odier, the psychoanalyst, in his book[4] contrasts "mental functions" with "values." It is encouraging that a strict Freudian should hold out a hand in this way to the world of religion by speaking of "true values," whereas Freudian doctrine claimed to reduce all spiritual values to the level of mental functions. I am told that he met with a very cool reception. One religious journal even refused to mention his book to its readers. I find this difficult to

[4] *Les deux sources, consciente et inconsciente de la vie morale.*

understand. There is no gainsaying the fact that the reason why so many people are forsaking religion today is largely because of scientific theories that have attempted to explain all moral and spiritual values as mere psychological projections. It is well known that Freud claimed to attribute all religious and philosophical concepts to the mere interplay of instinctive psychic functions. And now here is one of his disciples recognizing that there are "true values," and maintaining that they can be usefully served by learning how to use analytical technique to distinguish them from false values, that is to say, from those that are no more than illusions due to psychic functions.

I hope I will not be unfair to Odier if I give a theoretical example, in order to show in a few lines the thesis he himself develops in considerable detail. Two men become converted. Whereas one, whose mental functions are healthy, is truly obeying an inner call of the Spirit, the other, dominated unconsciously by an Oedipus complex, is motivated in reality by an urge to contradict his father, who is a professed atheist. The complex goes back to his childhood, when his affective attachment to his mother made him a rival to his father. But at the same time this very fact keeps him in a state of psychological dependence on the father. Not being strong enough to break free, he is unconsciously trying to put between his father and himself the ocean of a religious controversy. He believes himself to be as sincere a convert as the first man is. Technical analysis, however, reveals the personal psychological functions which in fact determine his behavior, and which are quite the opposite of a call of the Spirit.

Odier's thesis seems to me to be true. It would appear to provide an excellent meeting place for psychologists and Christians. Observing men honestly, I can see every day that they are often deluded by their mental functions, so that they take to be moral victories things that are in reality only psychological defeats. With Odier, I believe that analytical technique can be of great use to religion in disentangling genuine motives from self-deception in people's spiritual development.

I must only add that the question seems to me to be even more complex than Odier shows. His contrast between true and false values, helpful as it is in argument, seems to me to be too artificial in practice. It is a mental concept. In real life we would never find true and false values represented in the pure state in two distinct beings, as just described. Rather do we see them both at once, incarnate in each one of us. In our spiritual lives there are plenty of events, impulses, and inspirations that we attribute to God, when in fact they are the outcome of unconscious urges. Religious meditation, as well as technical analysis, can help us to recognize this. There are also real interventions by the Spirit. These are what Odier calls "values." That a disciple of Freud recognizes this so frankly, is in my view a major event in the history of psychoanalysis. He speaks of these values with respect. With so much respect in fact that he is careful not to touch them with his technique. Let us have the courage to do so, and we will find that, even in the case of the most genuine conversion, psychological analysis can determine the mental functions which dictate it. In other words, from the technological point of view it is all a matter of mental functions. But in the perspective of faith it is possible to see, behind the interplay of these functions, the great struggle between the Spirit and the Enemy. The divine and diabolical forces manipulate these mental functions in their struggle, like two chess players moving piece against piece, except that instead of each player having his own pieces, they both use the same ones, for in our earthly condition good and evil are mixed together in each of our psychic functions. It is just here that psychoanalytical technique can come to the aid of faith, in unmasking with ever greater penetration the false motives—pride, aggressiveness, egoism, jealousy, and so on—which come and insinuate themselves even into our sincerest attempts to obey God. In this way the honesty about oneself that is fostered by psychological analysis continually refines the spiritual life. Our values are never completely pure in this life. But the psychological functions can contribute continually toward the accomplishment of God's purpose and of our spiritual destiny, as well as standing in the way. The unconscious does not contain only base instincts, but superior instincts as well, which also control the mechanism of the mind.

A certain woman went to see a psychiatrist, who pronounced a serious diagnosis of her case. Afraid and upset, she went to see another psychiatrist. This one was a Christian. He recognized the religious aspirations that lay behind her troubles, and made her aware of them. All at once her depression gave way to extreme euphoria. She was so happy to have discovered that it was faith she had been seeking, and to have found it, that her excitement showed all the signs of mania. It is impossible to deny that this was a new manifestation of her sickness, rather than a cure. She realized this some time afterwards, when the period of excitement had passed. Nevertheless she remains convinced that she experienced something real and important despite the mask of disease that covered the whole episode. She writes: "The euphoria has gone. Still, I am better. The euphoria has gone. But I cannot deny the facts. I had an astonishing experience. It was almost like falling in love."

So in the perspective of the psychological phenomenon there are nothing but mental functions, in which the interplay of immediate cause and effect takes place in accordance with the laws of suggestion, projection, condensation, and symbolism. But in the perspective of faith one can see that the significance of this whole mechanism is that in it the drama of man's spiritual destiny is being played out.

Frank Abauzit, in a work to which I shall have occasion to refer later,[5] makes a distinction between the moral person and the individual. While the latter is egotistical and ruled by instinct, the former "seeks the realization of an ideal." But, as Abauzit very clearly shows, "the individual and the moral person are one." In order for the moral person—the "converted" individual—to make his appearance, there must be, as the permanent and indispensable basis, an egotistical and instinctive individual. The moral person pure and simple does not exist.

This distinction seems to me to fit precisely that of Odier's "functions" and "values." Although the functions seem to be to a certain extent the negation of the values, they are still their instruments. The consolidation of values requires a continual conversion, but even so, they will never in this life be freed from the functions which both serve and corrupt them.

Two theologians, one Catholic and the other Protestant, criticized me within a month of each other and on practically the same grounds, namely for expressing the joy felt at moral and medical cures that take place under the effect of spiritual experiences. They rightly fear that such testimony will arouse utopian hopes in readers. Even the greatest believers are never completely delivered on this earth either of all misfortune or of all sin. However decisive some of the victories won by faith, these never mean that a person is thereafter sheltered from constantly recurring combats and sufferings.

[5] *Le problème de la tolérance.*

The sole real hope of the Christian is in heaven, in the triumphant return of Christ.

Just about then there came to see me a woman patient who had been delivered from a lasting neurosis by her conversion. For years she had exercised a fruitful ministry, proclaiming the power of Christ that she had experienced. Her witness had helped many others to undergo similar experiences. All this activity had no doubt helped to give her a sense of well-being which hid a number of unresolved problems in her heart. One day her doctor had to prescribe for her a complete rest. She found herself alone, and was horrified to discover that a number of guilty or morbid tendencies, which she had believed to have been finally liquidated, had in fact only been held temporarily at bay. The blessings of grace we receive in this world are but installments of heaven, "the guarantee of the Spirit," as St. Paul says (II Cor. 1:22).

One can imagine the distress into which her disillusion plunged our patient. Her depression returned, but this time it was still more despairing. Was the witness she had borne to her liberation all futile after all? Would not her relapse into depression raise doubts in the minds of those who had heard her witness, as it was doing in her own mind? Her doubts, and these agonizing questions, only deepened her depression.

We are touching here upon the delicate question of how far these victories of faith are absolute, and how far they are only relative. None of them is definitive, in the sense that we are thenceforth impervious to sin, doubt, and suffering. Must we then conclude that they are no more than an illusion? Certainly not, for it is only in believing in their totality that we attain that level of faith which does not suffer from relativity. In fact both the absolute and the relative are present in the Gospel.

When John the Baptist sends to ask Jesus if he is indeed the Christ, Jesus replies: "The blind receive their sight" (Matt. 11:5). He does not say: "They see a little better for a while." "Our Lord," writes Henri Bon,[6] "expressly cites the medical miracle as proof of the divine power." "The proof drawn from the miracles," my father once wrote, " . . . is as conclusive for us as it was for the witnesses themselves," but it "concerns the intellect; it operates only indirectly

[6] *Précis de médecine catholique.*

for the conversion of the heart."[7] But after the miracles in Galilee there comes the solitude of the Cross. After the proof of God by success, there comes the proof of God in failure: a paradoxical proof, but how much greater, in fact, and more absolute, despite its apparently relative character.

Here again, on the level of our human logic, all is contradiction, because the limitations of our minds will not allow us to grasp the absolute and the relative at the same time. So at one moment we bear witness to the power of the Spirit, manifested in our decisive victories, and at the next we discover the even greater witness that lies in keeping one's faith despite the collapse of one's earthly hopes.

I had no message for my patient but that proclaimed by my two theological critics: In this world the tares will always remain mixed with the good grain. The final sorting-out will be done only at harvest time, in the world to come; the Gospel is quite clear on the point. Her cure had been a wonderful experience, and she could now bear grateful witness of God's goodness by keeping her faith when the days were dark. She had been able in the past to help people by witnessing to her victory. Now, having been tested, the help she could give would perhaps be even more effective. She must remember, too, that in the flush of victory she was herself in danger of stumbling, because of the self-satisfaction with which victory so easily fills us. For it is only by realizing how much there is in us that remains unconverted, how much is still mental function ruled by instinct and self-interest, that our moral person undergoes a purifying spiritual experience.

In this world, because of the very fact of the mystery of the incarnation of the Spirit, values are never absolutely free of functions. But these same functions, even when disturbed by disease, serve as the poor but necessary instruments of the values.

---

[7] Louis Tournier, *Des miracles dans le Nouveau Testament.*

CHAPTER · 4

Grace

A young student comes to see me in the throes of a psychological crisis. He has lost interest in everything, is becoming unsociable, and finds it impossible to concentrate on his work. We use technical methods in order to throw light on the situation. They reveal a crisis of retarded adolescence in a young man who has remained morally dependent upon his parents. But he is soon telling me that he is conscious that in reality he is going through a religious crisis behind the screen of his psychological crisis. The reason why he has been unable to detach himself from his parents is that he has no strength of personality, and he feels the emptiness of an impersonal religious attitude, which he has inherited from his family tradition.

A young woman displays certain functional disturbances. Analysis of their mechanism leads us to interesting discoveries concerning a whole mass of complexes laid down in her childhood, which have vitiated her reactions. She is intelligent enough fully to understand all these analytical findings, which she sees confirmed by the flood of childhood memories that rises to her consciousness. One day, however, she admits to me that the functional trouble first made its appearance at a time when she was going through a religious crisis. She had been reluctant to talk to me about it on account of my own religious belief. She had been afraid that I might not be sufficiently neutral on the point. Before the religious crisis came along, she had come more or less to terms with all the complexes we had spent so much time analyzing. Like so many others, she had learned to live with them, and would no doubt have gone on doing so had it not been for the trigger action of a spiritual combat. To go back to the analogy of the puppets that I was using just now, it was at the moment when the Spirit called her that the secret string was stretched. My patient suddenly felt that she was not free to answer the call, which was a call to her to commit herself, to have done with a certain cowardice she felt within herself, and to witness to her faith. Shackled by her unconscious bonds, she had not been able to do this in a personal and spontaneous fashion. She had fallen back upon a conventional make-believe, which made her feel she was acting a part rather than really committing herself. I was the first to encourage her to have done with this fake piety, and to seek instead an original and personal way of expressing her faith. When she found this means of expression in art, she felt herself truly liberated.

A case such as this seems to me to illustrate clearly the necessary relationship between the technique of psychology and the cure of souls. Everybody has complexes, and comes to some sort of terms with them. When they begin to cause real suffering, this is because they are standing in the way of the realization of a person's profoundest aspirations. Such aspirations are always religious in kind— taking the word in a nonformal sense. Technical means must then be used to break up these complexes, but the real purpose of this process is to allow the person to make a free response to his aspirations.

Technology of itself is negative. "Psychoanalysis," says a letter from a patient who herself has undergone it, "reveals evil, with its hundred faces and its thousand tricks. But where is good?" I am reminded of another patient who became frightened at the great number of problems which were brought to light by our technical investigations. "What am I going to do to solve all that?" she asked anxiously. "Please, don't do anything," I replied, "your efforts would only be futile and discouraging." I do not think that the analysts will contradict me if I maintain that, strictly speaking, no problem is ever resolved. We bring them out into the daylight in order to be honest about them, for to repress them is basically to be dishonest toward oneself. "I would point out," writes a Swiss doctor, "in order to avoid a confusion that is still too frequent, even among doctors, that to repress means, not to give up a thought or a desire, but to choke it back, to bury it, to thrust it into a false oblivion." This is a wonderful verification of the biblical affirmation that sin confessed is taken away, whereas if it is hidden it continues to weigh upon the mind. A repressed tendency poisons the mind and disturbs its functioning. On the other hand, the always humbling process of bringing it out into the light opens the door to a real experience of God's grace, even if no word of religion has been uttered by doctor or patient.

People come to me for my help in "solving" their problems. No one knows better than I do that all human effort is powerless to solve any problem. In fact, when I try to understand their difficulties, I discover nothing but insoluble vicious circles. Faith is needed in order to experience God's grace, and God's grace is needed in order to find faith. Forgiveness is needed in order to love, and love is needed in order to forgive. A child must free himself from his parents in order to stand on his own feet, and to stand on his own feet he must free himself. Belief is necessary in order to pray, and prayer is necessary in order to believe. Self-confidence is needed in order to succeed, and success is needed in order to promote self-confidence.

Our patients often tell us how unjustly hurt they feel when they are plied with exhortations and advice: "You only have to believe. All you need is will power. Just love others and forget yourself. It's only a matter of confidence." Psychology cures us of this oversimplified view of personal problems. It shows us that they are tenacious and terribly complicated. And these same people who, from the security of their faith and health, are so free with their "all you need is . . ." (which always means: "All you need is to do as I do") would soon discover, if they themselves were assailed by doubt and depression, that things are not so simple.

Why is it, then, that people still come to me with their problems? It is because, although I do not believe in their solution, I do believe in their dissolution. I do not believe they can be solved technically, like a problem in arithmetic, in which one starts from established data and goes through a logical series of deductions until one arrives at the final result. Such a process in psychology would be endless, because every problem leads on to another, and whenever one tries to solve one, it is seen to depend on another that has not yet been solved. This is why technical psychoanalysis so often becomes a labor of Sisyphus. And people with mixed-up minds get a certain pleasure out of this. They fill their heads with ill-digested psychology. They turn in upon themselves, and get farther and farther away from the things of ordinary life.

Without realizing it, under the pretense of increasing their self-knowledge, they are using this analysis of details as an excuse to avoid the real stocktaking that would bring them back to life—to avoid the discovery of the real obstacle that is distorting the working of their minds: rebellion against God, perhaps, or enmity against some person, or pride or impurity. They go on endlessly analyzing. The process takes on the character of a war of position in which tactical victories are always being won, but there is never a strategic victory unless the opening of a "second front," in the form of a spiritual revolution, comes to force a decision. In an impasse of this sort, a good moral rest, sound physical treatment, positive action, and an interesting occupation will often do far more than all the subtleties of psychology.

I believe that problems can be dissolved by grace, like a mist that is dissipated by the sunshine. One sees the Christian gospel of salvation quite concretely at work in the gradual dissolution of all these tangled problems, without any of them being solved in the usual sense of the word. In the climate of faith, a life that has seemed to be nothing but a tangle of problems looks quite different. The problems disappear without anyone actually solving them. This process of dissolution is all the more definite if one does not try to find human solutions, but relies rather upon God's grace.

Then the mind, instead of concentrating sterilely on the problems, concentrates on the grace it expects: "Let him who looks for miracles fortify his faith," Goethe says in *Faust*. Once the kind of life that depends on grace has been glimpsed, it is never forgotten. I am reminded of a young woman whose marriage had plunged her into crushing and difficult problems, and who then remembered a brief stay more than ten years previously in a religious colony full of lively faith. Amidst all her distress, she was comforted by the thought that the darkest clouds could suddenly part and allow the light to shine through.

This is the way that, in my experience, technology and faith work together. Psychoanalysis explores the problems in order to bring them out into the daylight. Grace dissolves them without our ever knowing exactly how.

The experience of God's grace cannot be manufactured, you see. There is no technique available that will lead to it. I am often asked for advice on the practice of soul-healing. I have none to give. I am always in difficulties when I am faced with a soul in search of God. I never know what to do to help. I sometimes think that it is best to do nothing, because to do anything in this connection is to rely on oneself instead of on God. This is the way to lose that spontaneity of heart which is the precondition of any growth in faith. It is the quickest way to repression rather than to liberation, to crushing moral constraint rather than to inner freedom.

Furthermore, we underestimate grace if we strive by all sorts of means to get it, as if we doubted that it would be given. One day a lady came to see me. After the appointment had been made for her to come, she had met an evangelist to whom she had been able to unburden herself, and who had helped her to bring all her cares to God. I sent her away, saying: "To begin all over again would be a lack of confidence in God."

The technique of psychology is learned, it involves methods which must be studied and applied in accordance with the rules. It is valuable in clearing the ground; it helps us to see clearly and frankly what are the problems in a person's life. I sometimes think it is like emptying an untidy drawer, in which everything has been so jumbled up that it is hopeless to try to tidy it without taking everything out. Or like a piece of knitting that has to be completely undone because of mistakes made right at the beginning in casting-on, so that, using the same wool, it can be started again properly. But the constructive work, the orderly replacing of the contents of the drawer, or the new knitting, if it is to be successful, must be done otherwise than before. And this "otherwise" is not a technical matter, it is a matter of a different climate. Any technique is good, provided it is exercised in a climate of faith. The ministry of soul-healing does not finally depend on what we do for a person, but on what we are ourselves. The victory of faith must first be won in me. I must myself believe in God's grace for my patient, I must believe in his victory, in the dissolution of his problems, which are insoluble on the human level. This is not easy! Too often one pretends to believe, in order to be encouraging, without really believing. But if we do really believe, and if we communicate that faith despite every objection and every failure, relying on God's promises and on the proofs we have ourselves received of His faithfulness in our deliverance, then we see His promises fulfilled once again.

So anyone who practices a spiritual ministry is constantly recalled from the "problems of soul-healing," that is to say, from the problems of others, to the only problem that really depends on himself, the problem of his own faithfulness, of his own honesty with himself and with others.

If I am myself in contact with God, and if that contact leads me, not to self-satisfaction, but to a deepening understanding of the wiles of my mind, in which false values are always getting mixed up with the true, it is when I am really humbled by these discoveries, when I feel myself unworthy in these circumstances to claim to help others, that those others find in me the climate they need in order to experience God's grace themselves. As far as technology goes, my advice may help them. But as regards faith, my advice is of no use to them. For when we claim to give advice in matters of faith, we are, by the very fact of doing so, adopting an attitude of self-satisfaction and not of humility. But analytical technique may very well help me to track down my own secret faults. I realized one day that I was beginning to sign my name with my Christian name in full instead of merely with an initial. Why had I been covering it up like that for so long? My knowledge of psychological analysis made it easy for me to understand the cause. I saw that in spite of all I had been saying and writing for years about the Christian virtue of the acceptance of suffering, there was within me a repressed revolt against my suffering as an orphan. It showed itself in this elimination of something that might remind me of it, of something of me that came from my father: the Christian name he had chosen for me. I talked about it to a friend, and he replied at once: "Heavens! I am the same!" He suddenly saw that the same thing in himself came from the same complex.

This constant stocktaking, this deepening of consciousness, which is one of the best fruits of the conjunction of psychological technique and Christian faith, brings also a change of perspective which I should like to help the reader see in this book. It takes one from the perspective of formal moralism in which religious people are apt to isolate themselves, into the prospect of true morality. I cannot describe this change better than by quoting St. Paul's famous words: "If I give away all I have, . . . but have not love, I gain nothing" (I Cor. 13:3). Formal moralism looks at what a man does; true morality at what a man is. Formal moralism criticizes, opposes, argues; true morality understands. Formal moralism sees external appearances; true morality sees deep into the heart. Here, as I shall show in my next chapter, psychology is a great help to us. It helps us to observe in others the true virtues of the heart hidden behind an external behavior which formal moralism condemns. It helps us to see in our own hearts guilty tendencies which we try to hide under a veneer of virtue.

In the perspective of formal moralism, there is only controversy and dogmatic opposition between the technologist and the believer. In the perspective of the heart these contradictions melt away. If we stop looking at conventional labels, and look into the heart, we find ourselves quite close together. We discover that a doctor like Paul Dubois, who called himself a freethinker (or rather a free thinker, because, as he said, freethinking is a system full of prejudices), was in reality a great believer, if we consider the understanding and love he showed toward his patients and the faith he was able to give in their cure. And when he wanted to suggest a moral ideal to them, he used the words of Christ: "Love your neighbor as yourself."

Yes, if we leave the realm of dogmatic arguments and theories, we find ourselves standing side by side in the realm of observation and experience. We believers recognize the harm done by religious formalism, which the psychologists denounce, and which Christ denounced just as vigorously before them. So vigorously indeed, that he aroused the hate that crucified him. He looked into men's hearts, he discovered in those whom society rejected impulses of faith that were lacking in those who were religious and moral, and who were satisfied with themselves.

We see too that Plato, who certainly cannot be suspected of giving technology precedence over spirit, gave a perfect definition of psychoanalysis, and even spoke of the analysis of dreams: "There is in each of us," he says, "a class of desires that are monstrous, wild, and unbridled. Those desires seem to some, however, to be quite normal. They are unveiled particularly in dreams."[1] We see that all believers have weaknesses running counter to the faith they profess, that they are much more apt to obey the natural impulses which secretly control their unconscious complexes than to give free and spontaneous obedience to God. We see that they are more prone than other people to hide their weaknesses for fear of scandal, and that this

[1] *Republic*, IX.

more or less conscious duplicity aggravates their repressions and keeps their spiritual life at half pressure.

Our colleagues who are devoted to technology find that it brings them to similar conclusions. Even those who describe themselves as unbelievers know well that all men are weak and wretched; that they construct fine edifices of reason, but when it comes to the point they are carried away by their passions; that they all have their noble ideals, but are powerless to conform to them; that they seek to appear strong, but have all sorts of hidden fears in their hearts; that they all have a need to believe in something greater than themselves, and that if they do not follow the true God they fall into childish superstition. Our colleagues also recognize that science, despite all its technical progress, when brought face to face with suffering, disease, and death, affords only a limited and precarious comfort; that it has still no answer to the great mystery of the meaning of life. They know that successful medical ministration depends more upon the moral qualities of the doctor than on his technical knowledge; and that these moral qualities are the integrity, the love, the self-sacrifice, and the dignity demanded by Christ; and that a living faith that springs from the heart, and not from the lips only, can give the doctor, as well as his patients, resources of which no technical examination would permit us to suspect the existence. "Sooner or later," writes Odier, "there comes a moment when the psychotherapist, however devoted he is to his scientific principles, must become human. Whether he wishes it or no, his faithfulness to his therapeutic task constrains him to be unfaithful to his ideal of objective neutrality."

I am going to try now to define more clearly the true morality, about which it is so easy for us to come to a common understanding provided we forget all about our formal labels as believers or skeptics. But I shall first conclude this study of the relationship between faith and technology by pointing out that it has an importance of a more general kind.

The reader will understand that while I have tackled the question from the particular point of view of psychology, because it is the one which daily forces itself upon my attention, this is but one aspect of a problem that is general to our times.

Science and technology have developed enormously, and in the last century they were even looked upon as a religion. Our own generation is turning back from that illusion, and is groping once more toward those mystic pathways apart from which science and technology produce more bad fruit than good.

"Humanity groans," writes Bergson, "well-nigh crushed under the weight of its own progress."

We are so accustomed, however, to looking upon faith as being opposed to technology, that we find it difficult to imagine a reconciliation, much less a synthesis of the two. Believers are too ready to despise technology in the name of faith. And technologists too often expect to be able to do without faith, thanks to their technical skill.

The same attitude may be observed in physical medicine as in psychology. On the one hand you have idealists, both the genuine and the quack, who claim that all that is needed for healing is faith. They see the calling in of the doctor and the taking of medicines or recourse to the surgeon's knife as moral abdication and a denial of the spirit. On the other hand materialists, both the scientist and the ignoramus, see in the sick organism only a machine that has broken down, and which can be repaired by purely technical means, with which faith has no connection.

Among the sick there are some who, disappointed with the failure of orthodox science to heal them, turn to the unorthodox, both religious and secular, and discover in them an outlook on life that is quite new to them. Others, who have long been wrestling vainly in prayer, derive immense comfort from the sudden realization of the mechanical causes of their failure.

I think there is another perspective in which this opposition between faith and technology vanishes—that of the heart. Whole nations have turned technology into a veritable mystique. We need not ask these people to turn their backs on technology in order to come back to God. All we must do is to ask them to believe with us that when it is applied by men of faith it will bear even more wonderful fruit.

It is not technology that is responsible for our ills, but rather the schism between technology and the spiritual side of life. The thought of Berdyaev is extremely penetrating and suggestive on this point.[2]

Technology is neutral. It can serve good ends as well as bad. It is neither good nor bad in itself, but only according to how it is used. From the flint axe which increased the power of our distant ances-

[2] N. Berdyaev, *The Destiny of Man.*

tors, and which they could use either to kill their neighbors or to serve them better, right down to modern science—chemistry, medicine, aviation, radio—every technique can be used for good or for evil. For good and evil reside not in things and ideas, but as Christ said, in the hearts of the men who use them.

The farmer sows his wheat in the gray days of autumn.

He knows in the springtime his field will be green with thousands of little shoots, and that in summer it will turn to the gold of harvest.

He knows this because from time immemorial this phenomenon has been observed. Science can analyze this: it can study every phase of germination, growth, and fructification. It creates techniques which will increase the yield.

Faith consists in the recognition that it is God who makes the grain grow, and in loving and glorifying Him in thanksgiving.

Impiety consists in deriding God while at the same time counting upon having bread next year.

Our gluttony has made us eat too much, and we have a headache. We know that the pain will disappear if we take a pain-killing tablet. Science can study the pharmacodynamic effect of the remedy, improve it, and increase its efficacy.

Faith consists in seeing this effect, which is still essentially a mystery to us, as a blessing from God—in our thanking Him for it and repenting of our gluttony.

Impiety consists in thinking that we can give free rein to gluttony, thanks to the miracles of science, which will preserve us from its uncomfortable consequences.

A spiritual experience frees us from some functional trouble which has been weighing on our lives, perhaps excessive shyness or an inferiority complex.

Science can study the laws of suggestion which have been involved in our cure.

Faith consists in thanking God for our deliverance, and attaching ourselves to Him. And impiety consists in taking advantage of our feeling of increased strength in life by throwing our weight about.

In the remainder of this book I intend to pursue the study of the relationship between technology and faith, keeping to my own ground, that of psychology and soul-healing. But the industrialist, the educator, the artist, or the economist will doubtless be able to apply what I have to say to the problems of his own field. This problem is, after all, the same for all of us in our respective disciplines. It is the spirit of our civilization that makes us set technology over against faith. We ought to be trying instead to unite them in our minds, so that in our professional activity we may be able to work for their reconciliation.

PART II

Moralism and Morality

CHAPTER 5

Nothing Is Good or Bad in Itself

I once wrote a book whose purpose was to depict the solitude of modern man. I wrote about my own experience, and that of many others, that through spiritual victories over individualism, one can rediscover the community spirit.

Having read the book, one of my colleagues who is a distinguished psychoanalyst invited my wife and me to come in and have a talk with him.

"I must have taken the opposite road to you," he told us, in substance; "I felt so acutely the meaning and the need of community life, that I was not myself. I had identified myself at first with my parents, and then with patients in whom I was particularly interested, to such an extent that I was unable to help them because I was unable to look at them objectively. It was only after experiencing serious failures that in the course of a painful crisis I realized what was wrong, and learned to manage without company, to have the courage to be alone, and to acquire a faith independent of my environment."

My colleague was speaking the truth. What is good or bad is not solitude in itself, or community in itself. The valuable thing is the experience, diversified in form but unified in its spiritual reality, of looking honestly at oneself in order to see what is false in one's attitude, whether this attitude be a spirit of independence and a liking for solitude, or social dependence and a fear of solitude.

In my book *The Healing of Persons* I emphasized the Christian virtue of acceptance. It too is fruitful when it is the result of a victory over oneself, of the difficult process of giving up a spirit of rebelliousness and self-assertion. But I also see people who accept their lot through laziness, weakness, and fear.

Take the case of a young woman, admired for her unbounded devotion to others. She evinces symptoms of serious nervous disturbance, extreme hypertension, and insomnia, because behind her apparent renunciation there broods a storm of unadmitted irritations and personal aspirations which she dare not express. Among the services she is constantly rendering, there are some which spring from her heart, but there are many more which are unwillingly rendered, because she is afraid of refusing, for fear of upsetting her domineering mother or of spoiling her reputation as a helper of other people. Often she feels convinced that she ought to be occupying her time differently, but she is afraid to say so. Or take the case of a religious-minded woman who, for twenty years, had allowed herself to be bullied by her husband. Every time she raised an objection to any outrageous thing he wanted, he would practice a sort of emotional blackmail upon her, which aroused in her such a fear of losing his love that she backed down at once. She lost her own personality, and did not make her husband happy, because he became a tyrant and quarreled with everybody, since he could not bear to be contradicted. She worked herself to the bone for him, never taking a day's holiday, and ruined her health both physically and psychically.

Another case is that of a man who longs constantly to leave his job as a bank clerk in order to set up in a profession on his own. We observe that what is wrong is that he is too weak to assert himself in his present employment. He is the "willing horse" of whom everyone takes advantage because he has no idea how to defend himself. He sees well enough that this is not right, and blames himself. His apparent self-sacrifice is merely inertia—an inertia which is bound up with complexes dating from his childhood.

So acceptance or self-assertion are neither good nor bad in themselves. It all depends on the spirit that informs them. This is the same "change of perspective" of which I was speaking in the preceding chapter, passing from the formal perspective to the spiritual. Every discrepancy between our outward behavior and our inner feelings is both a moral fault and a psychological injury to our personality.

"For a long time I believed that renunciation was the highest expression of humanity," a woman writes. "Now I know that it is love which gives the soul its length, breadth, and depth, and that renunciation is only significant when it is the expression of a great love." Indeed, true love is the only thing that is good in itself. But I would have you mark the word "true," because we all know that there are affections that are jealous and possessive.

So self-abnegation may be a victory over selfishness; it can also be an unworthy escape. Self-assertion can equally well be rebellion or obedience to stout-hearted conviction. The trouble is that these motives, legitimate as well as illegitimate, are always mixed up together in our hearts.

In 1937 I realized that God was asking me to break out of my comfortable professional routine and to undertake a new work of experiment and thought in search of a Christian view of medicine. In full agreement with my wife, I faced the risk of being misunderstood by many of my colleagues, lonely in my beliefs, criticized by many of my friends, exposed to financial difficulties and to the anguish of not knowing which route to follow among all the problems surrounding me. It was certainly an act of obedience, and it has borne much fruit. Nevertheless I was later to come to see that it contained, hidden within it, several of my habitual sins. My proud liking for doing something extraordinary; my readiness to avoid the simple humdrum routine of ordinary medical practice; in a word, what I call my complex against normal life.

So, in the Christian life—and this is what makes it a constant and thrilling adventure—we are always discovering new facets of our own minds. Secret faults are always coming and insinuating themselves into our most costly acts of obedience.

A certain young woman was obliged, in order to earn her living, to do work which was beyond her strength. She had real artistic talent, but her unjust hours of work left her practically no time to cultivate it, and when she might have had time, she was so overwrought that she lacked the calm necessary for success. For years I encouraged her to accept her trial patiently. If God had some other plan for her, I said, he would show it to her. Her acceptance bore much fruit in her inner life.

But a colleague who shared her treatment with me said to me one day: "Might this not really be weakness rather than self-abnegation? Is it right that she should always be sacrificing herself to employers who see it as quite natural that she should comply with whatever they demand?" These were useful questions, because they meant that the whole problem must be re-examined in prayer. I then perceived that this young woman had so thoroughly renounced the idea of ever changing her employment, that she now felt doing so would involve disobeying God. Now, God shows us the way we should follow when we are ready in our hearts to say "Yes," and also when we are ready to say "No," whether we are ready for patient acceptance or for the risks of combat. Two days later, in fact, that girl received an offer of a new job, in which more reasonable hours of work would leave her with the free time she had been deprived of for so long.

Another young woman, who lived with her parents, but only at the cost of continual irritations, was toying with the idea of leaving home. But she too supposed that I should look upon her departure as the coward's way out. An incidental question gave me the opportunity of undeceiving her. I told her that I had no idea whether God wanted her to stay or go. She was greatly surprised to hear this. The Bible commanded her to honor her father and mother; it said nothing about living with them. It was by no means certain that she honored them more by living with them rather than elsewhere.

We can see God's plan for us only if we get rid of all preconceived ideas about it, since they are likely to contain much more human prejudice than true inspiration. Then instead of asking ourselves, on the level of formal moralism, whether such and such a decision is good or bad in itself, we can turn to an examination of the underlying motives for the decision. In moving thus from conventional moralism to true morality, we can see that an action is, in general, neither good nor bad in itself, but only in relation to the sentiments that inspire it. It is clear that this "change of perspective" does not lead to moral relativism. On the contrary, it involves a much more exacting morality. For example, it often shows up so-called virtues as a cover-up for secret sins.

Such is the case with a young woman who seems to be completely submissive to her mother, and who will avoid doing anything at all that would displease her. She sees that this is nothing more than an external psychological compensation for a deep sense of grievance against her mother. Her apparent submissiveness does nothing to assuage her sense of grievance, which goes on gnawing at her subconscious, and disturbs her whole psychic balance.

Such, too, is the case with a mother who has a baby she does not want. Deep within her she harbors a secret resentment against the child. The unbalanced and exaggerated nature of the love with which she surrounds him is merely a compensation for her veiled hostility.

There are wives who poison their husbands' lives with their jealousy and constant suspicion, and end up by pushing them in desperation into adulterous adventures. But another will take such a liberal-minded attitude to her husband's infidelities, for fear of losing him, that he finds himself left alone in the face of temptation, and he gives in.

We are all very often insincere. But a certain young woman is so beset by doubts about herself that she becomes obsessed with the idea of being absolutely sincere. As a result, she loses all spontaneity.

We all commit sins of pride daily. A certain mother has a reputation for humility. She sees that it is only a camouflage behind which she hides in order to avoid the responsibilities of life.

There are husbands who avoid responsibility by escaping into a frivolous way of living. But I remember one who was such a slave to duty, social convention, and carefulness over money, that his wife found herself living in an atmosphere that was morally stifling. She would no doubt have preferred a husband who was less virtuous but had more warmth of heart.

A certain student is tremendously keen to be helpful. He comes to see, however, that the errands he runs for his mother are really just excuses for interrupting preparation for his examinations.

An idealist takes pleasure in high-minded meditation and humanitarian projects. But he comes to see that what he is really doing is avoiding action and the necessity of facing up to the realities of his life. As Spoerri says,[1] instead of making the spiritual incarnate, he floats comfortably between heaven and earth.

Lastly, there is the mother of a family who suffered in her childhood from the social disgrace her father brought on himself. She has never forgiven him; and now she sees that this is the underlying cause of her inflexible insistence on perfection, both for herself and for her children. They have got to the point where they can stand it no longer.

I could prolong this list with many more illustrations of all kinds. Generosity, for example, may be a spiritual victory over natural cupidity; but it may also be motivated by all sorts of false sentiments

[1] Théophile Spoerri, *Notre Père.*

—the vanity of maintaining a flattering reputation for disinterestedness, perhaps, either in general or in regard to some social activity through which one is seeking public favor; the desire to appear rich or the fear of admitting that one is not; the lack of a sense of responsibility; a spirit of contradictiousness in regard to a wife or a prudent father; a reaction of disappointment or vengeance over money; or perhaps an unconscious desire to reduce one's possessions in order to disinherit a hated child.

Even more disturbing is the examination of the motivations which may underlie even the most successful spiritual ministry.

I have seen a fair number of people founder in an illicit relationship when they sincerely thought they were pursuing a spiritual mission in trying to save some wayward soul, and have become too attached to the person in question. And when they realize that instead of rescuing the person they have been allowing themselves to be dragged down into the abyss, and I have recommended the complete breaking off of the relationship, they tell me that they still have scruples about abandoning a person in distress whom God has led them to encounter along the way.

A desire to dominate others can also creep into a vocation to a spiritual ministry. One often sees this in the case of new converts who, even before they have worked out the consequences for their own lives of their new-found faith—and sometimes in order to escape them—try to impose it upon all those around them, and get annoyed if they meet with resistance. Lastly, pride in brilliantly serving a good cause may also play its part. One recalls the remark of a great preacher when one of his parishioners, congratulating him on his sermon, said admiringly: "You were magnificent!" The preacher replied: "The devil has already told me so!"

On the other hand, when one examines people's lives honestly, one discovers good qualities hiding behind appearances that are universally condemned. So, a woman is constantly accused of coquettishness, and I find that it is really her innate liking for beautiful things. Evil be to him who evil thinks!

Another woman lives in a stiflingly conventional atmosphere, and her extravagance, which is severely condemned, is the expression of a need for healthy fantasy and spontaneity—which her judges could well do with more of!

A young man professes extreme political opinions which give deep offense to the other members of his family, but which have not for him, if one looks into the matter closely, the significance of rebellion and hate which is attributed to them, but rather a sincere and heartfelt aspiration toward justice.

A child is brought to me for persistent lying, and I find that it is his love for his parents that has led him into it—his parents are in conflict, and he has turned to dissimulation in the hope, albeit a vain one, of pacifying them.

We can say similarly that many of the events in a person's life are good or bad only in accordance with the spirit in which they are accepted or undergone.

On the formal level we classify events as being good or bad according to whether they are favorable to us or not. This is, of course, true. But on a deeper level, it is our underlying attitude to them that matters. We suffer an injustice: if we are made rebellious by it, it arouses evil in our hearts; if we can bear it unselfishly, it becomes, on the contrary, the occasion of a rich inner experience. We win a success: if it provokes us to pride, it is fatal for us; if it makes us work even harder, it is good. Seen from this angle, objectively, good events are sometimes revealed as harmful, while others, thought to be bad, turn out to have good results. Everything can be useful, and everything can be harmful, according to the spirit in which a person reacts. The spirit of formal moralism leads to the accentuation of external events, the spirit of true morality leads to the realization of personal responsibility. Both are right, because everything in this world has a twofold cause, external and internal.

But nothing is so useful as the discovery that our recriminations about external events have helped us divert our attention from our own inner unease. "I thought," a schoolgirl writes, "that it was my old classroom that was getting me down; it was so dark and dismal. Now I am in a different room, and it feels just the same."

A certain man has high moral ideals. He is afraid of betraying them under the impulse of his sensual appetites. So he launches prematurely into engagement and marriage. But his motive is fear, and fear blinds us. He recognizes this later on, when serious marital troubles crop up. Another man delays marriage because in his case he is afraid of material difficulties, and wishes to be in a steady job before he marries the girl he loves. But his capacity for love becomes exhausted and warped in a long bachelor life which has degenerated into a series of sterile and fruitless affairs.

People are always coming to us with questions of principle. Is it right to marry young or not? Are you for or against eating meat, dancing, or psychoanalysis? The most usual reply is that it all depends on the spirit in which one acts.

Take, for example, educational controversies.

Some people inveigh against the harmful effects of severity and authoritarianism, since it is only by feeling himself free, by undergoing even painful experiences, that the child acquires a sense of moral responsibility and learns to take the initiative in life.

Others point to the dangers of indulgence and liberty, since without solid habits of discipline, left at the mercy of every kind of bad influence, the child never learns self-control.

Both are right.

The same arguments arise over timetables, the balance between brainwork and physical exercise, and the giving of marks—which can distort the child's attitude, and yet without which he loses all sense of effort and of self-discipline in his work.

In every one of those who tell me their life stories, the analysis of their childhood memories throws light on their present difficulties, and shows the origin to lie in "faulty upbringing."

One patient is incapable of decision because his parents always decided everything for him. They chose his friends, his clothes, his career, and organized his recreation. Another is incapable of decision because his parents left him to himself and to his uncertainty and inexperience in face of important decisions about his future. He sees the pros and cons of everything.

One man is undisciplined because his parents weighed him down with so many rules and regulations, and surrounded him with so many prohibitions. Now that he is grown up he is taking his revenge in a reaction that is quite instinctive. He wants to try everything, even those things which his conscience condemns; he flies in the face of all the social conventions, and has such an appetite for fantasy that he is incapable of tackling anything methodically. Another is undisciplined because his parents gave his every caprice free rein, and allowed him to fall into habits of disorder, unreliability, and dissipation which he cannot now break. When the age of adolescence arrives, it is too late for his parents to act. The authority they abdicated when he was a child cannot be suddenly exerted now. The only thing is to send him to an institution where someone else will impose discipline upon him.

Most young people nowadays suffer from the abdication of paternal authority. Lecomte du Noüy, in his *Avenir de l'esprit*, has said that we ought to be strict with the small child, in order to allow him more liberty as his reasoning faculties develop. Most parents do the opposite: they allow complete liberty to their children in the early years, and even find their stupidities charming. When the child grows older and they see what their policy is leading to, they try to be more severe. But it is too late, and the child rebels.

One patient is timid because his mother was afraid on his account, and brought him up in a continual state of fear of all the dangers that might threaten him. Another is timid because he has lacked that feeling of being protected which the child needs in order to face the hostility and mystery of life.

One patient is vindictive because he has been brought up in an atmosphere of continual self-justification, criticism, and rebellion against all the injustices of life. Another is vindictive because, when he was the victim of some injustice, his parents never gave him the feeling that they were on his side. He felt misunderstood, or even that his parents were readier to believe other people's versions of the incident than his own.

One patient is sensitive because his parents made a great fuss over anything that hurt him, and encouraged him in an attitude of self-pity. Another is sensitive because he has not been shown sufficient sympathy. I remember a young woman, for example, who became very depressed as a result of the breaking-off of her engagement, thinking that she was having to bear her grief alone. In fact, her parents were weeping for her in secret, but in front of her they put on an appearance of indifference for fear of making her worse.

One patient complains of having been left in ignorance of sex, of having had to unravel its mystery on his own and of having been given a wrong attitude to it as a result of all the misunderstandings and dangerous, painful experiences which he might have been spared. Another's parents were so anxious to protect him from such experiences that they have implanted a fear of sex in him. The solemnity with which they laid before him the dangers of masturbation, of sexual perversions, or of venereal disease, the books they made him read, in which these dangers were explained in lurid detail, have implanted all sorts of obsessive fears in him—of woman as a sly temptress, of homosexuality, of unfitness for marriage after having fallen so frequently into the temptation of impurity, of his eternal damnation. A certain man had been persuaded by his mother, while quite young, to swear an oath to remain chaste until marriage, and to confess to her at once if ever he gave way to the temptation of masturbation. His oath had weighed so heavily on his mind that he had become obsessed with sex. His obsession had brought countless lapses in its train, and he had been unable to confess the fact either to his mother or to anyone else. The shame of having violated his oath undermined his moral resistance. Now married, he is impotent. Another, on the other hand, read a very well-intentioned book which set out to show the divine meaning of sex. It showed that the harmonious development of the sex life between husband and wife is essential to their physical, psychological, and moral health, and to the solidity of their home. The result in him of all this was such a fear of not being able to attain so high a standard that he became obsessed with the idea of impotence, and actual impotence resulted.

The parents of one patient were so worried about moral danger, that they kept a tight watch over all his friendships, forbade his attendance at dances, controlled all his activities, and refused to allow him to spend any holidays abroad. The result was that he was so naïve that he fell into the trap of the first adventuress he met. Another was corrupted when still a child by a perverted housemaid, undergoing all kinds of evil influences and degrading adventures.

One was so constantly warned against the faults of each of the girls he met that he lost all spontaneity and simplicity of heart. He cannot even trust the woman he has married. Another blames his parents for having carelessly allowed him to contract a premature marriage. He was blinded by his young love, and the inevitable disillusionment was catastrophic.

I could go on giving endless examples of this sort. The daily, objective examination of all these life stories convinces me that there is no principle or system of upbringing that is good in itself. All have their dangers and their advantages. Everything depends on the spirit in which they are applied. Thus an authority on the fundamentals of mental hygiene in early childhood writes: "Our advice and influence ought to be aimed less at the child than at the environment that educates and nurtures him."

One recalls the story of Aesop, whose master Xanthus had ordered him to prepare the most perfect dish on earth. Aesop served up a dish of tongue, for, he said, the tongue is the instrument of the mind, of the most beautiful poems and the noblest thoughts. But when his master ordered him to serve the most abominable dish possible, Aesop once more gave him tongue, saying that it was the poisoned instrument of calumny, falsehood, and blasphemy.

Jesus said: "Out of the heart come evil thoughts, murder, adultery, fornication, theft, false witness, slander" (Matt. 15:19).

CHAPTER 6

It All Depends on the Spirit

You give a child advice. Your state of mind is far more important than the advice itself. You may be inspired by fear—the fear that he is "turning out badly." In this case you will suggest the fear to him, even without formulating it. And your advice, however proper it may be, by turning his thoughts toward evil, gives power to the evil. If, however, you are inspired by prudent and trusting wisdom, this same advice will be useful.

You have to punish a child. You know well that you can do it in anger. You will then work out of your own system the irritation his misdemeanor has caused in you. Or you may be avenging yourself unconsciously for punishments you yourself received in childhood. In such a case the effect of the punishment will not be to correct him, but to arouse rebellion in him. But it may also be a proper sense of your educational responsibility which prompts you to punish him, without any question of your being angry. In this case it is your love for the child that inspires you, and the punishment will be fruitful.

Similarly, indulgence can be a form of moral abdication on the part of parents. It may, however, be a mark of their confidence in the child, by which he learns self-control.

There are fathers whose severity is nothing but tyranny, the means by which they get their own back for the tyranny they themselves suffer at the hands of their wives or their superiors at work. There are some, however, in whom severity is the fruit of a victory over themselves and over their naturally easygoing nature. In the first case severity is destructive, in the second it helps the child put his own inner energy to work.

The same thing is true of psychological perspicacity. The more we study the human mind and learn to know its secret motivations, the more sincerely, even, we try to recognize the real and often murky currents in our own hearts, the more do we develop in ourselves this psychological and moral clairvoyance. We discover in fact that sins are often hidden behind what we thought were good qualities, and that genuine treasures of the mind underlie what we have looked upon as failings. This perspicacity can, however, be used for both good and evil, depending on the spirit that animates us. It is for good if we use it in order to unmask ourselves and to understand others. It is for evil if we use it in order to justify ourselves, and criticize others. And so the study of psychology may wonderfully fertilize the ministry of soul-healing in a person who is inspired by a true vocation of love. It can also turn the practitioner into a misanthrope and a pitiless critic, seeing only evil everywhere, even in those who are most sincere and well-intentioned.

I know there are people who look in my books for a means of better self-knowledge and a road to a more lively faith. But I know also that there are some who are chiefly struck by some passage because it confirms the severe judgment they have made in the case of some relative or friend.

A young woman comes to see me. Straightway she asks me if I consider the movies to be compatible with the Christian life. You can guess my reply: It all depends on the spirit in which one goes to them. One can go from a pure and legitimate love of art; one can go in order better to understand the drama of human life, which the cinema often depicts with great truth; one can even go without any personal interest in the movie, but simply in order to accompany a friend—and that can be a more telling testimony of one's affection than grand phrases. But one can also go from unhealthy curiosity, from selfish passion, as an escape from reality, or through sensuality.

The same is true of dancing, and of many other analogous problems about which my opinion is often sought. In every case what one must do is to take these formal questions back to the real problems underlying them.

The other day one of my friends told me of how he had given the same book to several young people. In accordance with their inner dispositions, some had found in it only positive and uplifting thoughts, while others had dwelt upon the disturbing and depressing passages.

But let us take care not to draw from such observations a liberal doctrine which also could have very harmful effects. To allow a child to read a questionable book, on the grounds that he will see in it only those things that are in accordance with his own tendencies, could lead to moral disaster. To go to a questionable show, flattering oneself that one is impervious to its subtle poison, is to deceive oneself. For evil lies in wait in all our hearts, needing only to be fed in order to grow fat, and using all kinds of ruses to procure its food! That is why, in spite of everything, the Church, which is charged with the task of guiding us inconstant and impulsive human beings, must formulate morality. There are laws in life. "You know well," a friend of mine used to say, "that if you lean too far out of a sixth-floor window you risk falling into the street." Similarly, however sincere people may be, they risk the most serious disasters if their consciences are not enlightened by the Church's warnings. This has been clearly shown in the sphere of sexual morality in marriage by a doctor's treatise on the doctrine of the Roman Catholic Church on this subject.[1]

Never let us say, therefore, that nothing is good or bad in itself, without adding the rider that it all depends on the spirit which animates us! The aphorism that nothing is good or bad in itself is, I believe, true. But I know that it too can be used for evil as well as good ends. It can be the pretext for a moral skepticism which serves as a cover for all kinds of wickedness. But it may also be the expression (and I need hardly say that this is the sense in which I use it here) of a much more exacting morality than mere formal moralism.

For me, it is bound up with the absolute standard of biblical morality. One might say that from time to time in history this absolute standard is lost and then rediscovered. Under the guidance of the Spirit, believers become aware of it once again, and feel how hollow their petty conventional morality is in the face of God's demand for total self-giving and his concern with what is in men's hearts. Then all at once they are liberated from formal moralism, and are led to a personal discipline that is infinitely more severe.

[1] A. Maget, *Médecine et mariage.*

Then the flame of the Spirit gradually fades, and the living, burning, free morality which they have forged becomes crystallized once more in hollow traditions and a narrow formalism that crushes the spirit, and to which people submit without any real, lively conviction in their hearts. The Church slips back into scholasticism, and loses much of its influence upon society. What is needed then is the rediscovery of the absolute standard of the morality taught by the Christian Gospel.

Without wishing to oversystematize, since these problems are applicable to all periods of time, I believe that we are at a period in which the religious world stands in urgent need of this rediscovery. To our contemporaries, churchmen seem to be self-satisfied, content to observe a few formal principles, to engage in theological debates, and to practice traditional forms of piety, none of which has any influence on their real lives. They become lost in minor scruples and fail to observe their complete failure in large and all-important areas of Christian morality. They appear to put their trust in a doctrine of gradual improvement, and no longer look for the revolutionary explosion of the Gospel, which bursts wide open the compromises of society. Theodore Bovet vividly describes the distinction between moralism and the "salvation" of which the Gospel speaks. The former consists in "trying to be good by ourselves, that is to say, fixing ourselves the limits of good and evil . . . , but this very effort makes us self-satisfied, and turns us away from God." The second consists in a "change of heart," a return to God. These two levels are, he says, coexistent but always separate, just as on the radio one can go from one station to another by turning the knob, but one program will never of itself gradually change into another.[2]

Psychoanalysts have pointed out the enormous number of cases of psychological breakdown that are found to occur in religious families, and which are due to religious, moral, and social formalism. I owe it to truth, and even to the Church I love, to join my voice to theirs. It is certainly true that the majority of neuroses are found in "right-thinking" families. I could give some poignant examples. I have before me at this moment more than a dozen typical cases. Patients whose fathers or mothers were pillars of the Church or of society, and whose behavior in private—where the child could observe it at

[2] Theodore Bovet, *Sur la terre comme au ciel.*

leisure—was in flagrant contrast with what one would have expected of them.

The same pattern may be observed time and time again: religious formalism on the part of the father, social formalism on the part of the mother; in either case there is that fear of "what people will say," which overrules everything else, and kills all true feeling. You can imagine the damage done to the child, and the way in which such an upbringing deprives him of all moral bearings, doing lasting psychological harm. It is not difficult to see why they lose their faith. One of my patients confessed to me one day that her complaint against her father, a pious churchman, was not so much the irregular life he led, as the fact that because of it she had been turned away from the faith she would have liked to come back to, but could not, because of all the terrible memories she had. She could no longer bear to open her Bible, because she had so often heard it solemnly read after the most awful family scenes. And when these children rebel, and dare to show that they are not taken in by such hypocrisy, they arouse the anger of the father, who uses his authority to silence them. Or else the child tries to get away from home. He asks to be sent to a boarding school, only to meet a flat refusal on the part of the father. I have here an account of a child who, in similar circumstances, was so bold as to persist in her request, so awful had life at home become for her. Her father's reaction was to send her to see a priest, whom he had forewarned, and who then duly told the girl that religion required her complete submission to her father.

The father of one of my patients used to beat her because she refused to go to Sunday school.

One feels intense pity for those people whose lives have been broken by such childhood tragedies. And their parents go on being covered with social honors, presiding over charitable committees, surrounded by admiring men and women. In the name of their religious principles they forbid their children all recreation on Sundays, dancing, and theaters. The child either bows his head and becomes for the rest of his life a passive, shy "goody," lacking in personality and drive; or else he becomes a rebel, in continual conflict with society—with all authority and all discipline—and ends up as a failure.

It will be objected that these are individual cases from which it is unsafe to generalize. I agree. And as a doctor I can also imagine the pathological factors which lie behind the behavior of such parents. But these cases are too numerous for the doctor not to be struck by them. I do not believe I am mistaken when I say that this pattern is to be observed more frequently in religious families than in others. In any case, the flagrant contradiction between the behavior of the parents and the faith they profess and their official role in church life makes the emotive shock to the child much more serious. We know what conclusions our agnostic colleagues draw from these facts. It would not become the Church to blame them for this. We must be honest, and honesty here can only make us say *mea culpa*. These facts raise for the Church a serious problem of conscience, from which she cannot escape by pointing to their exceptional or pathological character.

But the tragedies of formalism are more widespread still. It is often a case of morally correct parents, in the conventional sense, who burden their children with all the "do's and don't's" which are the sum of their relationship with them. They never show any desire to stop and consider the subtle and moving mystery of these developing minds, or try to understand the reason for the reactions they are so quick to condemn out of hand, or to guess at their children's aspirations and disappointments. Others are so full of worldly and social activities that they never have time for serious conversation with their children. They are busy with good works, delivering lectures on education, but knowing nothing of the tragedies that are taking place in their own homes—children who are suffering sexual shocks due to brothers and sisters, to lodgers, to servants, or who simply have no one in whom to confide their little childish troubles, which to them are very great. Teaching their children how to behave "properly," and scolding them when their school reports are bad, is the limit of most parents' efforts at bringing up their children. They would, no doubt, be most surprised if one were to point this out to them, because they have never imagined that their children might have all kinds of thoughts different from their own, and in any case they are secure in the thought that their position as parents and as honorable members of society means they must be right. And so they never ask themselves any questions. And even where children receive a good education—I ought to say a good training—there comes a time when they realize that their whole life is regulated, not by personal conviction, but by a desire to please their parents. This is a moment of great crisis for such children. They have an overpowering urge to kick over the traces, merely in order to prove to themselves that they are themselves. When the thing has been done—and often it is some insignificant and silly indiscretion, though sometimes it is serious and compromising—they get no satisfaction from it, because it is not the expression of a free and conscious personal will. This is why one sometimes sees worthy gentlemen who occupy an honored place in society breaking out in some childish escapade on account of which they find themselves in the police station, or at the age of forty indulging in some vulgar sentimental adventure on the pretext that they have "never had any youth."

More often, however, they do not have the courage to throw off the yoke of their formalist upbringing in this way, so firmly has habit made them its prisoners. A young woman falls back on a modest symbolic act: she smokes a cigarette all alone in her room, without even enjoying it. It is her harmless way of protesting against her strict upbringing! But her upbringing has implanted in her such an exaggerated idea of "duty" that even her cigarette seems to her to be an irritating duty! She is quite astonished when I tell her to smoke if it gives her any pleasure, and not to smoke if it does not. In this connection, I have been told that at the meeting at Ermatingen in 1931, which marked the beginning of a great spiritual movement in my country, there were among those present two men: one threw his cigarettes into Lake Constance, as a concrete symbol of his will to break with all compromise and slavery; the other lit the first cigarette of his life, as a symbol of his liberation from the formalism which had been stifling all his spontaneity of heart.

The serious thing about religious formalism is that it is an unnatural behavior, a seeming morality, which does not spring from the heart. And so it becomes the source of all those repressions which the psychoanalysts denounce. "Even worse than hate," writes one of my patients, "is the pretense of forgiveness; even worse than immorality is the pretense of morality!" She describes the fruitless effort to obey a moral code, without grace. Feeling that one is not succeeding, one experiences an inner unease for which one compensates by a pretense of perfection. Thus one of my patients, a victim of depression, was assured by a friend that when we are "converted," as the latter claimed to be, Satan has no more hold over us. You can imagine the sort of doubt about her own conversion this raised in my patient's mind. Another of my patients, who quite recently underwent an important spiritual experience, told me of the strange impression made on her when she was young by the lady with whom she was in service. This lady was inordinately fond of discoursing on religion, and used to talk to her about the life of abandonment to God's guidance, but at the same time she used to consult clairvoyants and fortunetellers. I am always astonished to see into what childish superstitions educated people can fall—even teachers, university men, and others reputed for their piety, who when they come to see me will bring their horoscopes with them to help me in my investigations.

And then, what Christian does not go through periods when the flame of his true inner piety burns low? Unfortunately it is those who are looked upon as spiritual leaders—ecclesiastics, church councilors, and deaconesses—who are the least willing to admit it, for fear of causing others to stumble. They have to fight their battles all alone, and continue to officiate. These are the dramas of formalism, and sometimes they are tragedies indeed!

Every discord between form and substance, between what others see and the reality of the heart, is a denial of the Gospel and can only be a source of psychological trouble. "Being a Christian," Zwingli used to say, "is not chatting about Christ, but living as he lived." Obviously what we must do is not reject empty forms, but replenish them with the spirit, to rediscover the absolute demands of true morality. Simplicity means the harmony of form and substance. There can be nothing but insoluble problems and complexity in a life seeking to maintain the external structure of a superimposed moralism that does not spring from the conversion of the heart. Everything becomes simple once again when this essential harmony is rediscovered, even if the outer façade then looks much less imposing.

In our day this formalism is particularly prevalent in the domain of sex. We see religious people who are willing to hold out the hand of forgiveness and mercy to any sinner, to devote themselves with understanding love to the rescue of the alcoholic, but who have nothing but contempt for the slightest sexual misdemeanor. A pious wife, who would be ready to forgive all kinds of failings in her husband, tells me she could not pray with him until he has broken off a certain irregular association. And she sincerely believes that in this inflexible attitude she is obeying the commands of the Gospel.

Whereas Christ showed himself so severe in regard to disloyalty, self-righteousness, and hardheartedness, and so merciful toward prostitutes and adulteresses, most Christians behave in the contrary manner. They seem to be afraid of nothing for their children except sexual sins, and inculcate in them a negative attitude toward the whole subject of sex—God's masterpiece. Sex equals sin: this is the attitude drummed into them from early childhood, not only by words, but also by those mysterious silences and awkward moments which often have to do with the parents' own indiscipline in matters of sex. One cannot help noticing that those who live disordered lives where sexual morality is concerned are usually much more warmhearted, generous, and kind than all your moral rigorists. Let me not be misunderstood: in saying this I do not wish to encourage sexual immorality. But doctors have been horrified to discover how many tenacious complexes can be traced back to a formalist upbringing. One of my patients had been engaged to be married for a whole year without ever being allowed to see her fiancé unless her mother was there as well! It is not hard to understand why she did not find married life easy.

And then there is the formalism of certain religious institutions, in which everything is regulations and duties, with no warmth of heart or affectionate understanding for each other's difficulties. In that milieu, the person who confesses a fault, far from finding the acceptance which forgives and holds out the hand of succor, meets only inflexible condemnation, while the cunning one who keeps up appearances and hides his sins is held up as an example.

And there is the formalism of some charitable organizations, in which warmhearted zeal has given way to the rigidity of administrative regulation. From the social point of view we claim that the factory worker should no longer be treated as an anonymous machine, a mere number, but as a human person who should have the sense of his own worth restored to him. But nowhere, perhaps, do the disinherited feel more as if they were being treated as mere numbers, with less regard to their dignity as human beings, than in the offices of some charitable organizations.

"In the matter of social welfare," a friend of mine remarked recently, "it is not so much what one does that matters, as how it is done and in what spirit it is done."

There are philanthropic committees in which worldly vanity and intrigue abound. There are socialites who make a point of visiting the sick and the poor, without making any real contact with them. "The atmosphere is stifling," a woman writes, "amidst all these self-satisfied people who refuse to see that their privileges are paid for by the sufferings of the disinherited, and who cling to conventions from which all life has vanished. Yes, indeed, there is something rotten in Christianity." As La Rochefoucauld said, "Virtue would not go so far if vanity did not keep it company."

I have been the recipient of the confidences of countless social workers who have been going through terrible crises of conscience. Their idealism made them take up a career of service, and now they realize that the whole present system, despite its technical efficiency —perhaps because of it—condemns them to play the part of cold officials, in whom warmth of heart has no place, and is even frowned upon. You can see why so many people today feel they are being suffocated by our formalist society, in which technical organization kills life, so that they become rebels, unproductive nonconformists, persecuted by society. Even law is experiencing this universal crisis of our times. "The crisis of law is a crisis of faith," says one of our lawyers.

You can understand the grave reactions of doctors, confidants as they are of the weak, the neurotic, and the poor. Before the psychoanalysts, Dubois, of Berne,[3] inveighed powerfully against the pitiless spirit of criticism in which hypocritical society strikes at the neuropath, against the unjust and ineffective moral sermonizing which appeals uselessly to his disabled will, when a little love, understanding, and brotherliness would restore him to health. There is a certain piquancy in the fact that a doctor who declared himself to be an atheist, in speaking against all this formalism, at the same time as he appealed to scientific determinism which denies that these patients are more blameworthy than honorable burghers, invoked the teaching of Christ. Christ, in fact, is constantly appealing to faith, to love, to confidence, to inward truth; he liberates the soul from the yoke of moralism. Long before the psychoanalysts he was denouncing the wickedness in the hearts of the Pharisees—whitewashed sepulchers— which they kept hidden beneath their severe and impeccable exterior.

One day a young woman tells me that she feels an inner compul-

[3] Dubois, *Les psychonévroses et leur traitement moral.*

sion to declare herself once and for all for Christ and to seal her decision with a solemn promise. And this she does—in prayer. But a few days later I find her in a state of great distress. Timidly she confesses that she feels now that everything she does for Christ is done in order to keep her promise, and not from a spontaneous love for him. Nevertheless she loves him with all her heart. You can guess that I wasted no time in releasing her from her promise, only too glad to see her go from the realm of the law into that of faith and of grace.

CHAPTER · 7

True Morality

Obviously, however, in order to become a more lively Christian it is not enough merely to turn one's back on the moral law. What we must do is not to defy this law, but to rediscover its source in the person of Jesus Christ. It then becomes more absolute and consistent, losing at the same time its character of formal constraint. It stops being a system, a tradition, an end in itself, and becomes the spontaneous effect of a burning love for God and for men.

I have already pointed out that those who react against the hollow formalism of their environment by running counter to it are not thereby either freer or happier. They are not more free, because they are driven by their rebelliousness and antagonism against their environment; and not more happy, because there is an objective moral truth, which can never be violated with impunity. This destruction of moral standards and of the framework of society which occurs when people react against moral formalism is probably one of its worst consequences. On the grounds that one is fighting against formalism in morality, one can destroy everything—all law, all morality, and all tradition. The result is not the triumph of the spirit, but chaos. We can understand how all those people suffering from nervous diseases, of whom I have been speaking, are in rebellion against the moralism which has been such a dead weight on their upbringing. But this does not mean that they are not people of rich personal qualities. Having broken with traditional discipline, they are tossed about by their impulses and passions; they are negative and inconstant, in a perpetual state of distress and discontent with themselves, unless a change of heart comes to re-establish a firm basis for their lives. Then, in new

69

ways that are different from the empty traditions by which they have been hemmed in before, they rediscover in their turn the age-old demands of true morality. They understand at last what sin really is—not a catalogue of social conventions, but, as Spoerri says, "everything that hinders the advent of the kingdom of God." Then too they discover that the rigidity and austerity of the old traditions—I am thinking of my own country, of my own city of Geneva—are not without their virtue, for they were forged in their beginning, in spite of everything, by men who were led by the spirit. It is still the same spirit that must be rediscovered, so that morals will be given new life, and not destroyed.

There is a continuity in history, and nations which think they can build everything anew without taking account of it, only bring disaster upon themselves.

A man who is a leading figure in the movement for the reform of modern education once told me of the origin of his vocation, in his sufferings as a sensitive child in the old type of formalist, traditionalist school. He left school determined to give up study altogether, to qualify in life, and not in examinations. But he would have remained a lonely outsider if he had not relented. He took up study once again, went to the university, and was led into a fruitful, though revolutionary career.

The great danger in systematic opposition to social conformity is individualism, an incapacity to take part in anything at all. "I don't like that," was the reply given by one of my patients to all my suggestions as to the institutions, activities, and careers she might interest herself in, since she was bored with having nothing useful to do in life. And then, however much one may rebel against one's environment, one retains its marks. It remains the nursery ground from which the sap of childhood was drawn. If we are taken away from it, it always leaves an indefinable nostalgia in our hearts. How many men there are who have reacted against their environment by taking a wife from a quite different background. At first they are indignant when their wives are cold-shouldered, and they denounce such narrow formalism all the more vehemently. But as the years pass they come to realize that their wives cannot respond to the cultural and spiritual needs which their own upbringing, in spite of themselves, has awakened in them.

Perhaps if I touch upon the difficulty in which I find myself in the presence of a certain kind of marital conflict, I shall be better able to define this delicate process of conciliation between the inescapable, public, objective morality and the love, free of all formalism, which is enjoined upon us by the Gospel. A friend is getting a divorce. Naturally he takes a line critical of formal conventionalism in order to justify his action. He maintains that he is being more honest than all those who, through fear of what people will say, are morally divorced but dare not make the situation legal. I cannot approve of his course of action, because divorce is always disobedience of God. I should be betraying my belief if I were to hide it from him. I know that there is always a solution other than divorce to a marital conflict, if we are really prepared to seek it under God's guidance. But I know that this disobedience is no worse than the slander, the lie, the gesture of pride of which I am guilty every day. The circumstances of our lives are different, but the reality of our hearts is the same. If I were in his place, would I act any differently from him? I have no idea. At least I know that I should need friends who loved me unreservedly just as I am, with all my weaknesses, and who would trust me without judging me. If he gets his divorce, he will no doubt meet even greater difficulties than those he is in today. He will need my affection all the more, and this is the assurance I must give him.

Similarly, a young woman comes to see me, and timidly tells me about the irregular life she is leading. I talk to her about faith, about the strength one can draw from it, and which we need all the more at times when we feel ourselves to be most wretched. Shortly afterwards she sends me a letter canceling her next appointment with me. I insist on her keeping it. She then admits that she does not dare to come and see me before she has had the courage to break with her lover. But is that really the first act of obedience that God is demanding of her? I am not at all sure that it is. Perhaps she ought first to fortify her faith and her communion with God by means of a large number of other less difficult acts of obedience. One day perhaps she will find the courage she lacks now. She is astonished that a religious man should show himself to be more free of prejudice than she is herself! Some years have passed. Her liaison is broken off. She has recently written to tell me of her tremendous joy in finding faith once more.

I have also known people who through fear of formalism, and of being pharisaical, never dare to proclaim their convictions. They are unhappy, mixed-up people, since the truth is that the way to tap the current of grace is to commit oneself categorically, while at the same time remaining aware of the gaps in one's faith.

Our Church, despite all her formalism, her inconsistencies and her weaknesses, has nevertheless handed on to us the torch of Revelation. Without her we should not know Jesus Christ, who comes from age to age to lay hold on men's souls and inflame them with faith, and so to revive the dead forms of piety.

A few years ago I went on a cruise with my family. Early one morning, while the ship's cranes creaked as they unloaded some timber, I went for a walk in a small Greek village. An hour later, returning toward the harbor, I met the ship's chief engineer. He said there was time, and offered to take me to see a very pretty little old church. In the church stood the priest, still and silent, while the villagers came in, knelt down, kissed the icons, and departed. As we came out, my guide began to give me his views on the Church and on religion in general. Born in a little Croatian village, he had left his native land and the age-old customs of his family. One felt his pride in having broken free from the narrow traditions of his background, opened wider horizons for himself, and rubbed shoulders with the cosmopolitan populations of the seaports, and in having submitted to a critical revision the ideas which his family had accepted for centuries without argument.

You can guess all his bitter complaints against the formalism of his Church, which held the people in ignorance, and about which he told me several scandalous stories.

I listened without making any reply, while he warmed to his subject and poured out the accumulated bitterness of his heart against the Church. It was going through my mind that among us too there were many, many people emancipated from their traditions who thought the same, although in other terms, as this engineer.

We were nearing the harbor when he concluded with an exclamation such as this: "This Church, its priests, its formalism—that's not true religion!"

I then interrupted him with a direct question: "So what, for you, is true religion?"

He seemed taken aback. Obviously he did not know what answer to give. After all his criticism, he now found himself suddenly faced with the need to formulate a positive conviction.

Suddenly he thought he saw a way out by means of a clever piece of flattery: "Well," he said to me, "I've seen you for the last week living on board among the other passengers. When I see your family, and the peace and joy that reigns in it, and how charming and helpful your children are, and how fond all the crew are of them, I say to myself that this is what matters in life, and not the dogmas and rites that the Church teaches."

I answered: "It is the same God, of whom both your Church and mine speak, and whom they serve, who has made our family what it is. It is because we pray together, because we read the Bible, and because we help each other to put Jesus Christ at the center of our lives, that the difficulties of every day find solutions day after day. Good will by itself is not enough to do that."

My companion stood looking at me in astonishment. Visibly, he felt that his whole system of thought was being shaken by new questions. For him the doctor was the type of man set free from the obscure prejudices of tradition. Now it was no longer a question of the Church and its failings, of religion and all the questions it raises, but of Jesus Christ and his living activity in the man of today. This is the risen, living, active Christ whom the Church preaches.

I began to tell him of my experience as a doctor, of the awful wretchedness of men, of their anguish, and of the confidences I hear. Then the engineer said that all this was true enough; that everywhere he had been in the world he had seen conflicts, injustice, and hate; that it was all right to denounce such things, but it was not so easy to find the remedy for them. He talked to me about his family and his own life, of all the things that troubled him, and which he tried in vain to come to terms with. He agreed that men need more than intelligence, training, and energy to overcome their difficulties; they need a strength that goes far beyond that. . .

So, then, the truth does not lie either in the formalism of pure tradition, or in a scornful attitude to tradition; it is not to be found either in the utopian ideal of a serene life, untouched by sin or suffering, or in a passionate nonconformity which turns into a proud taste for high drama.

The popularization of the ideas of analytical psychology has given our contemporaries a false notion of life; namely, that in order to lead a normal life one must have had a normal childhood, free from all emotional shocks. One must have perfect parents, free of all psychological complexes, a spotless heredity, and first-class teachers.

First of all, this never happens. Secondly, we see plenty of people who seem to be the suffering victims of too perfect a preparation for life. They have had such wise and perspicacious parents, such a happy childhood, such a harmonious family life, an education so nicely balanced between authority and liberty, that they are lost when they come up against the difficulties of life. They have not learned to face them. They cannot bear their wives' little bad habits, and constantly compare them with their own exemplary mothers. They have no experience either of suffering or of sin and grace. The wise solicitude of his parents and God's providence may protect a child for a long time from any kind of accident. Nevertheless it is when he falls and breaks his leg that he has his first deep inner experience. That does not mean, however, that we ought to wish suffering, sickness, and difficulties on everybody!

But in reality, whatever a person's goal in life, it is not easy to achieve. Every way of life has its difficulties, whether rich or poor, married or single, in sickness and infirmity or in good health, full of failures and defeats, or of success and self-mastery.

A certain man has had a terrible childhood. He tells me a story of poverty, malnutrition, bullying psychopathic parents, and an atmosphere of systematic distrust on the part of his father as a result of bitter disappointment in an elder son. All this has hardened him. He has put into his career an energy which has carried him to brilliant successes in intellectual, financial, and moral fields. But his early experiences have also set up in him a constant inner tension, and even amidst all his triumphs he remains anxious, obsessed by fears for the future, and lacking in self-confidence.

The same is true in the case of the difficulties due to the conflicts that are an inevitable and necessary part of life. The very life of an organism is nothing other than its continual struggle against its environment. Even from the physicochemical point of view, Guye shows "that a living organism could not fulfill the conditions required for perfect equilibrium. If such were the case, everything in it would be fixed and rigid. . . . The organism would be as good as dead."

It is not a case of having a life with no difficulties, but of having the strength to surmount them. No one is exempt from conflict, which can strengthen a man as well as overwhelm him. There are physical combats with comrades who set upon us; moral conflicts with parents, with brothers and sisters, and with rivals; social conflicts;

conflicts with oneself and with one's own failings. All of them are both useful in the reactions they arouse in us, and harmful in the cowardly defeats and proud victories to which they lead. Only the spirit which we bring to them determines whether they are good or evil.

We never find ideal conditions of life and work. We always think that if only things were different, we could really show what we were capable of. How many charitable movements there are which, in their penurious beginnings when ardent pioneers toiled in attics with packing cases for furniture, did wonders which they no longer accomplish now that they have become large and richly endowed organizations.

The same is true of all kinds of affliction. Consider two of my patients. One is impatient at the time he is wasting. The other writes to me: "How nice it is to have time to spare, even if it is only the time to be ill." For illness relieves you of all other duties. One patient wears himself out in revolt and in insoluble arguments on the problem of evil; another writes: "I have learned to go beyond the question of 'why illness?' to that of 'what can I learn from my illness?'" One person learns patience, understanding, and compassion for others; another becomes unbearable. I read this line in the newspaper the other day: "I suffer acutely from my wife's rheumatism." A young woman who has undergone the severest trials in the midst of the horror of war writes: "Suffering is the great means used by God to transform evil into good."

A colleague who is a refugee in Switzerland writes: "What would Pascal have been without his sickness, in which he consciously and humbly desired to experience the agony of Christ; and Heine, without his slow descent to the grave; and Hölderlin without his madness, and Nietzsche without the disease which spurred him relentlessly onwards? Or ought we to wish that Poe, Baudelaire, Verlaine, Rimbaud, Leopardi, Lenau, Leonardo, and lots of others, had been cured of their inner conflicts by some psychoanalyst?" However, although disease can be fruitful, it can also destroy all a man's values, and as a doctor I shall not cease to try and snatch its victims from it. Nevertheless, the preservation of health never seems to me to be the supreme goal of life. There came to consult me one day a man of rather weak constitution, who had heavy responsibilities as a result of the war. He had accepted a task that was manifestly out of proportion to his natural strength, because he had felt that he was called by God to do so. The doctor in me, who ought to have advised him to resign, had to give way to the Christian and the patriot. I told him that Winkelried,[1] too, sacrificed himself for his country. But that did not excuse me from my technical task as a doctor, and together we sought how his life might best be organized to safeguard his health. Then we prayed that God would grant him the strength to fulfill his vocation. That was some years ago. He has rendered signal service, and his health is better now than it was then.

A serious illness never leaves anyone the same as he was before. According to the spirit in which we have accepted the illness, we come out of it morally either weaker or stronger, even if our physical resistance remains impaired. "Thou grindest me, Lord," cried Calvin in his sickness, "but it is thou who doest it, and that suffices me." The same is true of the trials of war, of captivity, and of martyrdom. You will realize that I could give many examples of this. I shall confine myself to quoting from two letters. The first is from a young prisoner of war: "Even in a concentration camp, where everyone is fighting for his life—many, often, to the detriment of others—one can be completely happy when one forgets oneself." The second is from a letter written to his father by a young Dutchman under sentence of death:

When I look back, I am profoundly thankful for my life—in the first place to God, who has guided me and shown me such wonderful things. I shall soon be happier than you, Father, happier than you all; do not be sad, but rejoice at God's mercy. I pray that my going will be accepted by you with serenity, without any feeling of rebellion, but that it will strengthen you to give yourselves up more wholeheartedly to the common task, in which each of us has to play a different part.

It is not for me, as a Swiss, and so until now spared the sufferings of war, to talk about the rich experiences of many men and women whom war has bereft of loved ones or of material possessions.

"Good health," writes a Swiss doctor, "prosperity, and a comfortable political situation are not the climate most conducive to serious philosophical speculations." A mother, after fifteen years of marriage, sees upon the death of her parents that she has built up neither her

---

[1] Arnold von Winkelried, one of the heroes of the struggle for Swiss independence, was killed at the battle of Sempach in 1386.

own life nor that of her home. She has had such a happy, carefree life, and such a perfect understanding with her parents, that she continued after her marriage to go and see them every day, to seek their advice in everything, to tell them about everything concerning herself, while her husband went to his work. Suddenly she feels that she has never yet learned to think for herself.

One can do harm with the best of intentions. Take the case of a neurotic young woman with whom her mother bears with angelic patience, without ever a word of irritation or reproach. Her mother looks upon her as a cross to be borne unselfishly. The daughter senses this, and it humiliates her terribly. She would like her mother to lose her temper with her just once, so that she would not always feel inferior to her. Others oppress those around them by their joy. Joy can be infectious and beneficent, but it can also get on the nerves of someone who does not share it. Especially if one is unable to win forgiveness for it by helping others to find the faith one declares to be its source. A certain young man's parents had made friends with people higher up the social scale than themselves. Whereas these friends were in easy circumstances, they themselves had remained poor. He soon took to stealing, and it was clear that this was a manifestation of rebellion on his part against society, exacerbated by the contrast he observed between his parents and their new friends.

At the time of my first great spiritual experiences, I had been caring for some years for an elderly foreign lady for whom I felt a profound pity. She came of a distinguished family, but had fallen upon evil days, far from her own country. She had boundless affection, gratitude, and admiration for me, because my visits brought her the sort of social contact she had known in the past. I can well believe that her unconscious was aggravating her symptoms in order to solicit my affectionate commiseration. In the name of sincerity I decided one day to try to make her see the workings of this complex. She misunderstood completely. She thought that I was suspecting her of an improper attachment, and was horrified at the thought. I looked after her until her death. But something was broken, and I never succeeded in re-establishing an openhearted relationship between us.

I remember one of my patients—one of several such—who was so virtuous that one could never catch her out in the tiniest fault. She was goodness personified. She would give wise advice to all and sundry, and was as strict with herself as with others. She was in despair that in spite of so much good will on her part, she only created a void around herself. Her husband wrapped himself up in his work; her elder daughter had been under psychoanalytical treatment for some years; and her younger daughter had left home and was living an irregular life, and shut the door in her mother's face when she tried to intervene.

Every grace has its dangers, and not only for others. Who would dare deny that there is a considerable amount of pride in the sense of well-being and exaltation felt by the person who bears witness to the fine spiritual experiences that have been granted to him? I once took it into my head to reform my handwriting, since my hasty scribble, although it saved me time, wasted that of my readers; it was a sign of lack of love. But recently I caught myself contemplating my writing with an improper self-love, and taking particular care with it in order to give a good impression!

I have met many nurses and social workers who were in conflict with their families. Their pride in having chosen a career of social service made them adopt at home a condescending attitude toward their brothers and sisters which set the whole family against them.

"God is the creative fire," one of my patients once wrote, "and the devil is the destructive fire!"

But just try to separate the destructive from the creative fire! It is all according to the use one makes of it. That same flame which is at the basis of the whole of civilization can, if we are not careful, start the most terrible conflagrations.

CHAPTER 8

"Striving to Better, Oft We Mar What's Well"

In the chapter devoted to "Flight" in *The Healing of Persons,* I described how our sincerest and most generous undertakings may sometimes be an unconscious pretext for running away from an unresolved problem. On several occasions I have been visited by a reader who was worried by that chapter. "I have come to realize," he said to me, "that the career I have been so proud of has only been a flight. I became a prospector in order to get out of the house. And so my vocation was not genuine! I have spoilt my life. What must I do now? Change my job?"

I set to work to reassure him.

Of course it is useful for all of us to learn to know ourselves better, to realize that sometimes the motives behind some of those acts we have thought to be among our finest were not very honorable. It is useful, because it makes us humble, and because it convinces us of our complete moral destitution. It is especially useful to be able to see honestly, *before* making a decision, the unadmitted factors that govern our inclinations in the secrecy of our hearts. Thus, if a student wants to change his course, I must ask him to try to see for himself whether his desire is inspired by negative or by positive forces, by a genuine vocation to the new career he envisages, or by disappointment at failing an examination and a desire to run away from the extra effort he ought to put into his work.

There is, however, no human decision that does not spring from an intimate mixture of both good and bad motives. It is impossible ever to disentangle them entirely. And even from a flight, a mistake, an illusion, and even more, from a fault, an act of disobedience, a sin, God can produce good. *Felix culpa!*

So even if a vocation has been taken up to some extent from wrong motives, it can be genuine and fruitful. Faith consists, in fact, in seeing the hand of God in it, and in following it in a spirit of service toward Him.

The quicker we are to discover our secret faults, the more do we need, if we are to avoid becoming obsessed by them, to understand the immensity of God's forgiveness. He asks us to recognize them, and humbly to turn away from them, solely in order for us to understand our poverty and His mercy, not so that we shall carry on in the utopian hope that we can ever act without sin entering into our action. "When we are in doubt as to whether we have offended God," says St. Francis de Sales, "we must humble ourselves, request God to excuse us, and ask for more enlightenment for another time, and forget completely what has happened and return to our accustomed way. For an inquisitive and anxious search to know whether we have acted rightly, indubitably arises from self-love."

In this world, our task is not so much to avoid mistakes, as to be fruitful. To be more and more able to recognize our faults, so as the better to be able to understand the price of God's mercy, and to devote ourselves more completely to him, makes our lives more fertile. But to become obsessed with the effort to recognize our faults, and to refuse to act for fear of committing some sin, makes them sterile. Our vocation is, I believe, to build good out of evil. For if we try to build good out of good, we are in danger of running out of raw material.

A serious fault can be the instrument of the liberation of him who has committed it.

It can also be the occasion for the salutary humbling of a person.

A husband who is fully in command of himself has always looked upon his wife with a certain contempt because she always gives in to her nerves. He thinks that she is very lucky to have found a husband whose character is more balanced than hers. Suddenly, however, he finds himself in a salutary situation of moral equality with her, because he has allowed himself to do an act for which his conscience reproves him severely. His wife at once feels less alone, and becomes less nervous.

Some of those persons whom I recognize as having attained the greatest spiritual authority are among those who have in their past seriously "blotted their copybooks." I use the familiar expression intentionally, to show that this is a matter of real life, and not an academic point. I have sometimes envied them the remarkable grandeur of their experience of repentance and forgiveness, and the decisive transformation of their lives. Moses had committed murder. St. Peter had been a coward, and St. Paul, the accomplice of bloody executioners. But of course I do not want anyone to have such experiences, any more than I want anyone to be ill, since the outcome could be quite different.

It is nevertheless true that the most wonderful thing in this world is not the good that we accomplish, but the fact that good can come even out of the evil that we do. I have been struck, for example, by the numbers of people who have been brought back to God under the influence of a person to whom they had some improper attachment. I once read the diary of a lady of good family, which was a poignant record of such a case. Another lady, long after she had acknowledged her fault and been forgiven for it, and having achieved a genuine sublimation of the passion that had been awakened in her, found herself being told one day: "You must have been very much in love with someone once, to be able to be so loving toward everybody without making any distinction." Love is so close to mysticism that even when it is illicit it can uplift the soul and lead to faith. Many people are disturbed by this. It disturbs them that adultery can bring true liberation to some people, because their own marital fidelity has been more a matter of convention and fear of "what people might say," than of love of God's commandments. The world is too ready to throw stones at such people, and to cast doubts on the genuineness of the faith thus rediscovered. But is it not of more value than the seeming probity of the respectable man who, so often, "commits adultery in his heart" (Matt. 5:28)? Moreover this new-found faith, provided that the Holy Spirit nurtures it, will not be long in bearing fruit in the form of a crisis of conscience, in which the sin that has been its cradle will be overcome.

I realize that I am touching on an exceedingly delicate subject here. It is appropriate once more to repeat that nothing is good or bad in itself. These lines could harm the reader who took them as an encouragement to do evil, or looked in them for a moral relativism which I am far from professing. He could snatch at them as a pretext for giving way to temptation—provided his intentions were good. Nevertheless he will permit me to express my doubt as to whether in thus interpreting my thought his intentions are really pure.

I hope that these pages will also bring liberation to people who are weighed down by their desire to do good and their tortured fear of committing some fault. I cannot keep count of the number of people in whom religion, the love of God and the desire to serve him, or even a quite secular ideal of perfection, lead only to a life of sterility, sadness, and anxiety. The fear of sinning has killed all their spontaneity. The subtle analysis of their consciences has taken the place of that childlike simplicity of heart which Christ demands. All joy has been replaced by the pursuit of duty. They have come to the point of doing nothing that gives them pleasure, as if God, who loves us, never required any but disagreeable things of us! They make incredible efforts, but win no victories. They are always comparing themselves with those they look upon as their betters.

What I said in the preceding chapter about the usefulness of moral traditions and the established framework of society will have warned the reader in advance that it is not the aim of these considerations to open the door to a complete unleashing of the passions. As Fénelon said, "Those people who have the misfortune to become accustomed to violent pleasures lose the taste for moderate pleasures, and weary themselves in an anxious pursuit of happiness." Taboos, much criticized by the psychologists, served a useful purpose in safeguarding people from moral anarchy. It is one of the tragedies of our time that on the one hand those who uphold the principles of morality do so on thoroughly conventionalist grounds, the dangers of which we have seen; whereas on the other hand, in the name of sincerity, or of a mission to remake the world, others set at nought the intangible laws of morality. It cannot be denied that the great increase in the number of cases of nervous disease is a consequence of the distress arising from being caught between these two extremes.

What we need, then, is to rediscover an austerity of life and a solid piety which spring spontaneously from the conversion of the heart instead of being a formal constraint. All those people weighed down by the obsessive fear of "doing something wrong," or who utter so many prayers that their very number suggests that the utterer has his doubts about their being heard, are not a very good advertisement for the way of God.

A friend of mine once told me he was astonished to find, on moving to another house, how many books he had accumulated in his library giving advice on psychology and morality. The fact that he had collected so many was a manifestation of his ceaseless anxiety. He had decided not to open them, but once and for all to come to terms with the fact that in this world, despite all the teachings of science and theology, we can never manage to avoid every imperfection of behavior. Henceforth he would try to regain true simplicity of heart and mind by trusting in God's grace.

The Gospel message of salvation was given us so that we might be freed from the weight of the law, but very often it is made no more than a source of anxiety. A certain woman never stops anxiously wondering whether she is really being guided by God, whether she has really seen what his purpose is for her. She worries so much, of course, that she can no longer see anything at all. God guides us when we trust his guidance, and often without our realizing it; not when we keep worrying about what his guidance is.

Similarly, dissatisfaction with self, which is the powerful motive force of moral progress, can on the other hand become a source of discouragement if we get to a state of never being able to forgive ourselves for backsliding into sin despite our best efforts. In reality, victory and an ever clearer vision of our moral destitution always go together, just as there is no sunlight without shadow. The greater our experience of grace, the more do we discover of the wickedness of our hearts, and the harder, too, it is to bear the wretchedness and slavery of our bodies. "Great Christians," writes a Swiss doctor, "have suffered all their lives, have gone through periods of nervous troubles, obsessions, scruples, etc. . . . without their inner spiritual lives being damaged or destroyed."[1]

Disease is a natural occurrence. I do not say that it is normal! We must fight ceaselessly against it as Christ fought ceaselessly against it. But we cannot forget that it is part of nature. Perfect health is an idea in the mind, and one which does, indeed, witness to our intuition concerning a perfect world, and so to our nostalgia for God. But on

[1] Georges Liengme, *Pour apprendre à mieux vivre.*

this earth we must accept that sooner or later we all have to pay our tribute to disease.

Similarly, sin is natural. Here again I do not say normal! We must also fight ceaselessly against it, and strive for perfection as the Gospel commands. But whatever we do, there will always be sin in our hearts in this world. "Conversion," writes Adrienne Kaegi-von Speyr,[2] "is never an act done once and for all, never an isolated, measurable fact. It is really growth, which needs time to develop—sometimes a long time. In very rare cases one can expect sudden transformations visible to the naked eye. The fruit that ripens altogether too quickly is premature, and soon falls."

This is just why we need a salvation that does not depend on our own efforts. The answer is grace. To those who are obsessed and humiliated by the vulgarity or the cruelty of the ideas that can take hold of their minds, we usually point out that such ideas are not for that reason a part of their true personality, since actually they fight against them. I have already alluded to this. That is true, but in general it does not pacify them. It has therefore seemed to me to be more valuable to say to them: "Of course you have horrible thoughts, because evil is woven into the heart of man, and he is utterly powerless, by himself, to subdue it. This is in fact what the Bible teaches. Everybody has thoughts of which he is ashamed. A man who was never ill and who had no sin would not be a normal man. We should all have reason to despair if instead of being required only to strive for holiness, we had to attain it. Besides, that would amount to claiming that we could manage without grace."

We must sincerely desire to follow God's will instead of our own. But if we want to be sure that on all occasions we are not mistaking our will for his, then we shall find ourselves floundering in a slough of despond that is far removed from the Christian ideal. I am interviewing a patient of whom I am very fond. I have spent a long time praying about him, and yet our interview goes quite differently from the way I had expected, and what I had prepared to say seems to miss the mark. I find I have become the prisoner of an overzealous preparation, and impermeable to the contrary orders of the Holy Spirit.

Thus I see many people whose spiritual zeal is so great that it

[2] *Schweizer Rundschau*, July, 1944, p. 245.

forms an obstacle to any peaceful and fruitful experience. They always remind me of people who have missed the train, and who, instead of waiting calmly for the next one that will take them to their destination, dash off frantically after the one they have missed, with no hope of catching it.

It is often the patients over whom I have taken most trouble that I have been unable to help. Whereas there are others who thank me warmly for what I have done for them, when I have been unaware of having done anything but listen to them. I believe, however, that if I tried to save myself the effort expended on the former, it would not be given me to experience the wonderful times I have with the latter.

I often think that the best things we do in this life are done without our intending to do them. I am on a journey, and let an old friend know that I am going to drop in and see him. When I get there he tells me of the great and wonderful experience he has had on confessing to his wife a fault he has been hiding from her for a long time. For a long time, too, he has felt called to make this confession, but has not had the courage to do so. The announcement of my visit sufficed to make him do it. And he thanks me warmly for the help I have given him in this way, and for which I can claim no merit at all!

In the same way our moments of greatest happiness often come quite unexpectedly, and if we tried to hold on to them or reproduce them, it would be in vain. A young wife is having some difficulty in adapting herself to married life. One day, through a somewhat mysterious concurrence of circumstances and intangible factors all her difficulties seemed suddenly to melt away, and she achieved unreserved communion. Now she is in despair because it has not continued. The pain of this disappointment certainly stands in the way of a return of the moment of happiness. "Striving to better, oft we mar what's well."

A woman had declined several offers of marriage when she was young, in the hope of "doing better." Now over forty, she has taken a husband with whom she has had nothing but difficulties. In the same way she has changed her job several times, always with the hope of "doing better." Now she finds herself alone and without stable employment.

This leads me to say a few words about the "all-or-nothing" types, the perfectionists. The doctor sees plenty of them, and I have before me a large file of notes on them. They are so full of ambition in everything that they are always disappointed with reality and with themselves. Among them are musicians who harbor such wonderful dreams of artistic perfection that as soon as they take up an instrument they are discouraged at falling so far short of their ambition, and they abandon their studies. These "all or nothing" types have such an intense need for affection that they have scarcely taken up acquaintance with someone when they break off the relationship because they are disappointed at not finding in him what they consider to be true friendship. They have such an unfulfilled longing to be happy because they cannot see what is lacking that will make them happy. They have such a desire to be perfect that they only see their failures. When one points to some real victory they have won, which they have assured one in advance could not possibly come about, they reply: "For all I did, I might as well not have bothered!" They will spend an hour telling you of all their cowardly defeats, and only on the doorstep, as they are leaving, will they admit to having won a success that is enough to fill you with jubilation. They have such a thirst for absolute solutions that they are in a constant state of irritation at the relativity of everything. "I am always looking for absolute answers," a young woman writes to me; "I really must come to terms with all the imperfections and unpleasantness I find everywhere. It is normal to seek the best possible conditions for one's work, but if one spends one's whole life in the search, one runs the risk of never getting on with the work."

They want to do everything, but choose nothing, and so never get started. Living means choosing one thing rather than another, but these people will give up nothing, and so lose everything. There is always plenty of time for what God wants us to do if we do not spend it on other things.

A young woman took it very hard when the man she was in love with married someone else. However, she managed to sublimate her disappointment in an artistic career. Suddenly she receives an offer of marriage from the same man, now a widower. But instead of being glad, she is upset and worried at the prospect of having to give up her art.

These "all-or-nothing" types are always dreaming of being entrusted with important tasks, and meanwhile they neglect the humbler duties whose accomplishment would carry them forward. I listen to the account of many such lives: permanently provisional lives, one might call them. People who are always waiting for the circumstances to come along in which they can show their mettle, but the right circumstances never come. "Perfection," St. Bernard said, "consists in doing common and everyday things in an uncommon manner, and not in doing great things, nor in doing many things."

These people, on the contrary, do everything with such intensity that they fatigue themselves, and the doctor has to stop them. When they at last undertake something they have longed to do, they are so emotional about it that they make themselves ill, and one has to forbid their carrying on with it. They make such a tremendous effort to control themselves, to concentrate, and to forget nothing, that the effort itself absorbs and distracts their attention, with the result that they make stupid mistakes, and this impels them to even more frantic efforts. In their despair they do just what they were afraid of doing. I call this a "fusspot complex." They are so fussy about getting everything done properly, even the finest details, that in the end they neglect what is essential, and fail. Or else they dissipate their efforts in so many different directions that they do nothing useful in any.

Amid this all-pervading activity they are not happy, for happiness depends on the state of our minds, and not on what we do. Their minds are always anxious. They would like to be friends with everybody, but do not manage to agree with their neighbors, whose smallest faults they perceive. At first they arouse enthusiasm with the originality of their views, their scintillating personalities, and the superabundant life they bring to everything they do. But their relentless activism ends up by becoming wearisome. First they are described as geniuses, and then as bumptious charlatans. And so they are worshipped at one moment and opposed the next. In the end everyone is on the defensive against them, and they are left alone. They remind one of a remark of Rilke's: "People who let their feelings overflow, like blood spurting, make me tired."

People like this are always having extraordinary adventures, and incredibly good or bad luck. They take everything to heart, and suffer intensely. Their illnesses are all serious, their case is always exceptional. As those around them, including the doctor, end up by minimizing their complaints, they are impelled unconsciously to inflate themselves continually in an attempt to compel sympathy. They feel people becoming more and more skeptical, and this hurts and embitters them, and in the end they are less well looked after than would otherwise have been the case. Or else they go from one doctor to another, and each one puts forward some vague and soothing diagnosis so as to be done with their innumerable questions and so as not to hurt them by telling them he can find no objective sign. All these Latin medical terms frighten them. They ask about each one of them, and all the answers set their terrified minds in a whirl. In this anguished atmosphere, suggestion does its inevitable work and creates new symptoms to make matters worse. If one tries to reason with them, to bring the whole thing back into proper perspective, they think they are being accused of pretending, and exclaim: "All I want is to get well again, but I have never yet found a doctor who understands my case."

When they become engaged to be married, they are filled with boundless enthusiasm. Their fiancée has every good quality, and no faults. No one has ever understood her as well as they do. They are indignant at our unjust suspicions if we venture to put them on their guard against possible difficulties. But when, in marriage, they come up against these difficulties, they lapse into despair. They have been deceived, and are indignant about it. They think we are very naïve if we suggest that divorce might be avoided. No half-baked compromise for them: they have too high a conception of marriage to live a married life that is just a lie, as it would be without perfect communion.

They remind one of those species which have become extinct in the course of evolution because they were overdifferentiated. Such as, for instance, the machairodont, a carnivore whose teeth had developed so enormously that it could no longer eat. This illustration from natural history strikes me as especially apt. It is in fact through the development of his mind that man has raised himself above the animals. His inquisitiveness, his eternal dissatisfaction, his yearning for the absolute, have given rise to philosophy, science, and theology. His emotional yearnings have given rise to society, and from them spring his spiritual experiences. But let this differentiation of his intelligence and his feelings get out of proportion, and man becomes unsuited for life, unsociable, incapable of loving, of being happy, of doing any useful intellectual work. What he needs is a new birth that will give him the soul of a child once more.

I have also often seen cases such as that of a wife who desired so keenly to convert her husband that she kept nagging him about it. The result was that though he would talk freely to others about his religious worries, he took good care to say nothing about them to her. Or a mother who was so anxious to inculcate a habit of religious observance in her child that he eventually rejected all religious practice. I have seen parents immunize their children against prayer and meditation—every time the child had been naughty they would tell him to go and say his prayers!

Sometimes, too, husbands and wives have given up meditating together, after practicing it for a long time, because it has become the occasion for one of them to sermonize the other, and air all his grievances. In another case, the wife felt an inner call to declare herself for Christ. She hesitated, knowing that her husband would not follow her, and for fear that her spiritual decision might become an obstacle between them. But true communion between them was in any case to become gradually weaker, for want of the blessings that only come from uncalculating obedience.

Some people are so overjoyed at having experienced a sudden conversion that they want at all costs to make other people have the same experience, and exercise a veritable tyranny over them to this end. They cannot conceive that anyone can come to faith by any other means.

Finally, here is a very delicate problem. A woman has been brought up in an atmosphere of strict and very formal religion. During a period of mental depression she was treated by one of my Christian colleagues, for whom I have the highest regard. Her contact with this exceptional personality has opened her mind to a higher and broader religious concept. She has realized how far removed the strict formalism of her childhood was from the Gospel, and at the same time how much it had to do with her illness. She goes back to her familiar background, and is full of criticisms of it. She can no longer accept the dogmas and rules which her family insists upon. The other members of the family feel this, and take it out on her. Her suffering now is far worse than before. The trouble is that the core of the nonformalist religion, the religion of the heart that has been revealed to her, is love of one's neighbor. For her, her neighbor now is this family with which she finds herself inevitably in serious conflict. And then, notwithstanding all its mistakes, this narrow background in which she has been brought up is the one in which she first found faith. She is still attached to it despite all the criticisms of it that fill her mind. Though her faith has evolved, this is where her early faith was sketched and molded; there is still something of it left. Now she is uprooted, separated spiritually from that to which she remains attached emotionally.

Of course it is not my purpose to blame my colleague. He most certainly never tried to set his patient against her family. I entirely share his spiritual breadth of vision. No doubt it has also happened to me that I have brought unhappiness to someone when I thought I was helping him back to health. But having seen tragedies of that sort, I take as much care as I can to take the possible contingencies into account. Everything that sets up an inner conflict in a person's mind, even if it is some godly thing, can serve the purposes of the devil, the prince of the kingdom of divisions. That is why I tremble as I hand my publisher the manuscript of a book. It could happen to do harm, however good my intentions. I can only ask my readers' forgiveness, and the forgiveness of Jesus Christ. When all is said and done, after all our efforts and our mumblings, the only thing we can ever count on is God's grace, which ensures the triumph of good, which blots out the ever-present evil and even sometimes turns it to good.

In trying to do everything for the best, we do not avoid all mistakes. So the Christian life is not a huge effort to do good, but abdication and a prayer that God will guide us through all the reefs.

PART III

Against the Spirit of Dogmatism

CHAPTER · 9

Tolerance

"Life is short," wrote Hippocrates, "and the Art long; the occasion fleeting; experience fallacious, and judgment difficult." It is perhaps in the sphere of psychological and spiritual medicine that we can most readily verify the truth of the great practitioner's wise words. It is easy to build theories, to pursue one's adversaries with implacable logic, and to collect enthusiastic followers when one develops a corpus of doctrine that is coherent and intransigent. But when it comes to daily practice, how many impenetrable mysteries, how many paradoxes, how many failures and equally unexpected successes! I am always discovering more of the complexity, the subtlety, and the delicacy of the human mind. One makes a few experiments. But as soon as one tries to build a theory upon them, one finds that life refuses to be bound by them, and the same results cannot be obtained again. On the other hand, it is often just when one feels helpless, perplexed, and in despair when faced with the disaster of a person's life, that there takes place suddenly, one does not know how, a living "experiment." With doctrines that are false, muddleheaded or contradictory, people who are convinced of their truth sometimes obtain surprising results. Great scientists can fail despite the most rigorously scientific methods. Great theologians can lose souls despite their scrupulous orthodoxy.

How is it then that so many medical men, despite the fact that they are fully conversant with the difficulties of daily practice, can argue so bitterly, hurl anathemas at one another, and maintain their personal point of view as if it were not in the slightest doubt? It is because the spirit of dogmatism is a grave and widespread disease.

Charles Baudouin, who cannot be suspected of hostility toward psychoanalysis, is quoted[1] as making the following wise remark on the subject of the doctrinal controversies between Freud and Adler: "Each has his theory, and the explanations (of the disease) that are given to the subject vary with the analyst. Nevertheless the practical successes are a fact." If such be the case, is it not because success does not depend, as the authors believe, so much on the particular system they employ, as on moral factors which they introduce without realizing it, and whose efficacy is independent of the system? I think so. The sincerity, affection, and confidence which the analyst brings to his task do more than anything else toward his success with the patient. Both patient and analyst attribute this success to the excellence of the theories and techniques used, and see it therefore as the proof of that excellence. But different techniques and different theories, applied with the same honesty, affection, and trust, are equally successful, and serve their authors as a demonstration of the superiority of those techniques and theories. I should not wish to carry this argument to extremes, for that would involve me in asserting the equivalence of all techniques and all doctrines. On the contrary, I think that as doctors we must try to find for each case the technique that is best suited to it, but without making the mistake of attributing an absolute value, a monopoly of truth, to any particular theory or technique.

Ferrière makes a pertinent comment on the successes of Emile Coué: "His is a philosophy for people who are well!" To those who demur that it was nevertheless "the sick who went to Coué," he replies:

We do not deny it. But those who came away cured, and definitively cured, were those who had in themselves sufficient perseverance—sufficient imagination, according to Coué; sufficient will power, according to Marden; sufficient faith, according to Christian Science; sufficient detachment, according to the Stoics—to make the forces of health get the better of the disease germs. . . . Now, we believe that in fact that perseverance which underlies all the moral techniques, is a sign of "moral" health.[2]

I fully subscribe to Ferrière's observation, and take it even farther. Thus Baudouin criticizes the theories of Dubois when the latter called

[1] In Adolphe Ferrière, *Le progrès spirituel.*
[2] *Ibid.*

for the education of the will, for modern psychology has demonstrated the impotence of the will when it is not supported by the imagination—that is to say by faith, in the psychological meaning of the term. But if one looks into the matter more closely, one sees that it was really faith in the possibility of getting well that Dubois was arousing when he assured his patients that sound self-training would surely restore them to health.

So, under varying labels, which lend themselves to endless theoretical argument, we are really always releasing the same constructive forces of the mind, and it is they that bring about a cure, rather than the particular doctrine with which they may be associated.

A patient has been liberated by means of a course of psychoanalysis conducted on Freudian principles. He is persuaded that all psychological disorders come from the false fear aroused by social constraint in regard to sex, which is a natural and healthy force, the free development of which is the source of all genuine personal dynamism. On account of the conclusive experience he has had in his psychoanalytical treatment, he accepts the whole of the teaching of Freud and his school. He defends it against all comers with the same zeal that a man will put into the defense of the truth against anyone who denies it. He displays, moreover, a certain condescension toward his contradictors, and thinks they cannot possibly understand the workings of the mind without undergoing a course of psychoanalysis.

Another man undergoes the same liberating experience in the course of psychoanalytical treatment by a disciple of Adler. He concludes from it that the whole trouble is due to feelings of inferiority resulting from mistakes in his upbringing. He adheres to the body of teaching professed by his analyst.

Another has been treated by a follower of Jung, and he concludes from his liberation that the whole trouble arises from a failure to recognize the intuitive ancestral spiritual forces which lie dormant in all of us, and which bind us to the universal dynamism of the spirit.

Yet another has experienced the power of suggestion under the influence of Coué or Baudouin. From this he concludes that suggestion is really the only thing involved in the successes which some attribute to the Christian faith, and others to science, to drugs, or to any other agent. He thinks that the success of any technique is due solely to the fact that its practitioners firmly believe in it, and that they are really making use of the law of suggestion, like M. Jourdain[3] who spoke prose without realizing it.

Another man has found his life similarly transformed as a result of following the advice of, say, Dubois or one of the American advocates of self-education and the cultivation of the will. He concludes that this is the only certain road to success. He thinks that all those who have been hurt or defeated by life have simply failed to appreciate the virtue of a proper method of training in self-mastery, which would lead them to certain success.

Yet another has experienced the sense of well-being which followed upon his reforming his diet in accordance with the advice of a school of naturists, and he is convinced that there are people suffering from all kinds of diseases who fail to realize their real cause, and that they would be set free if they could be enlightened on the laws of healthy eating, according to nature. He links with the study of these laws a whole philosophy of life which seems to him to be the only true one.

Another has read the Stoics, or Leibnitz, Le Dantec, or Karl Marx, and in his reading has found illumination which has brought him a personal experience of liberation. He adheres with no less fanaticism to the philosophical system of his master, and sees in it a complete and exclusive exposition of the truth.

Thus the spirit of dogmatism impels each to attribute the merit of his personal experience to the excellence of the doctrines professed by the person who has helped him to have that experience. Human beings have so great a need to believe in something that even those who affect the most disdainful religious skepticism adhere in this way to some philosophy, take up the cudgel for it, and are capable of evincing the greatest intolerance toward anyone who does not adopt it wholeheartedly.

It is the same where religion is concerned. One man has had a living experience within the framework of the Catholic Church. He has experienced the virtue of abdicating his own personal criticism in favor of the age-old authority of the Church, and of humble submission to its teaching. He concludes that outside the efficacy of the sacraments, of which that Church is the historical guardian, there is no possibility of salvation.

Another has experienced within the framework of Protestantism the

---

[3] The hero of Molière's comedy *Le Bourgeois Gentilhomme*.

liberating power of religious sincerity. He concludes that no doctrine can bear fruit if it is imposed on the mind from outside, and that grace is bound up with the complete spontaneity of the soul answering God's inner call.

Another has had a personal experience through the preaching of Christian Science. He concludes from it that evil exists only because one believes in it, and all that is needed is to understand the nature of universal harmony in order to find it within oneself.

Yet another has come under the influence of the Oxford Group, and has experienced meditation and the complete confession of one's life in front of a friend. He concludes that this is the necessary road to the transformation of any man's life.

Another has had an experience of conversion while reading Swedenborg. He concludes that without an understanding of the symbolic meaning of the Scriptures and without the key to the mysterious correspondence of the spiritual world, one can grasp nothing of the truth.

Yet another has come into contact with the Plymouth Brethren, and has known the liberating experience of a strict personal discipline. He concludes that the reason why so many souls are straying in suffering is solely that they compromise with the world and its deceitful pleasures.

Another has been tremendously helped by reading the works of the Indian sages. He concludes that detachment from earthly realities, and long meditations in which the individual self is absorbed into the universal mind, are the supreme road of infinite spiritual progress. Or else he has had a personal experience of tolerance in the Sufi movement. He has realized that all religions share essentially in the same verities, and he therefore concludes that to look upon Jesus Christ as the exclusive divine mediator of salvation is to deprive oneself of the genuine religious treasures which have been presented to mankind by all the other great inspired teachers.

Another, however, has found liberation in personal encounter with Jesus, and in the salvation received through the faith that recognizes God in him. He concludes that to compare him with thinkers, however great, is to deny him and to slide down the slippery path of human pride which claims that it can ensure its salvation through its own wisdom.

One man quotes some scriptural text to prove that apart from the strictest doctrinal orthodoxy we cannot come into fellowship with the risen Christ; and another will quote a different text to prove that such an attitude misunderstands the good news brought to all men by Christ, who wanted to liberate them from all theological constraint.

Thus each of us deduces from his personal experience a system of thought, which he sets up as the truth against all other systems of thought.

Each of us calls to witness his personal experience in support of the system to which he considers it to be due. Each maintains the truths which the system he favors has revealed to him, and concludes that those who disagree with him are in error. As Adrienne Kaegi-von Speyr rightly says, any attempt to lay down a method of reaching God involves the danger of "reducing the immensity of God, who remains essentially immeasurable." She takes me to task myself on this score, and I keenly regret having given such an impression to my readers, for I have the liveliest sense of the immeasurable greatness of God, in comparison with which all our mumblings are of no significance.

Each of us hides his secret weaknesses, and the painful failures which still persist in his life, for fear that to admit them might call in question the system he holds to be true. And each points to the errors of others, and uses their inconsistencies and wrongdoing as a demonstration of the worthlessness of their teaching.

The apostles of tolerance show themselves to be quite intolerant toward those who refuse to have anything to do with their universal tolerance. The orthodox violate the law of love which their orthodoxy enjoins upon them, in persecuting any who do not share their dogmas.

In Leibnitz's celebrated words, all systems are right in what they affirm, and wrong in what they deny.

But be careful! Does it not follow, then, that all doctrine is equally true, and that there is no objective revealed truth? I do not think so.

I think one can be both orthodox and tolerant. In general, people are either orthodox and intolerant, or tolerant and agnostic. I have long felt an inner call to try to conjoin orthodoxy and tolerance. By orthodoxy, I understand a personal evangelistic faith completely subject to the authority of the Bible; and by tolerance, I mean a definitive renunciation of any attempt to propagate that faith by doctrinal argument or controversy. Such a conjunction is difficult; it is contrary to our natural inclination, but we can work toward it, and it bears fruit.

In his fine book on this subject, Frank Abauzit[4] has shown that true tolerance is not moral cowardice, but none other than Christian humility, faith, and love. Humility, because it gives up any pretensions to possession of a monopoly of truth, and to the domination of others in order to indoctrinate them. Faith, because it trusts in the action of God, who draws men's souls to himself, even through the byways of doctrinal error. Love, because it interests itself in people as persons, in order to help them find their own way, and not in their ideas in order to combat them. Trust awakens in them the moral person, which will lead them eventually to the truth, while controversy drives them more deeply into their error, by arousing their opposition.

The spirit of dogmatism insinuates itself into my heart as soon as I feel sure of myself:

1. When I draw that assurance from my experience of the power of Jesus Christ, the spirit of dogmatism sets up an impenetrable barrier between me and the person to whom I am speaking. The account of some victory I have won, far from encouraging him, actually discourages him, because instead of uniting me with him as a brother in distress, it puts me in the position of an expert who claims to have preceded him along this road. Just at that moment I am farther away from the spirit of the Christ of whom I am speaking to him, than he is himself in confessing his distress. The spirit of dogmatism is the source of all spiritual tyrannies, and spiritual tyranny is the worst poison of the mind. "A person who has had a particular religious experience," one of my patients once remarked to me, "always wants other people to have the same experience, because he is sure it is what they all need" Now all true religious experience is nothing if not spontaneous. I have seen many people suffering under this sort of spiritual tyranny, and they have struck me as being nearer to the Gospel in their distress than were their tyrants. On several occasions I have seen a real mental breakdown occur in people who were the objects of religious tyranny of this kind on the part of those around them or of some ardent proselyte. Such mental crises would appear to be a sort of instinctive defense by the mind

[4] *Le problème de la tolérance.*

under attack, illness being the only remaining route of escape open to it.

2. And when I base my doctrinal assurance on the biblical revelation, I may then convince a person intellectually, but I cannot bring him to personal knowledge of Jesus Christ. As Frank Buchman said, "One can win an argument and lose a soul." Theologically, the upholders of orthodoxy are right, but in practice they are in danger of betraying the spirit of Christ in the intransigence to which their conviction of their own rightness can lead them. Christ calls for an orthodoxy of the spirit instead of an orthodoxy of the letter.

It is often their self-love, agressiveness, and will to power which drive people to polemics of all kinds, especially on the subject of religion. I would certainly not wish to write in a spirit of polemic against the theologians! I accept that if there is a revealed truth it must be proclaimed. I myself should never have received it if faithful servants of God had not passed it on to me, or if the struggles they had to make against error had not helped me understand it better. Once more we are brought back to the truth that nothing is good or bad in itself, but only according to the spirit which animates us. To remain silent in the face of error may be a cowardly betrayal of the truth received from God. But into the defense of truth there may be insinuated pride in defending it, and in possessing a monopoly of it. In meditation before God each of us can discover the underlying motivation of his actions, and whether it is inspired by God or by his own will. Self-love can be involved, too, in preaching denominational peace—in claiming to be above theological controversies!

The proclamation of the truth, truly inspired by God and by love of our fellow men, is infinitely fruitful. But when it is inspired by a spirit of controversy and by personal motives, it divides the Church and troubles men's minds. There are no more bitter controversialists than those new converts who criticize the errors of the church they have left, and the psychologist cannot but note the personal factors which underlie their ardor. For example, their conversion is often seen to be a projection of a revolt against their background, their upbringing, their parents, and a whole mental outlook which has crushed them, and on which they are now taking revenge.

Lastly, when I am sure of myself in my judgment about a patient, even if my decision is founded on my Christian faith, I say to myself: This patient is suffering from blocking due to a grudge against his father; when he is reconciled with him, he will find Christ. Or else: His intellectualism is what is stopping him; when he gives up arguing so much, he will find faith. Or again: The false doctrines he has imbibed are leading him astray; when he recognizes their falsity, he will realize that they have been serving to hide his despair from him, and he will grasp the grace that is offered! All this is doubtless true, but by the very fact of my thinking it, I am placing myself in the position of a judge in regard to my patient. I cannot help him any more. He feels himself neither understood nor loved. I must bring all these preconceived ideas to God in order to be set free from them, so as to become ready once more to trust. Then there can spring from our conversation experiences which are not always the ones I have foreseen, but in which I shall always find, in one form or another, the same inner movement which is the mark of the intervention of Christ in a person's soul, namely, the conviction of sin, confession, repentance, grace, dedication, and also, lastly, theological truth. What we say to people matters less than the attitude of mind they see we have toward them. Neurotics, by the very fact of their distress, are egoists. When we doctors, pastors, or nurses begin to pass judgment on them, to find them too demanding, too preoccupied with themselves; and even more, when we tell them so, when we describe their complaints and criticisms as self-conceit, we can no longer help them. The result is that, feeling themselves rejected, they become even more demanding and bitter. In the same way, in marriage, when one of the partners begins to list in his heart all the faults of the other, and to pass judgment, the effect is only to make the faults worse.

The spirit of dogmatism ossifies thought and sterilizes life. The person who is satisfied with one experience loses the dissatisfaction which could be the source of fresh experiences.

I have had a close friendship with a group of French pastors who conducted evangelistic missions with wholehearted zeal in various parishes. After one of these, they were received, in the late evening, by one of the notables of the parish. The latter was expressing his enthusiasm for the spiritual message they had brought. He added: "As a matter of fact, I too have had a religious experience." And turning to his wife, he said: "Would you mind going up to the attic and getting it? You remember I wrote it out and framed it. It must be in the big chest at the far end. These gentlemen would be interested to see it." A moment later the wife came back with the famous religious experience under her arm, but she had to beg pardon for producing it in such a condition, because the rats had been at it and had left it in a lamentable state!

The spirit of dogmatism is the source of the party spirit which so often sterilizes political life. Auguste Lumière, writing on education, also sees in dogmatism the greatest obstacle to the development of science. He calls for "the restoration of doubt in science, as Claude Bernard defined it. . . ."

In the book to which I have already referred (*Le problème de la tolérance*), Abauzit writes excellently of the contrast between the spirit of dogmatism and the spirit of pragmatism. But pragmatism also has its dogmatism, when it adopts an antagonistic attitude toward speculative thought in the name of the primacy of experience. The reader will have guessed that I propose rather to contrast them both with what I shall call the philosophical spirit. The spirit of dogmatism, whether it is intellectualist or pragmatic, is a spirit of systematization which claims to formulate truth, to comprehend it in a coherent whole and defend it; which claims to have found truth rather than to be seeking it; which is less critical of itself than of its opponents. The philosophical spirit, on the other hand, has a sense of wonder, a sense of the limitations of knowledge and of the poverty of the human mind. It never gives up the quest for truth, but determines to go on pursuing truth even though it knows that it will never completely attain to this in any sphere. It knows that there is no greater obstacle to the truth than the conviction that one possesses the truth. It has a sense of true criticism, which is not only compatible both with faith and with science, but also necessary to both. Laberthonnière contrasted[5] this true criticism with the false criticism of "freethinkers and of unthinking dogmatism."

The spirit of dogmatism is the proud aspect of thought; the philosophical spirit is its humble aspect. The type of the first is Aristotle or Spencer, and all those who claim to lay down absolute certainties, and build on them a system which banishes all mystery. The type of the second is Plato, who is continually calling in question his own theories; Socrates, who "knows nothing unless it be that he knows nothing"; Pascal and his "endless despair of obtaining knowl-

---

[5] In Frank Abauzit, *La pensée du Père Laberthonnière.*

edge of the beginning or the end of man"; and Montaigne with his wonderful intellectual honesty.

These two types of mind, these two currents, can be observed throughout the whole of history. The line of demarcation between them does not coincide at all with the usual division between those who accept religious faith and those who reject it. There are dogmatic minds among unbelievers as well as among believers. Similarly there are in both camps minds that are animated by the intellectual respect which inspires scientific doubt in the scientist, and also the realization of the unfathomable greatness of God in the believer.

In the eighteenth century the "spirit of certainty," in Volney's phrase, was the possession chiefly of religious circles, and the naturalists protested against it in their zeal for unprejudiced research. But in the nineteenth century it was the other way round. It was science that became dogmatic with its rationalist philosophy and its claim to explain everything. The same two attitudes are to be found among doctors. "You are always trying to explain to your patients what you can't even explain to yourself," said Axel Munthe to his colleagues.[6] Nothing is more difficult than to distinguish between true culture and false, or at least to define the distinction. It does not reside in the culture itself, but in the underlying moral factors. Intellectual varnish causes a conceited intoxication whereas true culture makes a man humble. "Knowledge without conscience is soul-destroying," said Rabelais.

The spirit of the true faith and that of true science have an evident kinship. Both go forward with awe, and in the doubt that comes from the consciousness of the unknowable and of the smallness of man in the face of the great mystery of the world and of life.

[6] *The Story of San Michele.*

CHAPTER 10

On Making Distinctions

The spirit of dogmatism is based on the making of distinctions. In every instance it sets out alternatives and proceeds to determine which is true, and which false. Either the scientific view of the world, with its rigorous determinism, is true, in which case there is no point in talking about moral responsibility, and thought itself, to use Carl Vogt's words, "is to the brain, more or less what the bile is to the liver or the urine to the kidneys." Or else God acting in accordance with his good pleasure, Spirit, and Ideas are the sole reality, and our whole vision of the real world and its laws is a mere illusion—a mental concept. In this way materialists and spiritualists oppose each other in an argument that has no end. But they have something in common: the very fact that they oppose each other's ideas, and are seeking the truth, the fundamental reality, not in the whole, but in one aspect of things, isolated from the rest by the operation of a false distinction.

Thus a mutually exclusive distinction is constantly made between a religious and an atheistic view of the world; the idea of a transcendent and personal God and that of an immanent God; that of the strict God of law and the merciful God of grace; that of a salvation exclusively tied to orthodox doctrine and that of a tolerant theism which approaches God by many different paths; technology and faith; social conformity and nonconformity; the idea of a divine Creator who has established immutable laws in nature, which man can study and use, and that of the God of miracles who violates those laws, and whom to know is to render unnecessary all other knowledge.

I meet people who have all these doctrines and concepts. Their doctrines are all opposed one to another. One has devoured Le Dantec, and repeats to me all the classical arguments of nineteenth-century atheist philosophy. Another has been reading Karl Barth, and he challenges all logic with the massive affirmations of a paradoxical faith. One is a liberal individualist; for him the sole function of society is to provide the conditions for the proper development of the individual person, who alone is capable of moral experience. Another is a collectivist, and allows no purpose for the individual-other than to forget himself and become integrated into society, which is a moral entity greater than he and will survive him. One is a pragmatist, and takes concrete reality as the measure of truth. Another is a speculative thinker, and takes intellectual reality as the measure of truth. One believes in the salvation of all men, another in the election of the saints. One wishes to wait only upon God, and rejects all personal initiative as an act of self-will. Another says, "Heaven helps those who help themselves," and claims that he is glorifying God in the efforts he makes to improve himself. One believes in the absolute permanence of spiritual victories, and casts doubt upon the authenticity of a faith in which these victories are only temporary in their effects. Another sees the spiritual as no more than relative, and considers all men to be equally sinners, whether they believe or not.

There is something of the truth in what each says, provided he is sincere. I learn a lot from them all, especially from those whose opinions are the most opposed to mine. There is something worthwhile in each of the systems of thought, the ideologies which divide mankind. Experience has taught me that without denying anything of my Calvinist Christian faith I can communicate with each of these people, because there is always a vital personal experience behind their ideas. If a certain man favors liberty, that is because at a decisive moment in his life, crushed under the weight of a rigorist upbringing, he has met a sincerely liberal person whose message has broken into his heart with the dazzling brilliance of new-found truth. If another favors discipline, that is because just when he was slipping, through lack of constraint, on the downward path of disorder, a salutary call to self-mastery broke in upon him with the same ring of truth.

Behind men's ideas lie experiences. Instead of arguing about their ideas and setting one up against another, it is more valuable to try to understand them by finding out what those experiences are. And then one sees that, although on the level of dogmatic debate there is nothing but antagonism, the living experience brings men together. This man who tells me he has no faith, I find to be quite close to me when we talk about our real lives. Like me, he has known difficulties and victories, advances and retreats; for men's real problems are all alike, and very simple—fear, covetousness, revolt, and despair. He has the same need to believe, and the same waves of doubt as I. The reason why the work of an atheist philosopher has had such an effect on him is that the religious formalism in which he was brought up has prevented him from meeting the true God. And as he had so great a need to believe in someone he has given himself wholeheartedly to the teaching of that philosopher. He is, of course, a false prophet, but our man has experienced through him something which, did he but know it, is really quite close to faith.

He who claims never to have doubted does not know what faith is, for faith is forged through doubt.

So then, behind every system of thought there is a living experience. It would be easy to show this in the history of philosophy. Similarly, one can read the autobiography of an author in all the novels he writes. To set up one system or doctrine against another impoverishes the mind by freezing it in a partisan attitude which obstructs the evolution of its life. How many upholders of orthodoxy seem to have fossilized minds, through having lost that unquenchable disquiet and curiosity which are the precondition of every advance in the spiritual life! As soon as one believes one possesses the truth, and encases it in a system, one shuts out other horizons. The mind is so made that it cannot formulate any affirmation that does not also imply a negation. The individualist runs the risk of failing to appreciate the mystical reality of the community, which is no less important. In upholding the value of the community one runs the risk of failing to appreciate the incomparable value of the individual personality, the chosen ground of all decisive spiritual events. The believer runs the risk of failing to appreciate the riches of doubt and of scientific research. The skeptic runs the risk of not appreciating the incomparable power of faith. In Chapter 3 I developed the idea of double causality—if one sees the immediate cause of events, one risks missing their deep symbolic meaning. When one discovers this meaning, one is in danger of underestimating the importance of the immediate causality.

A person's attitude at any given moment has a large number of meanings at once. A patient breaks away from his family background. It is perhaps pride which impels him to do so. Or perhaps it is a defensive reaction against the authoritarianism of his father; or maybe he is doing so in compensation for an inner disquiet. Lastly, he may be responding to a real call to break out of the debilitating comfort of his life and face up to the adventure of life. His decision may have many more meanings besides, and all of them may be true at once. I understood this when the psychoanalysts taught me that a dream was always susceptible of various interpretations, all of them true. It is our intellectualism which keeps on asking which is the true one. All of them contain something of the truth, and each enriches our vision of reality. The moment I think I have understood the cause of a given piece of behavior, I have closed my mind to the possibility of research on other aspects of the behavior. The moment I think I have understood someone, I stop helping him, because I am no longer in an attitude of seeking. Man is an inexhaustible mystery. He fits into none of our categories of thought.

Men are infinitely diverse. They travel along many different roads. There is always something new to be learned from each one, so long as one retains the spirit of seeking. But they are also diverse within. Several contradictory beings are at war within them, often without their knowledge, and their reactions are constantly overlapping. There are their father and mother, their forbears, something of all the teachers that have molded them, and of all the influences to which they have been subjected. This explains why we can have so much sympathy for people whose ideas seem wrong to us, and so little for others who share our beliefs. While they are developing one thesis, there is in them a being who is representing the opposite thesis. If they talk a lot about the value of the community, that is because there is at work within them a strong tendency toward individualism against which they are defending themselves. Inner harmony is the aspiration of all.

The spirit of dogmatism simplifies, opposes, and systematizes. The philosophical spirit has a sense of the endless complexity of things.

In their lives, too, people are constantly making distinctions that get them nowhere. They set the demands of their vocation over against those of their family; those of their conscience against those of society. They oppose their inner lives to their concrete lives, meditation to action, Sunday to the rest of the week, work to holidays, religious to secular activities, patient and methodical study to the sudden overflowing of genius, classicism to romanticism, reason to sentiment, optimism to pessimism, intuition to logic, reality to fiction, form to substance, flesh to spirit, *agape* to *eros* (i.e., love in fellowship to sexual love), training to education.

In the same way a false distinction is always made between faith and prudence. People say, that is, that when they perform an act of faith they do so without calculation of the possibilities, taking no precautions against evil: to take such precautions would be to betray their faith. But the Gospel, which preaches the "folly" of faith, speaks also of calculating the price of a building before undertaking the work, and of not giving meat to a child who cannot yet take more than milk. While talking to a clockmaker once on this subject, an illustration occurred to me: we take very little trouble with a cheap watch, whereas we treat a fine marine chronometer with the utmost care. People also say either "I trust other people and so get taken in by all and sundry," or else "I bear their wickedness in mind and trust nobody." Confucius laid down what I consider a remarkable precept on this point: "Never to suppose in advance that men are deceivers, nor to presume that they are full of suspicion, but to perceive their bad faith at once, this is wisdom."

Or again, in explaining his dilemma of conscience to us, a man sets his ideal of purity over against his ideal of charity. "If, out of fidelity to my Christian faith," he says, "I make a break with the woman with whom I have long been attached in a love in which she has given me a great deal, I shall leave her distressed and rebellious, and in doing so I shall be placing an extremely serious obstacle in the way of her spiritual progress." God always has a solution for us which is positive for everybody, and in which all duties are reconciled.

God alone can help us to build the unity of our lives in all their richness and complexity. For everything is contained in God, who gives each idea its meaning and its place in the whole complex of ideas. As long as we make these exclusive distinctions between them we shall go on shutting ourselves and others up in mental impasses. There is law in the Gospel, and also grace; there is God's judgment as well as his forgiveness; there are the follies of faith and also the wisdom of prudent foresight; there is the Cross and the Resurrection. Our minds are too small ever to grasp more than one aspect of the truth at a time; and then they make artificial distinctions between the different aspects. Jesus Christ is the unique and total incarnation of truth, the only way, the only life, and yet we betray his spirit of love when we build a wall between Buddhists, Jews, or Moslems and ourselves. He is our only Master, and yet without betraying him we can learn from the Greek philosophers, the sages of India, the philosophers of China, or the sacred texts of ancient Egypt. And I see so many people torn in two between Catholicism and Protestantism! The more priests and pastors they consult, each denouncing the errors of the other's church, the more are they pushed into opposing the one to the other in their minds, thus sterilizing their spiritual life; and so the unity of the Church, which Christ commanded, is in spirit destroyed. Also, many people are torn in two by the dichotomy between the doctrines of some sect or religious movement to which they have been attracted by its fervor, and those of the traditional Church which denounces its errors but lacks its zeal. So many people are torn in two by the arguments of the theologians. Long ago Johann Tauler of Strasbourg wrote concerning the Trinity: "Leave your arguments about it, but see to it that the Holy Trinity is within you."

However, just as at the beginning of this book I took care not to deny technology in the name of faith, so I do not want now to reject the making of distinctions in so far as it is an aid to fruitful thought. As in the case of technology, I shall say that it is useful on condition that we do not allow ourselves to become circumscribed by it.

To try to reach grace without passing through the law would only be to end up in disorder. Similarly to try to arrive at a synthesis of thought without first going through an analysis would only be to end in nebulous inconsistency. The making of distinctions seems to me to be an indispensable requisite of intellectual thought.

Let me take the evolution of the world as an illustration of what I mean. On its first page the Bible shows us God creating the world, starting from a primordial whole "without form and void," and proceeding through a series of "separations": he separates the light from the darkness, the waters which were under the firmament from the waters which were above the firmament, and then the waters from the dry land. This is fully in accord with science. For science too, creation is a succession of differentiations of opposites within a primitive whole, after which the complex whole tends to revert to its primitive uniformity, in accordance with Carnot's principle. Modern physics rests, in fact, on the basis of the second law of thermodynamics, or the Carnot-Clausius-Boltzmann principle. It establishes that a closed physicochemical system—and the universe can be considered as such—necessarily evolves in an irreversible direction, toward the increase of its entropy, that is to say toward a state of equilibrium, a sort of final leveling-out of the potential energies which were the source of physicochemical reactions. What the genius of Carnot discovered was that an engine for converting heat into power needs not one source of heat but two. The difference in their temperatures causes the physicochemical reactions which release energy in evolving toward a new state. But this new state always has an increased entropy, that is to say, less potential energy. So that the whole system is evolving continuously and necessarily toward a sort of physicochemical death.

It is clear that if this is the state of the world about us, if it is evolving in an irreversible direction, there must have been, before this, an opposite phase in which there took place within it the differentiation of these energies which are now being gradually exhausted and leveled out. The physicochemical laws of the universe cannot explain its creation, because they are irreversible. So, in the light of modern physics and chemistry, the history of the universe comprises two distinct phases: one of differentiation, and one of leveling-out; one in which entropy diminishes, and one in which it returns to its maximum, as a stretched piece of elastic returns to its original dimensions.

Where the evolution of species is concerned, creation proceeds here too by progressive differentiation of the functions and organic structures within the primitive undifferentiated living being. In the primitive state, all the functions are performed by a single cell. Then the organs gradually become specialized, right up to the most complex being, which is man. At first the reproduction of life is effected by simple cell division, and then sexuality appears, as a differentiation infinitely rich in possibilities through the laws of heredity which it brings into play. At first, sensitivity and memory belong to the primitive cell and, so to speak, form an integral part of its material reality. Then the mind is differentiated, permitting consciousness to develop in man.

In the same way, primitive thought is formless, global, and undifferentiated. By the making of a succession of distinctions, there gradually develops apperceptive or logical thought, which defines each concept with reference to its opposite, in the same way as light in the beginning was separated from darkness. This differentiation of thought continues, and becomes scientific analysis, which increasingly fragments reality into a number of partial realities each defined with reference to the others. The living being is determined only by contrast with the inanimate world, metals only in comparison with metalloids, an electrical resistance only in terms of current, the unconscious only by contrast with the conscious, and *vice versa*.

In the same way, the individual is conceived of only by contrasting him with society, authority with liberty, faith with doubt, sickness with health, scientific cognition with intuitive cognition. This analysis would seem to be the *sine qua non* of thought, while at the same time marking its limitation. For reality always contains all things, so that the more we analyze the more do we lose sight of the sum of reality. The trouble is that we cannot help hoping that this analysis will reveal to us the fundamental truth, the essential reality, the absolute value. We wonder if faith is truer than doubt, the individual more real than society, authority good and liberty bad, or *vice versa*.

The result is that culture wears itself out in futile arguments between systems of thought which are all right because they have all grasped one aspect of reality, but which, because of their very exclusiveness, make the grasping of the whole impossible. This is the present crisis of our rationalist and analytical civilization.

This is why I say that the making of distinctions is an indispensable requisite of thought. What would intellectual life be without Aristotle? Should we ever have a clear idea of the transcendent God if we did not contrast him with the immanent God? At this very moment is it not necessary for me, in order to be understood, to contrast the spirit of dogmatism with the philosophical spirit, and technology with faith?

It is impossible to arrive at the mathematical syntheses of the integral calculus, or of the quantum theory, without having first learned to distinguish a triangle from a square.

But just as in nature the phase of differentiation in creation is succeeded by the phase of standardization formed by the reciprocal reactions of all the disparate elements, so it seems to me that in thinking, the analytical phase is succeeded by a synthesizing phase.

Having made a distinction, in order to conceive of them, between liberty and authority, the unconscious and the conscious, or the technical and the moral aspect of things, thought then aims at the resolution of all these antitheses.

Thus I have no more intention of repudiating the spirit of dogmatism than I had of rejecting technology. We need it in order to help us to think clearly. Without analysis, synthesis is impossible; without it there is only a whole that is "without form and void." But I urge the thinking man not to stop at this first phase, but to pursue with the utmost zeal the aim of synthesizing all these artificial antitheses which have been the cradle of our thought. Having analyzed man; having distinguished, for purposes of study, his body, his mind, and his spirit; having entrusted this study to three distinct disciplines; having fractionalized our science more and more in order to penetrate the infinite mysteries of nature; our aim is to come back to a synthesized concept of man. It will show us that his spiritual destiny is not worked out *in abstracto,* but in his body and his mind, in his physiology and his psychology; that his "functions," to use Odier's term, include spiritual "values," and that in the perspective of faith one can appreciate the true riches of all the systems of thought that divide men.

Pure science has already firmly started on the road of synthesis. The theory of relativity lays down a relationship between time and space; the calculation of probabilities applied to physicochemical laws reconciles determinism and randomness; the granular concept of matter is resolving the dichotomy between it and energy. And while the public at large, fed on the popularizations of science of the last century, continues to believe that religion and science are inevitably opposed, scientists are coming to the world of the spirit via the laboratory. Lecomte du Noüy writes:

Those who, without the slightest proof, have systematically set about the destruction of the idea of God have acted in a base and antiscientific manner. And I assert it all the more forcefully because I do not possess the Faith, the true Faith which springs from the depths of the being. . . . Far from being, like other scientists whom I envy, supported and helped by an unshakable belief in God, I started out in life with the destructive skepticism which was the fashion. It has taken thirty years in the laboratory to convince me that those whose duty it was to enlighten me, even if only by admitting their ignorance, had deliberately lied to me.

CHAPTER · 11

☙

Sin and Disease

I can now tackle the mental antithesis we make between sin and disease, between moral responsibility and determinist irresponsibility and seek its solution on the deepest level. The reader will have realized that like the chess player, I have placed in position, one after another, a certain number of pieces—the relationship between technology and faith, between analytical psychology and soul-healing, between immediate and transcendent causality, between formal moralism and true morality, between tolerance and dogmatism—in order to come now to this subject. Not, indeed, in the hope of a decisive "checkmate," since it is in fear and trembling that I broach this infinitely delicate subject, but at least in order to try to make clear how it strikes me in the daily practice of my double ministry, medical and spiritual.

The spirit of dogmatism can only set up an irreducible antithesis:

1. We believe that we are, as science continually tries in minute detail to demonstrate, determined in all our reactions and all our physical, psychical, and even our intellectual and spiritual behavior. The components of our heredity, the physical and moral influences to which we have been exposed, the deficiencies of our body, the secretions of our endocrine glands, the influence of climate, diet, age, etc.—all these have made us what we are. It is therefore absurd to speak of moral responsibility for our acts. The idea of sin, or of moral defects, is an invention of men to explain the mystery that gripped them before science had enlightened them. The specific anguish of mind which they call the conviction of sin is merely the psychological projection of the metaphysical anxiety which, in a distant age of

ignorance, gripped them in face of the unfathomable mysteries of the world. This fatal notion of sin has been weighing on them for centuries, and has had a much worse effect than their unease in the face of the unknown forces of nature. But now that science has shown that what seemed to be unforeseeable cataclysm, or the workings of the occult, is nothing but the inevitable effect of the physical and psychical laws it studies, it is important to free men from the outmoded idea of sin. If they commit some act that is condemned by society, that is because they have been driven to it by physical and psychical causes for which they are not responsible. They are ill, and therapeutics ought to take the place of repression and condemnation.

2. Or else we believe that men are free and responsible in their behavior. Moment by moment they have a choice between obedience and disobedience to God, to the good, to the truth. Disorder, disease, and suffering have come into the world because men have disobeyed. But they try continually to escape the conviction of sin which would bring them back in repentance to God. The scientific theories they erect, these determinist ideas which they try to hide behind, are suggested to them by Satan, who uses this supreme ruse in order to sap men's morale and lull their consciences. Men use their all-powerful instincts as an excuse; they use their inevitable explosion under the compression exerted by society and its unnatural morality to explain their conduct. But only by being shown that they are guilty, responsible for these ills that they invoke as excuses, will they be made to take stock of themselves, to return to God, and recover a harmonious and healthy life.

Thus the dogmatism of determinism and the dogmatism of religion confront each other in two incompatible systems. When a scandal breaks out, when a churchman commits some outrage against morals, the first group wishes to treat him in order to correct the ill effects of heredity, hormones, and psychological repressions, while the second wishes to punish him in order to uphold morality and bring the guilty man to repentance.

Dubois, of Berne, devoted five lessons in the first part of his course on the treatment of psychoneuroses to protesting against the absurd notion of moral responsibility which makes it possible to hale poor sick people before the courts. If their iniquitous accusers had found themselves in the same condition of heredity, upbringing, and sickness, they would not—could not—have behaved any differently, and they would have been in need of love, understanding, and treatment, not condemnation. He shows that in the last analysis it is only the fear of the collapse of traditional morality that leads to such injustice; and this injustice, which is against all the evidence, prevents the logical conclusions being drawn from the irrefutable fact of scientific determinism. The supreme morality, he adds, is to love men and deal justly with them.

Faced with this "scientific" thesis, the idealists cling to the notion of moral responsibility, feeling that to undermine it is to take away from man that which makes his grandeur, that which is specific to him, distinguishing him from the physical and animal world. They maintain that to tell men and women that they are not responsible for their actions is to open wide the door to individual and social disorder, the danger of which is already demonstrated, moreover, by the general lowering of moral standards in the modern world.

Hence the undeniable vacillation of public opinion in our day, which so far as the law—civil and penal as well as international—is concerned, shows itself in recurrent arguments which give rise to compromises such as suspended sentences, but which come to no clear and satisfactory conclusion. The contemporary world, shaken by science in its ancient ideas of justice, goes on applying them, but without conviction, with attenuations and deferments which weaken and hybridize the law. Some say that we must have done with sentimental generosity, become strict once more, punish evil so as to re-establish social and international morality and law. Others assert that we must have done with legal pharisaism, and turn exclusively to trust, to love, to understanding, and technical organization.

I once attended a session of a court of law as a witness, along with several Christian colleagues, in a case in which a churchman was on trial for a moral offense. Two psychiatrists' reports were in flat contradiction of each other. The "scientific," "organicist" doctors maintained that there was absolutely no legal responsibility: if the accused had committed an offense, it was because he was ill. To condemn him would serve no useful purpose; it would only be a meaningless act of vengeance by an offended society. Castration would be more efficacious, because it would deliver him from impulses which were condemned by social prejudice. This was a clear and coherent argument, but one which the law hesitated to adopt because it might involve a denial of its own function. On the other side the "idealist" doctors spoke of "diminished responsibility." As doctors, they all recognized the physical and psychical factors which argued for leniency; but as moralists they wished to safeguard the principle of punishment for a crime in a man whose life ought to have been an example to others.

It seems to me that this expression "diminished responsibility" to which people so often cling corresponds to no clear concept. It is the expression of that vacillation of outlook in the modern world, between classic moral dogmatism and the new scientific dogmatism which is undermining it.

Faced with these two opposing views of the case at hand, it seemed to me that on Christian grounds it was possible to arrive at a perfectly clear conclusion: complete absence of legal responsibility, but complete personal moral responsibility. Let me explain:

If we cast aside all prejudice, if we divest ourselves of all pharisaism, as the Gospel commands us, we can do no other than agree unreservedly with the "scientific" doctors, and reject all legal responsibility. I told the jury that I myself suffer from a physical abnormality—I am color-blind. There are certain colors which I have difficulty in distinguishing; but fortunately for me, this abnormality does not bring me into conflict with the law. I am no more responsible for it than is the accused for the perversion of his sex instinct. To condemn him for that perversion—and that is indeed what is suggested in the name of justice—would be as unjust as to punish me for being color-blind, or as punishing people for being over six feet tall, or having red hair. Complete absence of legal responsibility, therefore.

On the other hand, when a man feels in his heart that he is completely responsible for his behavior, that is when he may undergo a decisive moral experience which changes his life, frees him from the tyranny of his passions, and rebuilds his personality. But this is a totally interior matter, with which the law, society, or *other people* have nothing to do. It is exclusively a matter between himself and God. Before God he feels responsible, not for the physical and psychological facts of his life—his heredity, his complexes, and the deficiencies and illnesses engendered by circumstances—but for the use he makes of what he has got. That responsibility is the same for all men: I am as guilty before God of misusing my normal sex instinct as the accused is of misusing his perverted instinct. Sin is not being ill; it is disobeying God, whether one is ill or well. Those who are well sin as much as the sick in the light of the Gospel, which pays attention to the disposition of the heart, and not to external appearances. And those who are well have less excuse for sinning, and more difficulty in recognizing their sin. Jesus Christ was more severe toward them than toward the sick, to whom he held out his hand in succor. Complete moral responsibility, therefore.

A distinguished colleague who is often called on as an expert witness in psychiatric matters, after reading these lines, has expressed his concern to me. He assures me that he unreservedly approves of the fundamental attitude I adopt in this book, but on this particular point of responsibility before the law he fears that if my views were pushed to their logical conclusion, "we should have in the end to look upon no criminal as being responsible for his criminal acts. For every criminal is abnormal to some extent—in his heredity, in the circumstances of his life, in his endocrine functions, etc. Even supposing he is in the sight of God not so great a sinner as the judge who pronounces judgment upon him, the judge must nevertheless formulate his opinion in the light of different considerations. In effect, the laws were not made . . . in order to establish first and foremost the moral guilt of the delinquent, but to ensure social and human order, to protect the weak, the young, and so on. How often, in fact, has not punishment set in train an inner transformation? How often has it not prevented the criminal from committing fresh crimes?"

I give great weight to these considerations. I have taken pains to quote them in order to avoid all misunderstanding. What I am trying to do is to resolve the flagrant contradiction which we are constantly coming up against between the scientific and the moral points of view in the matter of responsibility. I should not want an ill-considered systematization further to undermine the precarious position of human justice. I recognize that beside these two points of view there is a third, the practical social point of view, and that in the law courts society is defending itself against those who threaten its order. The trouble is that the Law does not approach the question from that point of view, but from the angle of responsibility. It does not ask: "Is the delinquent dangerous? Ought he to be condemned in order to protect the young and the weak?" It asks: "Is he responsible?"

In a study group of doctors and theologians of which I am a member, several doctors have recently expressed a desire to discuss these questions not only with doctors and theologians, but also with lawyers. They think that, in some cases at least, the best means of "protecting the young and the weak" would not be to sentence the offender to several years in prison—after which he comes out unchanged—but to give him medical treatment.

Here is the paradox. As long as a man is accused by the law, by society, by *other people,* he defends himself; it is a universal reflex. This defensive attitude prevents him from "coming to himself" and undergoing a moral experience. In the belief that it is leading him toward such an experience, society is in fact leading him away from it. But as soon as *other people,* instead of casting stones at him, recognize that in the perspective of the heart they are as guilty as he, he accuses *himself,* he repents and undergoes that moral experience which the Gospel calls salvation.

So where others are concerned: total absence of responsibility. Where we ourselves are concerned: total responsibility.

I believe that in thus formulating my views I am being true to the spirit of the Gospel. When our Lord's disciples asked him if a blind man was born blind because of his own sin or that of his parents, Jesus replied categorically: "No" (John 9:2–3). Similarly, he asked his disciples, on the subject of an accident: "Those eighteen upon whom the tower in Siloam fell and killed them, do you think that they were worse offenders than all the others who dwelt in Jerusalem? I tell you, No; but unless you repent you will all likewise perish" (Luke 13:4–5). So, when it was matter of the sins of *others,* he denied their responsibility; but where *their own* sin was concerned, he affirmed it.

It will perhaps be objected that this distinction between two opposite standpoints (when we are looking at others and when we are looking at ourselves) is oversubtle and illogical. It is, however, a distinction which is daily made the other way round. Where others are concerned we are outraged at their behavior, and consider them responsible. Where we ourselves are concerned we plead that we are not responsible, and point to all the external causes which have determined our conduct.

The reader will recall the illustration I used in Chapter 3, concerning the Matterhorn. Similarly, if I hold a coin between another person and myself, each of us sees one side of the coin only, either the head or the tail, whichever is facing him, and not the other. In the same way, each of us sees our own responsibility and not that of the other person. And yet, like the coin our infinitely complex human life is one single reality, although with our limited minds we cannot grasp this fact in its entirety. Depending on the side from which we approach it, we see its objective, scientific, technical, determined, nonresponsible aspect, or, on the contrary, its personal, subjective, moral, free, and responsible aspect.

Odier attributes to me a thought that I do not think I have ever entertained: "In his writings," he says, " 'sin' and 'morbid' seem to be the same." In other words, sin equals disease. That I shall never say, because it is false. It is contrary to the Gospel, and it is contrary to an honest and objective observation of the facts, which is the law of the doctor. Lavaud stresses the same point in his article on my work, and I cannot but give him my wholehearted approval. He reminds us that many great saints have suffered greatly from disease. I may add that some of the men for whose nobility and holiness of mind I have felt the most sincere respect suffered from physical or psychical disease. Like St. Paul, after he had thrice asked God in vain to deliver him from his "thorn in the flesh," they had to be content with the reply he received: "My grace is sufficient for you" (II Cor. 12:9).

I also see every day, unfortunately, how a neurosis or mental ill-health can damage the spiritual life, producing unconscious guilt feelings, the veritable "psychological monster," in Odier's apt phrase. I see also how they can give false feelings of salvation—a maniacal euphoria which is a caricature of the joy of forgiveness, or a distortion of the ego which is an unhealthy caricature of the true inner drama of the Christian as St. Paul describes it. I recognize the sign of the "superego" of the psychoanalysts in this kind of religious delirium, which, instead of enlightening the conscience, blinds it.

I recognize that if disease entered the world with sin, if they are both the sign of the curse consequent upon the Fall, we cannot forget, either, that human solidarity is such that one person bears in his sickness the consequence of the sin of others. This forbids any objective identification between sin and disease. Did not Christ bear the sin of mankind to the extent that his body was marked with it in the physical stigmata? Does disease come from Satan or from God? asks Pastor Schütz.[1] There is some truth in both views. It is like asking whether the Cross came from Satan or from God.

I have been told that a German-Swiss deaconess once came into

[1] Alfred Schütz, *Glaube und Gesundheit*.

the bedroom of one of her patients, with whom she had already had heated discussions, brandishing my book, *The Healing of Persons,* and exclaiming: "See! I was right! Read this book, and you will recognize that you must be a great sinner because you are ill!" You can understand how pained I am at hearing such things.

I have, on the other hand, reported the experience of many people, both the sick and the healthy, who where they themselves (and not others) were concerned, found improvement, healing, or deliverance from a physical malady or a psychical disturbance after the occurrence of an inner spiritual crisis. And this crisis has sometimes been, in particular cases, the discovery in the light of the Spirit of a sin that was obstructing healing. A good man whom I much admire informed me how much his deafness had been improved by the reading of my book. He had suddenly seen how much pleasure he took in deafness as a means of cutting himself off from the world.

So we return to this fundamental distinction between others and ourselves. A certain patient is in a bad humor, and I see that it is because his liver is upset, because of a hereditary nervous weakness, and because his employer has upset him unjustly. And I can also see the physical and psychical factors that govern the employer's behavior. But if I am ill-humored myself, I see that it is because of my self-will, my selfishness and lack of love—in a word, because of my sin.

I have referred to Dubois and his ringing indictment of the spirit of criticism which crushes the sick under the outworn notion of moral responsibility. He describes how, when "a rather overbearing father brings you his daughter as if she were a criminal," you assert that it is "a diseased state," in order to make him more understanding and charitable. But a few pages further on he writes of "a strapping young man, a little soft in his dress, who announces to you that he is neurasthenic," in order to explain that he is incapable of work. Dubois shows this young man "the value of moral courage, and of the continual tendency of our moral personality toward perfection." What does this mean, if not that the atheist doctor and the Christian doctor arrive in practice at the same conclusions: where others are concerned, to talk of disease and deny responsibility; where oneself is concerned, to talk of sin and assert responsibility. Lastly, although Dubois so ardently pleads mental determinism, he shows no less eloquently that in fact our inner development, our moral life, and our sense of responsibility for ourselves are mechanisms by which this determinism operates. In his eyes the behavior of man is determined by a group of factors; and among these are the moral influences he undergoes—his inner experiences. Lead him, therefore, as this doctor himself is constantly doing, to moral victories, and the very laws of determinism will make the victories, in their turn, the basis of a new behavior and a new life. This new quality of life is the same as the grace preached by Christianity, and Dubois, despite all his bluster against it, leads his patients to it along the same road of honesty with oneself, understanding love, and trust.

So disease does not equal sin. To suspect that sin is the cause of a person's sickness is to adopt in regard to him a formalist attitude which is contrary to Christianity. But where oneself is concerned, to examine one's conscience—whether one is well or ill—and recognize one's sin, is to rediscover the current of grace which very often (but not always!) improves one's physical and moral health by bringing new factors into the determinism which is studied by science.

"Although the body is not the immediate subject of grace," writes St. Thomas Aquinas, "nevertheless the effect of grace flows from the soul to the body."

Here is the case of a patient who had been treated for a long time by a distinguished psychoanalyst. I talked to her one day about the two opposite attitudes, the formalism which makes a healthy person say to a sick one: "Do as I do! Show some will power!" and in so doing misuses the idea of moral responsibility, and on the other hand the attitude of psychological understanding which recognizes the unhealthy sign of lack of will power, but rejects the idea of moral responsibility. Without hesitation she replied: "Both are necessary! There is truth in both." And she went on: "My psychoanalyst's moral neutrality was a great help to me in relieving me of the weight of formalism that had been crushing me. But I remember the no less lively feeling of liberation I had one day when I was talking with you, when I realized once more that I was personally responsible for an act for which the psychoanalyst had always said I was not responsible. It was as if a road out of my illness was being opened out in front of me. You see, as long as I was not responsible for anything, there was nothing I could do to help myself get out of it. It was as if I was locked into it by its very inevitableness!

A friend puts this question to me: "I have been seeing a rather sensual man whose wife denies him any sex life. Am I right to suggest to him that he should see his wife's sexual blocking as a disease and accept it as such, understanding her and caring for her rather than complaining to her about it, or ought I rather to recognize, with him, that she has her faults and her responsibilities in their marital conflict?" You can imagine my reply: "If you are seeing the husband, help him to see his wife's complex as a matter of ill-health, and his own sensual claims as a manifestation of his selfishness which is damaging the happiness of his home; but if you are seeing the wife, help her to see her husband's sensuality as a natural instinct or a need to assert a virility of which he is doubtful, and her own refusal as a lack of love toward him."

As my patient said, there is truth in both attitudes. Thus one sees a Christian psychoanalyst like Weatherhead[2] carefully describing the psychological mechanisms of rationalization, condensation, symbolization, and repression, and then adding: "Sin and selfishness are at the root of so many psychological troubles." Analytical psychology is in full agreement with the Gospel when it points out how clever our minds are at creating false problems so as to be able to turn on to them the excessive emotion generated by real problems which there is a tendency to leave hidden in the dark. This is the mechanism of obsessions and overscrupulousness. The real problems, which are highly charged with emotion, are often faults or sins which we are afraid to look in the face. The false problems are like bushes behind which we unconsciously play hide-and-seek with our consciences. Similarly, unjust criticism is seized upon as a ground for self-justification rather than as an opportunity to find out what our real faults are. Men's real problems are generally very simple: rebellions, rancours, passions, and fears. They always make me think of a theater in which some passionate conflict is being acted on the stage, while in the auditorium a couple in discord sits sulking and having intrigues with other spectators. The fictitious drama is well-lit and clearly seen by all. The real-life drama is in shadow and passes unnoticed. Thus the objective, external causes of man's behavior are immediately obvious and widely discussed. The inner causes most often remain hidden even from the person concerned himself. Science, being objective, is extremely valuable as an aid to the understanding of others. But as

[2] L. D. Weatherhead, *Psychology, Religion and Healing.*

regards oneself, it is often misleading concerning the real roots of evil. "I think," wrote one of my patients, "that only a detailed individual confession can dissipate the veil of ignorance which separates us from God." And she adds: "All our faults, all our psychic and physical ills, or almost all, are, so far as I can see, the symptoms of one single trouble." In medicine we like to make the "synthesis of a case," that is to say, to find the diagnosis which fits all the symptoms. It is rare in psychology for this synthesis to be arrived at by technical means, which tend on the contrary to give an infinitely complex picture of the mind. It comes rather through confession, which brings to light the common root of a number of facts that have no apparent relationship.

"The exterior is the signature of the interior," wrote Jacob Boehme. The reason why external events, such as unjust criticism, hurt us so much is that they find an echo in our own malaise. The person who has doubts about himself is extremely sensitive to the criticisms of others. The self-confident person does not even notice them. We are afraid of the external enemy because of the "fifth column" we are aware of in ourselves. We are very ready to look upon external events as bolts from the blue which come to upset the normal course of our lives. The day comes when we look upon them as the necessary instruments of a destiny ordained from within.

Nothing is more calculated to give us this feeling of fate than the determinist view of man to which science leads. All the elements that go to make up his being seem bound in an inescapable process of cause and effect. Every present is conditioned by the past, and every future is conditioned by the present, by a sort of inner fate. Grace, which touches man at the center of his being, introduces an entirely new element into the process, and gives it a new direction. An unknown woman wrote the following to me, on the sacraments: "Little by little, my discontent and my constant dissatisfaction (which the psychiatrists told me came from my complete lack of sexual satisfaction in marriage) disappeared. I feel a real sense of happiness and intimate satisfaction. . . . This completeness, which I thought I should never attain, comes from the approach of Jesus Christ." "The kingdom of God is nervous equilibrium, liberation, health, harmony, the perfect development of the person, which permit him to put out his feelers, to recover his intellectual, artistic, emotional, and religious sensitivity," another woman writes. And

Weatherhead: "An experience of Christ, the experience which follows upon as complete an abandonment and dedication of oneself to him as possible, is the most powerful force that the human personality can ever know, and the greatest transforming energy that has ever existed." "So," he adds, "since psychological determinism makes all men suffer from their past, what they need most in order to suffer less, is to realize that this 'past' has been rubbed out by God."[3] He is giving an answer there to the woman who wrote: "To begin my life again. . . . But will it be in my power to blot out the past?"

Here, in the profoundest and most moving manner, disease and sin find a common level: anyone who maintains at the back of his mind the false notion that something in his past separates him irremediably from God is doomed to despair, with all its psychological consequences. No technique can free him from it unless it is accompanied by God's forgiveness. One of my patients still feels that she was a coward and ran away when God called her, and that her chance will never return. All our psychological analysis, interesting and useful though it is, goes on endlessly and round and round. But as soon as she admits her fears to me, the admission brings her a sense of reconciliation with God. A few months later she writes to me of her joy at being able to pray again. Another woman has been jilted by her fiancé, and her despair has made her ill. I try to encourage her to face life once more, but it is in vain, until she confides in me that behind this admitted anguish there is another that is the real source of its despairing intensity: she is blaming herself for having given in to her fiancé when he insisted on her terminating a pregnancy. And now, having obtained God's forgiveness, she is able to forgive the man.

Dynamic psychology refers all the activity of the mind to its instinctive drives, which are considered to be the only active forces. Ought we not to liken the Holy Spirit and the thirst for God to instincts? For like instincts, they are powerful drives in the working of the mechanisms of the mind.

[3] *Ibid.*

CHAPTER · 12

Reversal

The next question that arises is how to acquire this spiritual strength —how to turn it from a potential force into an active one.

This, of course, is the effect of the grace of God breaking into a person's life, and we shall never succeed in defining it in intellectual terms, nor in laying down any method of procuring it, since it is God's doing and not ours.

But at least we can try to describe some aspects of the reversal of attitude implied in what the Christian tradition calls conversion.

In *The Healing of Persons* I quoted a passage from a lecture by Frank Abauzit, describing the distinction to which I have just referred between the scientific aspect and the moral aspect of an event. In his book,[1] the implications of this antithesis are developed with all the clarity of thought and vigor of the true philosopher—whereas I describe it rather as a painter of life. His view of morality is as follows:

Instead of considering things from the scientific point of view, taking, that is, the facts of my own life as mere facts whose causes I could analyze and whose nature I might modify in some small measure by modifying those causes, I rid myself of all such considerations, and abandon all my preoccupation with the crisscross within me of efficient causes, actions, interactions, and influences. I cast all these aside, and content myself with saying, in respect of all the actions for which I consider myself responsible: "It was I who did it." I concentrate my mind on that, and pay no attention to all the rest. I look only upon myself as a cause—not a link in an endless chain of events, but a starting point, something like the first beginning of which the philosophers speak, something like a creative

[1] *Le problème de la tolérance.*

125

cause. . . . If I live with the idea that it is always something other than myself that is to blame or responsible, which is the cause of my actions, I shall spend all my time in recrimination against things and people. I shall say: "It is not surprising that I did not succeed in this or that project; it is not surprising that this child I am concerned with turned out so badly. . . ." But for myself, I shall remain what I was: weak and inadequate for the great tasks that are before me.

Abauzit shows in the final part of his book that it is always when a man adopts this moral point of view of liberty and personal responsibility that he finds his moral personality developing at the expense of the egotistical individual, and spiritual power becoming the essential motive force of his life.

I am in full agreement with him. The reader, however, has probably felt that this antithesis leads us once again to a view of the mechanistic aspect of life as opposed to its moral aspect, to a dichotomy between science and religion. We may indeed disregard the scientific point of view when we are in the midst of an inner crisis—and with profit. But we cannot thrust it altogether from our thoughts forever, because it is also an aspect of the truth. For my part, I cannot bring myself to accept that the condition of conversion is to deny one side of the truth, yet it is an opinion commonly held both by unbelievers and by believers. Both cling to their own view of the truth. The argument between them is incapable of resolution.

I believe, however, that there is another aspect of this reversal which, instead of accentuating the dichotomy between science and religion, helps to resolve it. It is this:

One can, of course, as Abauzit shows, use science and psychology as an excuse for oneself, pleading the inevitable determinism of a chain of cause and effect in the influences one has been subjected to, in order to escape any conviction of sin and all sense of moral responsibility. But where other people are concerned, one can use the insights provided by scientific psychology to help one understand and forgive their faults, since one then sees the objective causes of their behavior in the ills that have befallen them, and the complexes that have resulted. In this way, thanks to the scientific view of things, one can lay aside all one's moral indignation at other people's acts—all one's tendency to judge, criticize, and condemn them.

Secondly, one can of course, as Abauzit shows, use morality to accuse oneself of the wrongs for which one feels responsible, in order to repent and ask for God's grace. But unfortunately one can also use morality in order to judge others, to crush them with a moralistic indictment, denouncing the sins for which one holds them responsible and condemning them on the grounds that morality and religion must be defended.

Again, one can use psychological analysis to tear away one's own mask and discover, behind one's so-called virtues, guilty intentions of which one has been unaware. But on the other hand one can use it to unmask others and to arouse the suspicion of all kinds of perverse tendencies in them. To accuse them of these things would be unfair, since they are quite unaware of them.

It is a natural attitude in men to make use of science or religion, psychology or morality, for the purpose of excusing oneself while criticizing others. However, using them to understand others and to bring oneself to repentance is the "reversed" attitude, the attitude of conversion, of true morality, and of the Gospel.

Thus, instead of making an exclusive distinction between the scientific and the moral views of the world, each of which contains part of the truth, we recognize that both can serve either our natural or our transformed attitude, according to our inner disposition.

The daily observation of men and women shows me that believers and unbelievers are much closer to one another than one would think if one judged by their dogmatic controversies. There are determinists who call themselves unbelievers on account of their scientific philosophy, but who have hearts of gold and use their determinist ideas to help them understand their fellow men; and so they act with gentle humility toward others while at the same time being extremely strict with themselves. There are hardhearted orthodox believers who use their moral view of the world for little else than to hurl anathemas about, without observing their own faults. "Not every one who says to me, 'Lord, Lord,' shall enter the kingdom of heaven," said Christ, "but he who does the will of my Father who is in heaven" (Matt. 7:21).

For example, I have several times received visits from a religious woman who announced at once that she had not come on her own account, but "for her husband." She wanted to bring him to faith. She had noted all his faults, and she described them all to me, at the same time expressing the hope that an inner transformation would free him from them. Interviews of that kind scarcely ever do any good. But if one day that wife returns, not now on behalf of her husband, but on her own account, having resolved to seek before God to find out what changes are needed in her, that will be much more fruitful.

Returning to the example of the coin which I used in the previous ·chapter, if I look only at the side representing my psychological determinism and absence of responsibility—which hides the side representing my moral responsibility—and show the other person the side representing his moral responsibility—which hides the side representing his psychological determinism—then my attitude is that of natural, unconverted man. If I see the side of my moral responsibility—which hides that of my psychological determinism—but see the other person's determinist side—which hides that of his moral responsibility—then my attitude is that of a disciple of Jesus Christ. The turning over of the coin which shows me first the one side and then the other represents the reversal which is brought about by conversion.

In an intellectual discussion, for example, we can examine the opinions and actions of others for everything of which we do not approve, in order to criticize them, and in our own case, look for all the good things we think and do, in order to boast about them and use them as a weapon against others. This is an attitude that impoverishes and embitters, and leads only to sterile argument. We can also examine what others say for a side of the truth that has hitherto escaped our notice, and for what God wants through their witness to show us is wrong with ourselves. This is an attitude that enriches discussion, making it joyful, fruitful, and purposeful. If one spends a little time listening to the general run of conversations, of which at least 80 per cent consists of denunciations of what is unjust, scandalous, badly organized, wicked, or defective in the world, one gets some idea of how much mental energy is wasted in arguments which lead to no real change. A reversal of our attitude makes us see that we can play a more useful part in the healing of the world by putting right the wrongs about which there is something we can do— those that we have ourselves committed. As Goethe said, if everyone swept outside his own door, the whole town would be clean.

Abauzit also describes this aspect of reversal:

Each of us has in himself two opposite tendencies, each of them in its own way natural, instinctive, and legitimate: a tendency toward severity, and a tendency toward benevolence and indulgence. Only—as Pascal might have said—we have turned things upside down: we apply severity where we ought to use indulgence, and indulgence where we ought to be severe. We are full of indulgence toward ourselves, and full of severity toward others, when we ought to be full of indulgence toward others and full of severity toward ourselves. . . . The egotist condemns others and approves of himself; he who is born to the spiritual life begins by condemning himself—which is made possible for him because he knows that his salvation is at hand—and he is full of indulgence toward others.[2]

This is clearly seen in marital conflicts. As long as each is denouncing the other's faults, they get nowhere. As soon as one of them begins to see and understand the struggle, psychological as well as moral, which is going on within the other, he stops seeing the other's behavior as personally offensive to him, and becomes a peacemaker. Here I must make a correction to the oversimplified distinction I have made between Odier's "functions" and "values." To see the behavior of a man as a "function" is to see the psychological determinism which governs it; to see it as a "value" is to see in it the battle being waged in that man between good and evil, between God and the devil. It follows that in the idea of "values" we must see a positive value, God's call, and also a negative value, the call of Satan. If the patient who comes to see me is obeying the good call, I must consider him from the point of view of "values" and not of "function." But I should be adopting a censorious attitude toward him if I did this when he is answering the call to evil. In that case I must see his behavior as a "function."

This reversal of attitude has many other aspects besides. One is struck by the number of people, believers as well as unbelievers, who look in the Bible for just those passages which do not apply to them. Those who are tortured, crushed, and in despair pick out the hard words that Jesus addressed to the smug Pharisees—the passages in which he speaks of God's judgment, of the sin against the Holy Ghost which will not be forgiven, or of the gates of heaven which are closed against those who arrive too late. Those who are optimistic, superficial, and self-satisfied, however, pick out the words which Christ addressed to outcasts and sinners to assure them of God's forgiveness which blots out every sin. The effect of the reversal of attitude that I

[2] *Ibid.*

am describing is to make us look in the Bible for the things that apply to us personally!

The tragedy of our Western world is that it remains impregnated with Christianity, but has in general ceased really believing in it. The same man, for example, who declares that it is not possible to be honest in business, scolds his son sharply if he catches him in a lie. If we were frankly pagan we should be—perhaps—more immoral, but we should be less sick. The reason why there are so many sick is that this dichotomy in our Western civilization is reflected in the minds of all our contemporaries. Any inner cleavage between two contradictory tendencies gives rise to psychological troubles. There are always two ways of resolving an intrapsychic conflict, which is like disequilibrium in a balance. To overload the side that is too light is what the psychologists call overcompensation—the erection of a whole façade of virtue, morality, and respectability, which is intended to hide from oneself and others one's inner malaise and shame. But to lighten the side that is too heavy is Christian sacrifice, the honest recognition of one's own sin in order to take it to God so as to be forgiven and set free.

This giving up of sin is also a reversal, a change of direction, in that the mind, instead of proceeding from the outside inward, in order to bring everything into itself, assessing every event according to the good it can extract, or the harm it might do itself, proceeds from the inside outward, in order to forget itself and assess everything according to what it can give of itself to others.

Then the truth of the paradox of the Gospel can be verified, that whoever seeks to gain his life will lose it, and *vice versa*. It is what John Stuart Mill said about happiness, that the only way to achieve it is not to seek it. "The more I try to leave my brother and sister-in-law in the intimacy they are so jealous of," a spinster writes to me, "the more they press me to join them." And here is the nice story of a young woman on the day after she had experienced this radical reversal of attitude: "I went for a walk in the country, and found some excellent little wild fruit on a bush. I was thinking that it was a sort of present from God, when I heard the sound of approaching footsteps. My first reaction was to move away so as not to reveal my find to anyone else and so have to share it. At once a battle took place in me—my new attitude meant sharing everything. I spoke to the lady who had come up to me, and she replied, to my delighted surprise:

'Just over there you'll find a lot more even better ones!' " A patient writes: "I am not yet mature enough for the complete self-sacrifice of Christianity." Which of us, indeed, could claim to be so? And yet the day comes when we realize that the more we give up the more we receive.

Spoerri refers to this reversal of attitude in connection with the Lord's Prayer:

The shape of the Lord's Prayer distinguishes it from all other prayers: it begins in heaven and comes down to earth. All other prayers move in the opposite direction. They begin on earth and go toward heaven. . . . But Jesus Christ goes in the other direction. He reverses the heavenly ladder of all the Pharisees in the world." Instead of asking God to do what we want, the Lord's Prayer puts us at His service, listening for His instructions.[3]

I see so many people who want to "protect their personalities," and who in reality are trampled upon by everybody. I often feel that I am being asked to visit a person's life like a guest being invited to take a walk on his host's property. Every path off to right or left bears a notice saying "Keep out," so that the visitor is obliged to remain in the uninteresting central drive. Something begins to happen only when the conversation begins to stray away from the subjects that have been expected and provided for in advance.

Reversal has taken on yet another meaning for me. It was when a friend asked me: "How many souls have you brought to Jesus Christ?" I realized then that my spiritual ministry was still so poor, not because of any lack of zeal and activity on my part, but because my own life did not shine out as an example, and that this was because of the compromises I still tolerated in myself while I was quite ready to denounce them in everyone else.

Before we can hope to bring Christ to others, we are required to dedicate ourselves totally to him and accept his rule in our hearts. This demands a definite decision, but it demands no science, no formula, no set method. It is an inner attitude. A young man in great distress tries to put an end to his life, but makes a mess of it, and lies for some hours injured, helpless and alone in his attic. Suddenly a great calm spreads over his mind, and to his surprise he finds that he is praying. There are no words; it is more like a sigh, but it expresses

[3] Théophile Spoerri, *Notre Père.*

the reversal that God is bringing about within him. He sees a way out that he had not seen before, in his tense and despairing distress.

In defining this new inner attitude as the acceptance of the rule of Jesus Christ, I take the phrase in a sense that excludes all formalism. All those who have preached a true spiritual message to mankind are at one in this attitude, which is incarnate in Jesus Christ. Listen, for example, to Confucius, whose words are astonishingly similar to those of Christ: "What I do not wish others to do to me, I will not do to others." And again: "If someone is not capable of directing himself, how could he direct others?" And Pythagoras: "What is below is like what is on high." All come in the end to the paradoxical message which runs right through the Christian Gospel. Man, that paradoxical being, has found, one might say, a paradoxical God in Jesus Christ. What a strange God! He gained the affection of the unlearned, strangers to spiritual matters, whereas he was in constant conflict with the theologians. He readily associated with the most immoral types of people—prostitutes, shady public officials, and neuropaths—while hurling the strongest possible invective at the most honored and distinguished representatives of respectable society. He remained silent before the powerful Pilate, but was prepared to spend time sitting with his arms round the kids, or talking to a despised foreign woman who was drawing water. He asserted that he was one with the Father, and admitted that he had been so sorely tempted by the devil that the battle had lasted forty days. He talked about perfect joy, but was sweating blood a few hours later. He said he was going to his Father, and soon was crying: "My God, why hast thou forsaken me?" He had come to save men from evil, and yet he remained passive in face of the supreme triumph of evil.

Attachment to the person of Christ means avoiding both moral dogmatism and moral anarchy. The reader will realize that all I have been saying against despotic dogmatism could well open the door to a no less dangerous individualism, subjectivism, and amorality, if all we had to guide us was a moral code, instead of a living person. If man is not to look upon himself as a god, or a sovereign interpreter of God, he needs an objective criterion of truth: and this we have in Jesus Christ. We may do anything at all provided it is done with Christ. He alone frees us both from passive conformity and from rebellious nonconformity. If we think of him in every circumstance of our lives; consult him on every point; seek him in every person we meet; and whenever we are faced with a decision, ask ourselves what he would do; ask ourselves in every affliction and every blessing what he is saying to us in that affliction or that blessing; then we shall be passionately interested in everything and everybody; we shall take everything seriously but nothing tragically; we shall unify our lives and our personalities, through giving them one single axis. Above all we shall find ourselves daily taking the road that leads to the reversal of our attitude, which we can never achieve by ourselves.

People often say that the sudden, uniquely decisive character of Christian conversion does not fit in with the necessity of going through it, as it were, daily. Either this reversal is really a radical change of attitude in life, so that the whole process ought to be completed at once, and for good; or else this new attitude is arrived at little by little, experience by experience, in which case it is a slow progress toward perfection, not a sudden reversal. Here again, both are true. God brings every man to a moment in his life when there takes place within him—often over some quite minor act of obedience—this inner debate as to which of the two attitudes, resistance or acceptance, he is to adopt. This moment cannot be artificially created, nor can it be escaped when it comes. I have met many scrupulous souls who have thought they ought to present themselves—quite artificially—with the same choice as they have heard someone else say he had faced. In their case they are acting merely imitatively, and not on account of personal initiative, and the result is a false debate which will lead to no genuine conviction. I remember, however, one of my patients who, feeling that she had a real problem of conscience to deal with, went to see her pastor. He disappointed her by trying to minimize the importance of the conflict, and to reassure her: "You are torturing yourself unnecessarily; you are a very good Christian; stop worrying about it."

The solemn moment of decision sometimes comes on the occasion of an illness, which one sees as a warning sent from God; or of a moral conflict, which shows up the disorder in one's mind. But this renunciation is quite as necessary in the healthiest and most evenly balanced lives, for no man does it by nature. Sometimes it is quite a simple matter, and seems to be given by grace, and sometimes it is a heroic struggle. Sometimes it results from quite orthodox preaching; sometimes it happens amidst dogmatic assertions the error of which one later recognizes; sometimes it is helped by something said by a person with no pretensions whatever to religion. It matters little how one finds God, or that the field in which the discovery is made is a limited one. The experience is always accompanied by the feeling that something absolutely new has come into one's life. It is in substance a new quality of life which will gradually penetrate all the other fields of one's activity. We are sometimes put off by the immense complexity of human problems, as if one had to deal with every fruit on a tree separately in order to ripen it. Now at last we realize that all we have to do is to plant the tree, water it, and protect it against parasites, in order to have each fruit ripening of itself in its own proper time. One of my patients writes: "I remember that an important decision—to give up a love affair—had at once made all my other feelings and thoughts clearer. Until then, I had been sick with indecision in every department of my life."

One further point is that this decision, while it brings new life and hope, does come into collision with one's old, ingrained habits. In biology everything is habit, and the repetition of this reversal causes new habits to be substituted for the old.

So the reversal is qualitatively total from the first. It is God that is found, not "a little bit of God," whenever the heart turns toward him. But the new attitude, which is contained virtually in the first act of obedience, is only realized through a continual examination of the conscience.

For the Greeks everything was immutable. They had a static conception of the world.

The Jews conceived of God as intervening in history; hence they looked forward to a future golden age.

The Indian religions see this perfection as the end of a gradual process of spiritualization.

For the Christian all is accomplished in Jesus Christ. The center of history, the decisive intervention of God, is behind us, and so we are delivered from the hopeless problem of how we are to scale the heights of heaven. Nevertheless we have an inborn feeling of our own perfectibility.

It seems to me that evolution, as presented to us by science, provides a useful illustration of this difficult question. At each stage of evolution—the appearance of life on the earth, for instance—a quite new fact intervenes, unexplained by the determining factors that have gone before. This new fact, however, will take many centuries to realize its many possibilities in all the multitude of increasingly differentiated living creatures that will make their appearance; and yet all those possibilities were already contained in the very first appearance of life.

In the same way Jesus Christ is a historical reality. He marks the beginning of a new stage, the reign of the Spirit. This reign was fully contained in its first appearance, but God incarnates it gradually in all these new appearances of the Spirit, as each of us experiences the reversal of his inner attitude, following in Christ's footsteps and receiving his grace.

PART IV

Faith

₩

CHAPTER 13

Suggestion and Faith

We have just seen that Christian conversion involves a psychological reversal of one's attitude. The person who has been continually criticizing others—holding them morally responsible for wrongs done to him, while finding excuses for himself in the determinism which controlled his own conduct—from now on applies his severity to himself, and keeps his indulgence for others. Instead of constantly defending himself against the injustices of the world, instead of living with all the psychic and functional troubles that fear and doubt bring in their train, instead of claiming attention, benefits, and charity from others, he attaches himself personally to Christ, and tries to obey him in order to inspire in others the confidence, justice, and love that he draws from him.

This reversal of attitude, however, comes about only as the consequence of conversion and would be quite utopian without faith and fellowship in Christ. It is the psychological significance of the Christian faith. This significance, however, this psychological aspect of faith, is inseparable from its true spiritual significance.

Where the psychological significance of faith is concerned, doctors and psychologists of differing schools are generally in agreement. Like us, our agnostic colleagues underline the important part played by fear, despair, and doubt in the genesis of psychological troubles, functional disorders, and even certain organic diseases. They also recognize that the restoration of confidence is a decisive healing factor, when a patient feels himself to be loved, understood, and upheld by our own faith.

Even atheist doctors honestly recognize, as a result of long experience, that religious faith is the most powerful means of restoring the serenity and confidence of a troubled mind. They sometimes send a patient to a Christian colleague, with the thought that he is the one best able to help him, through his witness, and that nothing will contribute more to his cure than religious faith. The patient's mystic contact with the divinity; the relieving of his conscience that will come with forgiveness; the feeling of being protected by Providence; the beneficent suggestion that with heaven's help he will be able to win victories where hitherto he has failed—all this will have a beneficial psychological effect on him. The assurance of being able to establish contact with God in prayer will give him a sense of security.

One of my patients told me that once when she was taking a little girl for a walk in the woods she asked the child: "You aren't afraid, I hope?" And the girl replied: "I'm never afraid when you hold my hand."

Is it not itself a confession of faith to have confidence in the power of faith? Nevertheless religious circles do not always give such tributes the welcome they deserve. They are afraid of a misunderstanding of their beliefs. They are afraid that the very agreement which is expressed in this way on the psychological value of faith contains an insidious threat to the true faith. They are afraid that it means bringing it down to the purely human level of a therapeutical method, a psychological phenomenon, mere suggestion. They are afraid that to recognize in this way the psychological effect of religious faith is to insinuate that its action has nothing of the supernatural in it, that it has nothing to do with God's intervening in a person's soul, but only with a belief—an illusory one—in the action of a fictitious God.

I thoroughly understand these fears. Since the time of the Greek philosophers—when the Pythagoreans saw all natural events as manifestations of divine forces, whereas the Eleatic School considered the gods to be merely a human invention—two currents have confronted each other. One, with Plato, starts from the invisible realities in order to explain the visible world, while the other, with Aristotle, starts from the testimony of the senses, and sees in the world of the Spirit nothing more than a product of human thought.

The positivist philosophy of the last century, the age of materialism which grew out of it, and organicist medicine, which refused to see, even in psychological disorders, anything but the effect of anatomical and physiological changes in the nerve centers, separated the two camps once more, drawing between them a continuous front line which turned their antagonism into a war of position.

This thoroughgoing materialism, however, was so contrary to the facts that a split took place in the scientists' camp: "When one studies only the physical sciences," Count Arnaud de Grammont wrote, "I can just understand how one can be a materialist, although it seems to me to be difficult. When one studies biology, it seems to me to be impossible." Emile Boutroux demonstrated that examples of indeterminacy can be found in the laws of nature.[1] William James[2] pointed out that spiritual or religious phenomena are undeniable facts, a matter of experience. If a man, after praying, conducts himself differently from before, there is a causal relationship here which science ought to study and recognize.

If I may put it so, the spiritual was in this way being rehabilitated on scientific grounds, as a fact of experience. The School of Nancy— Bernheim and his pupils—set about the scientific study of the phenomena of suggestion. Suggestion, Baudouin wrote,[3] "is the subconscious realization of an idea."

Their work, like that of the psychoanalysts later, had considerable repercussions. They rehabilitated the mind as a cause of phenomena. They demonstrated abundantly that many of our actions—individual as well as social, normal as well as pathological—have as their necessary and sufficient cause, not the material, anatomical, physiological, and geographical facts of positivist philosophy, but ideas. When one thinks of the static, intellectualist conceptions in which psychological medicine was imprisoned at the turn of the century, one realizes the magnitude of the revolution wrought by psychoanalysis— and especially by the School of Zurich—in rediscovering the dynamism of the mind.

Marcel Sendrail has pointed out[4] the philosophical importance for medicine of the study of those functional disorders which did not fit into the framework of the triple definition of disease in vogue in the last century: "A lesion, an accident, an entity."

I shall not stop to demonstrate the power of suggestion and

[1] Emile Boutroux, *De la contingence des lois de la nature.*
[2] W. James, *The Varieties of Religious Experience.*
[3] *Suggestion and Autosuggestion,* translated by E. and C. Paul.
[4] "L'homme et ses maladies" in *Revue des Deux Mondes,* Jan. 15, 1943.

autosuggestion. The reader will find pertinent proofs set out in numerous books, notably that of Charles Baudouin. Montaigne had already drawn attention to the power of suggestion: "Place a plank of wood on the ground," he said; "you will be able to walk from one end of it to the other without overbalancing. But put it at the height of a church steeple, and you will be incapable of walking along it."

At the turn of the century public demonstrations of the power of suggestion became so popular and caused such a stir that the authorities had to prohibit them, because of their disturbing effect on people's minds.

All ideas of history and psychology were suddenly transformed. The phenomena of crowd psychology, nervous contagion, panic, and all forms of superstition were given a completely satisfactory scientific explanation. Fontenelle had already written: "Give me four people persuaded of even the absurdest opinion, and through them I shall be certain of similarly persuading two million more."

Followers of Bernheim, Dubois, and later Coué,[5] cured hundreds of patients whom materialist science had failed to cure, simply by succeeding in communicating to them, by means of suggestion complete confidence in their cure.

All these studies and experiments established incontestably that the mind is not only a cause of ideas, but also of material facts. In the same experiments, however, unbelief could also find new arguments. The war of position, to which I referred just now, was succeeded by a war of movement in which the forces of the two sides became embroiled. The basic positions of the believers were attacked. The facts which they adduced as proofs of the supernatural—the miracles and healing acts recounted in the Bible or in the stories of the saints—could they not all be explained quite naturally in the same terms as the successes of witch doctors and other nonreligious healers, who made scientific use of the power of suggestion? Might not faith be reduced in its entirety to a matter of suggestion?

Many people honestly believed this. And so, with equal sincerity, religious people faced this new danger threatening their positions. They gave a cool reception to the whole of this movement of renewal in the realm of the spiritual, including even the philosophy of Bergson and the Zurich school of psychoanalysis, which they saw not

[5] Emile Coué, *Self-mastery through Conscious Autosuggestion.*

as allies but as the most treacherous of enemies. They reacted by attempting to deny that any analogy existed between religious experiences and the scientific experiments in suggestion.

I believe that the time has come for us to put an end to this new argument, in a spirit of mutual frankness. This is one more example of the mental distinction I have described between technology and faith.

The science of suggestion does not take all the religious facts into account. A new discovery always becomes something of a craze. It is treated as if it were of general application, as if it could explain everything. But the scientific outlook itself, to which the technologists claim to adhere, obliges us to preserve our criticial sense. While some of the cases of healing in the Gospels or in the history of the Church may legitimately bear comparison with those of Emile Coué, it is impossible honestly to see suggestion as a satisfactory explanation of many other miracles, such as Christ's virgin birth, his bodily Resurrection, his Ascension, or the very fact of his unique life, inconceivable as it is within the framework of classical psychological determinism. "From a certain point of view," writes Friedel, "the grand miracle may be said to be the person of Jesus Christ himself." Similarly, there have been in history a large number of well-attested miracles which it would be intellectual chicanery to attribute to the power of suggestion. Henri Bon writes: "The manifest character of many of the miracles observed, and the verifications accumulated by the Church for less striking cures, impart to the miracles admitted by the Congregation of Rites a credibility at least equal, and more often superior, to the medical facts accepted as basic to the whole of medical science."[6] And were there but one such miracle, that would be sufficient to make it impossible to reduce the supernatural to the natural. Moreover, even if in the natural order the study of the power of suggestion throws some light on the "how" of a religious fact—on its mechanism—it has nothing to say about the "why"—about its final cause.

But at the same time it would not be intellectually honest to refuse to see in various genuine religious facts the action of psychical reactions which science describes as the phenomena of suggestion. Fortunately there is no need for faith to stoop to such a proceeding in

6 *Précis de médecine catholique.*

order to defend itself. The fact that these phenomena obey the laws of suggestion does not detract in any way from their religious significance. By faith we recognize the action of God in natural events as they unfold in accordance with laws he has established, as well as in the unfolding of supernatural events, which are not subject to those laws because of his miraculous intervention.

One thing we must avoid, as Lavaud has quite rightly pointed out to me, is the wrong use of the word miracle. It is a misuse of language to apply it to cures brought about by suggestion, whether they are religious or not. It should be reserved for supernatural events.

I have therefore no hesitation in saying—for I can observe it daily—that the majority of the psychological effects of religious faith are the effects of suggestion. This is a matter of their mechanism, which science investigates and calls the law of suggestion: that ideas tend to turn into facts. But do not let us confuse the mechanism with the cause. Whereas the law of suggestion explains the mechanism, it takes no account of the cause. Faith recognizes the intervention of God as the cause of the suggestion.

Like all natural laws, the law of suggestion is neutral in itself. It can be the source of the most terrible suffering, as well as of the most wonderful deliverances. It lies behind the chain reaction by virtue of which the ills as well as the blessings in a person's life tend always to increase. One misfortune suggests the fear of a new misfortune, and the fear precipitates the person into the very thing he fears. One stroke of good fortune suggests the expectation of another, and this attitude of expectancy brings it about. Christ was obviously alluding to this effect of the law of suggestion when he said: "To him who has will more be given, and he will have abundance; but from him who has not, even what he has will be taken away" (Matt. 13:12).

Christ also said: "He that is not against us is for us" (Mark 9:40). I believe, therefore, that I am being faithful to him in stressing what brings us closer to our agnostic colleagues rather than what divides us. It is undeniable that the solid bastion of materialism has been breached by the work done by numerous doctors who, though not believers, have been convinced of the power of the mind, so that the way lies open to a spiritual renewal in medicine. The love shown by these doctors in their dealings with patients suffering from nervous complaints has done much to ensure that these sufferers are better understood and more justly treated.

They have demonstrated the decisive part played by suggestion in pathology—that it is the sole cause of countless illnesses, pains, and physical and moral sufferings. Well before the introduction of potato flour into bread in Switzerland, the announcement of this measure had set going an epidemic of digestive troubles in certain people who had not properly understood the notice, and thought the measure was already in force. A woman once came to me in a very debilitated condition. She finally admitted that for several months she had been taking purgatives every day, because she had gotten it into her head that she was susceptible to cancer, and someone had suggested to her the strange notion that purgation was a suitable preventive treatment. One can have no idea of the stupid things intelligent people will do the moment some suggestion is made concerning their health.

Our sense organs send neutral signals to our brain. It is our conscious mind which colors them as pleasant or unpleasant, beautiful or ugly, according to the suggestions we have received from society. We all know how close the most intolerable irritation is to voluptuous pleasure. Hence all those pains that are truly painful, but purely psychological. In moral matters, *a fortiori,* the same is true. Suggestion is a determining factor in great passions and disappointments in love. The Stoics, in Athens, maintained that death would not be frightening if the whole of society did not suggest fear of it.

When an illness or discomfort is due to suggestion—a stomach pain, for example, or fatigue or vertigo—the mechanism is not realized by the patient, since it is unconscious. The result is that it is extremely hard for him to agree that suggestion is the cause of what is wrong with him. He really believes that we are mistaken in interpreting it in this way. His mind, in accordance with the law of rationalization, always finds an illusory objective cause for the trouble—he has eaten something that disagrees with him, or else it is the hot, dry wind that makes him ill, and so on. This idea in turn becomes a source of suggestion, so that the symptom will reappear if he eats the same food, or when the same wind is blowing again. The patient will see this recurrence as an objective, experimental proof of the correctness of his false interpretation. Often he will say: "It can't be suggestion, because I did not want to believe it. But I had to give in to the evidence." His obstinacy in persisting in his honest belief bars the road to a cure, because the first condition of a cure must be the recognition that the sole cause is suggestion. Erotic sensations, because of the strong emotions connected with them, are of course an unending source of false interpretations.

The power of suggestion lies behind the appearance and persistence of all functional disorders, that is to say, all those maladies that interfere with the proper functioning of our organs without affecting their structure. They can affect the mind itself (causing obsessions, phobias, and anxiety) as well as the body. We have nerves in all parts of our bodies, governing the operations of every organ, accelerating or slowing down the rhythm of the heart or of the movements of the intestines, modifying the blood pressure or the allocation of blood in the body by means of the dilation or constriction of the blood vessels, and stimulating or inhibiting secretion by the glands. The nerves modify the tropism of the integuments or the metabolism of the body fluids, and produce or annul sensations of pain or pleasure. It follows that functional disorders of the most varied kind, even when quite objective—that is to say, verifiable by chemical analysis or physical examination—can attack any organ in the body, and provoke sensations of all kinds, often extremely painful ones, such as spasms, palpitations, migraine, dizziness, dermatitis, insomnia, cramps, tics, diarrhea, neuralgia, and sexual or urinary disorders.

Often, unfortunately, medicine itself (official or otherwise) is the cause of a pathogenic suggestion. Large numbers of cases of this type can be traced back to the descriptions in a popular medical dictionary, the reading of pharmaceutical prospectuses, a remark—often misunderstood—made by a doctor or nurse, sometimes a wrong diagnosis or a preconceived idea advanced without a proper medical examination in the rush of a hasty consultation, a treatment which the patient knows to be frequently applied in more serious cases— such as insulin, for example—and lastly the pretentious and wrongheaded explanations of quacks.

The truth is that everybody suffers from functional disturbances— for example, blushing when one hears oneself flattered. But very suggestible people are more prone to them. They only need to hear of a person having a heart attack to have palpitations themselves.

The starting point of these disorders is always an association of ideas; and the fact that this association is unconscious, and therefore its mechanism is concealed from the patient, makes the distress all the more serious and persistent.

Everybody experiences functional disorders, but in normal people they disappear of their own accord. What fixes them, prevents their disappearance and so turns them into morbid symptoms, is always emotion, or more exactly "super-emotion," of social origin, to which I shall return in the next chapter. Thus—coming back to the example I used just now—blushing can happen to anyone, for example in the stress of the emotion caused by joining an intimidating group of people. The thought that to blush like that is ridiculous only aggravates the reaction that has begun to take place. It gives rise next time to a fear of blushing, which through the power of suggestion creates a tendency to blush. But in spite of everything, in most people the distractions encountered in society gradually turn the attention away from this preoccupation with blushing. For the fear of blushing to turn into an obsession, and become a really functional disease, there must be behind the ordinary emotion an unconscious super-emotion, always linked with a personal complex which has been set up as a result of a formalistic upbringing.

All sorts of ideas can cross our minds: "If I were to fall . . ."; "If I were to make such and such a mistake. . . ." Generally we pay no attention, and the thought passes away, to be replaced by another. If, on the other hand, it arouses a false emotion, because of some psychological complex, the idea becomes fixed and turns into an obsession. Furthermore, when an emotion cannot be discharged because it remains unconscious—like a repressed feeling of aggressiveness toward someone one loves, for example, or an incestuous desire, or an unconscious fear of life—its force transfers to the pathogenic idea, which is thus kept alive.

The following is an illustration I often use with my patients. In a large house there are many bells, each operated by a push button. If some practical joker—an association of ideas—comes in secret and mixes up the wires on the main indicator board, the result will be continual misunderstandings. The ringing of a bell—in the form of a symptom, a sensation—will be wrongly attributed to the pressing of the corresponding button, whereas the call will be coming in fact from a different room—a quite different source of emotion.

Fostered by the disorder caused by these disturbances, the symptom will soon be making its appearance in response to the most varied stimuli. And the more it is repeated the more tenacious will it become.

This is the way in which Pavlov's conditioned reflexes are set up.

The Russian scientist rang a bell every time he gave food to a dog. Soon it was only necessary to ring the bell in order to bring about in the dog an abundant secretion of digestive juices—the false contact had been established among the wires leading to the bells. After a few days, however, the reflex acquired in this way disappeared, just as a functional disorder disappears of its own accord unless it is maintained by an emotion.

Several emotions contribute to the maintenance of functional disorders. First there is the emotion resulting from a false interpretation, to which I have already referred. Then there is the false shame which these patients always feel, arising from the fact that their trouble is "nervous," a word that always has a pejorative connotation. To say of an illness that it is nervous, functional, due to suggestion, is still (wrongly) to many people the same as saying that it is "imaginary," and that all that is required to rid oneself of it is a little will power. The efforts of will made by nerve sufferers are always the very thing that makes a nervous disorder even worse, because the mind is then concentrated on the trouble, which only increases the suggestion. This is particularly true of insomnia. Normally we go to sleep as much through suggestion and habit as through tiredness. We expect to sleep, and sleep comes. Let some unusual occurrence, such as a worry or an illness, bring on a period of sleeplessness, and the habit will be lost and disquiet creeps in: "I only hope I can get to sleep!" Along with the fear of not sleeping comes the suggestion which prevents sleep. As one of my patients wrote: "The fear of not sleeping keeps me awake." The person then makes a special effort, taking all sorts of precautions, trying various dodges, and insisting to himself that he must sleep. All this aggravates the negative suggestion, because it merely demonstrates his doubt of his ability to sleep. So true is this, that Vittoz succeeded in curing some cases of insomnia by advising the patient to try the opposite—to take steps to stop himself falling asleep! The truth is that nobody ever died of insomnia. Sleep is a natural phenomenon which necessarily returns of itself, and the less one does to bring it back, the sooner it comes. For instance, I have known several impatient people whose insomnia was a protest against the waste of time spent in sleeping. Another could not sleep because a doctor had let slip the word "encephalitis" during a visit, and this had aroused in him a terror of falling asleep. Another patient had been told by the doctor that she was not very strong; and so she prevented herself from going to sleep just to prove to herself that she could hold out against odds. In other cases insomnia may be due to a badly regulated life—for example, one that is too intellectual for a practical temperament.

Another cause of emotion resides in the knowledge that the patient to some extent has of the symbolic meaning of these functional disorders. For example, a spasm in the throat is symbolic of fear of a constricted life; a paralysis of the legs is symbolic of a refusal to go forward in life. Agoraphobia, that is to say, a morbid fear of going out alone into an open space, is symbolic of a desire for independence repressed in childhood by domineering and possessive parents.

Then there is the emotion due to disease. If the latter involves an interruption of work, if it causes the loss of a secure employment, if it causes a conflict with the family, for whom a "nerve" case is always something of a dishonor, the resulting emotion reinforces the pathogenic process. This is why a patient suffering from a functional disorder ought never to allow it to stop him working, however difficult that may seem to him to be. He must live as if he were quite well, and he can always do so if he is not afraid.

To this must be added the difficulty these patients have in explaining what they feel. The sensations they experience are strange and impossible to describe. They are always suspecting their family and their doctor of not understanding them. They give more and more details, so that the doctor becomes irritated and tells them that the details are unimportant. And then the persistence of the trouble also upsets the doctor. He is disappointed at the failure of all the various treatments he tries. The patient, being sensitive, perceives this irritation and this heightens his emotion. Fear of not being cured comes to complete the blockage of the road to healing.

When some improvement has taken place, the slightest relapse or fear of relapse—the slightest return of the symptom through some ordinary emotion, joyful as well as sad—sets going the whole chain of cause and effect; the patient's disappointment is all the worse because he thought he had escaped out of the vicious circle. When one has known the tempest one begins to be afraid at the slightest breath of air that stirs. One of my patients confessed to me once that on the occasion of a relapse she had "tempted fate"; that is to say, in order to savor her new-found liberty and have the pleasure of assuring herself of its stability, she had deliberately toyed with the ideas that used to set going her functional trouble. She had suddenly been afraid that it might reappear, and this fear at once brought on the trouble itself.

Lastly there is the quite ordinary part played by habit: everything is habit in biology. The body and the mind adopt false habits, which take a long time to disappear. "In order to cover up the indignities to which I was subjected," a young woman writes, "I adopted a mask of cowardice, contrary to my true nature. Now I realize that though I should like to throw it off, it sticks to me through force of habit."

All this shows the tenacity of the functional disorders that weigh so heavily on so many people's lives and require so much patience on the part of both patient and doctor.

Nevertheless doctors, even non-Christian doctors, have shown that a disorder due to suggestion can also be removed by suggestion. Dubois writes:

The neurotic is on the road to recovery as soon as he is convinced that he is going to recover; he is healed when he believes he is healed. . . . Religious faith could be the best prophylactic against these diseases of the mind and the most powerful means of healing them if it were sufficiently living to create true Christian stoicism in its adherents. In this state of mind—too rare, alas, in orthodox circles!—a man becomes invulnerable. Feeling that he is upheld by God, he fears neither disease nor death. He may fall victim to a physical disease, but morally he remains upright amidst his suffering. He is inaccessible to the pusillanimous emotions of the neurotic.[7]

I must recognize, with Dubois, how rare this victorious attitude is among the "adherents" of our Christian churches. I must confess that this is a terrible verdict on the poverty of our faith. Christ did not hesitate to use his healing power as a proof of his authority. If, instead of criticizing the public for its unbelief and exhorting it to come back to the Church, we were to give it more demonstrations of the power of the Holy Spirit, it would come back of its own accord.

Truth compels us, on the contrary, to recognize that functional disorders are more numerous and frequently more tenacious in religious people, even the most orthodox:

First, because sensitive, profound personalities, with intense reactions, are more open to the things of the Spirit—more concerned

[7] *Les psychonévroses et leur traitement moral.*

with religious problems, more apt to look in religion for an answer to their inner disquiet. It follows that the proportion of anxious people is higher among church people than among the rest, as is also true in the altruistic professions—doctors, ministers of religion, nurses, educators, artists, and social workers.

Second, it must be said, because the Church, instead of the liberating message of grace, has more often proposed the hopeless course of reliance on moral effort. According to the Bible, moral conduct is the spontaneous result of the inner transformation of the being by the Holy Spirit. For us, however, it is too often an effort to lift ourselves by our own shoestrings. A certain woman despised her husband because she found him "dull." She had violent reactions against him. Then she experienced conversion. It did, indeed, give her a quite new love for her husband. But also, in order to live up to her conversion, she repressed many a sudden surge of aggressiveness that still shook her. The inner conflict between what she really was and what she most sincerely desired to appear to be became the source of functional disorders which she did not have when she gave free rein to her hostility—and which she will no longer have when her inner regeneration is more complete, and she is really set free from her aggressiveness.

CHAPTER 14

Where Is the Truth?

Having considered some medical implications, we shall now broaden the discussion. Suggestion is not only the cause of many diseases; it is also the cause of innumerable false ideas.

People believe what they are told much more than we think. "Human suggestibility is limitless," wrote Dubois. This is clear in the case of those who have been brought up by people suffering from mental disease. All their ideas may be distorted.

Modern man has been told that chance alone presided over the evolution of the world and of the species. Incredible though it be, men have accepted the idea. As a result their philosophy of life has been reduced to a philosophy of chance. Everything that happens to them is a stroke of good or bad luck. The good luck is quite natural, and the bad luck is unfair, and so men come to demand good luck as a right. If a "good chance" presents itself, it must be seized even if to do so would not be altogether right; they would be fools to let it go: after all, it is their turn, after so much bad luck. And then it would benefit other people! We know how often "good chances" turn out to be bad. But in that case people blame bad luck again, and not the fact that they have acted in violation of morality.

Modern man has been told that the idea of God is a bogy invented by a clergy whose interest it is to keep men subject to their authority. He has been told that science explains everything, including the rise of religion; that the age of religion is over, thanks to progress and the spread of knowledge; that piety is an opium designed to keep the people quiet; and that prayer is nothing but autosuggestion. Without asking why the world exists, and why it obeys laws, men accept the teaching of these new prophets, and think they are being less credulous than church people.

Being deprived of the true God, they accept everything they are taught. Printing becomes the great weapon of suggestion. At the lakeside one day I overheard the following dialogue between two little boys on the myth of Icarus:

"You know, there was once a prisoner who wanted to escape. He stuck some sparrows' feathers on himself and flew. But he went up so high that the glue melted and he fell in the sea."

"Is that a true story?"

"What do you think? Of course it's true! It's in my history book!"

Whole nations adopt the picture of other nations that their newspapers have given them. The members of one church accept the picture of another church that is presented to them in their own.

Lastly, the most naïve superstition—for example, the vogue enjoyed by water divining, spiritualism, astrology, and magic—reigns over our modern age, which claims to have grown out of the religious prejudices of the past. I am continually seeing evidence of the power of suggestion exercised by these superstitious practices, especially when the fortuneteller persuades his client that the latter secretly desires the things foretold him.

The oddest sects, propagating the most extraordinary theological ideas, seem to spread without encountering the slightest opposition from people's critical sense. If you knew all the things I hear, you would be appalled at the confusion in which the modern mind is wallowing, a prey to all sorts of contradictory doctrines, all of them invoking the authority of science, experience, or revelation.

Even within the traditional framework of our great Christian churches, all kinds of suggestions arise to distort the spiritual life of the faithful.

Men are full of contradictions because of the power of suggestion. Even when they are intelligent and well-instructed, or animated by a fervent and genuine faith, they remain in bondage to erroneous ideas and false impulses, the seed of which has been sown in their minds long before. They may have studied psychology, and yet be incapable of controlling their own conduct. They may have had the most wonderful religious experiences, and yet relapse into the most ordinary sins. Yet they may combine this sin—whether it be carnal lust, jealousy, or pride—with a truly sincere spiritual ministry. They may go together to church, and yet have the most awful quarrels when they come out. They may make the most strenuous efforts to put their lives in order, and yet these lives may go on being a chain of disasters. They believe in the grace of God, and yet they cannot escape from the anxiety of all their past weighing on them. They think they are under a curse due to some spell, or on account of some sin of their youth which they have nevertheless brought in penitence to the Cross, in whose sovereign virtue they say they believe. So they expect only catastrophe, and the suggestive power of this idea impels them into it. The very effort to avoid disaster seems to be what brings it on. Someone has suggested the following excellent definition of neurosis: any state in which an instinct leads to the result opposite to that to which it tends.

On top of all this, pathological feelings of guilt, rooted in psychological complexes, arise to give them a false notion of sin as something that forgiveness cannot ever efface. A woman tells me she cannot pray, cannot even open her Bible, without a feeling of indescribable anxiety. Her mother died in bringing her into the world. I perceive that various reactions in those around her sowed in her mind when still a child the idea that she was "guilty" of her mother's death. The result has been a pathological feeling of guilt which disturbs her whole religious life. A real sin can lead a person to the liberating experience of grace, whereas a fictitious sin, a suggested guilt, has no such religious result. Another patient is unable to pray. She eventually tells me that while still a child she was once horrified to hear her father say to her mother in a fit of anger: "That child ought not to have been born." The remark had haunted her whole childhood, and had suggested to her the idea that she was not like the others, in that her life had not been willed by God. Later on, at Sunday School, she had asked her pastor if it was God who willed that we should come into the world, and if he willed it for everybody. But the pastor had replied that she was too young to be asking such questions.

Society, because of all the formalism with which it is impregnated, is a potent source of suggestions which distort the idea of sin, especially in the domain of sex. Formalism in this domain is the reason why so many of our patients regard sin that has to do with sex as being in a class by itself. They can believe in forgiveness for all other sin, but find it hard to believe in the case of sexual sin. This formalism invests the whole subject of sex with a particular emotion, a "super-emotion," on account of which any pathogenic suggestion in this field has unparalleled power. Suggestion is the fundamental cause of most sexual disorders, such as impotence, frigidity, and all kinds of perversion. Now, the healthy emotion of guilt for sin, which leads to repentance, leads also to the wonderful experience of grace and liberation. The super-emotion however, which is associated with formalist social criticism, and does not arise from the sin itself—the sin of impurity, whether perversion or not—but from the idea of *Neurosis* perversion, is fatal: it prevents liberation. For the criterion "against God," the super-emotion substitutes "against nature." This is the source of a false sense of guilt which, unlike true guilt for sin, finds no relief in repentance and grace.

All kinds of words heard in childhood can, helped by false emotion, exert a tyrannical influence on a person's life. One of my patients used to hear her mother constantly repeating: "Little children, little worries; big children, big worries." We cannot be surprised, when we consider the way the law of suggestion works, that this patient rushed as if impelled by some hidden force into the very kind of behavior that was calculated to cause her mother the greatest possible worry. Then there was the girl who was told that she was a "moral monster," and who felt as if she was being driven to become just that.

Such words can be spoken with the best of intentions. A young woman is troubled about her religious life. She eventually admits to me that it all began one day when one of her relatives said to her: "I am always very careful when I talk to you about religion. I know it could do you harm; you are so weak."

While on this subject I must refer to the spiritual disasters I have seen resulting from the failure of attempts at faith healing. A boy is in revolt against religion. He has a persistent dermatitis. I learn that a religious relative had taken him to a healer, who had tried in vain to cure him by prayer, and the failure has had a disastrous effect on him.

A neurotic woman, after years of unsuccessful treatment, went to a pastor who had a glowing reputation as a faith healer. But he failed. To cover up his failure he said to her: "You are possessed by infernal spirits. That is why you cannot be cured." You can imagine the effect of this remark! I have seen several other cases in which healers described morbid symptoms as diabolic manifestations, or said to the patient: "It is your lack of faith that is preventing me from healing you."

Nevertheless, the laying on of hands is often referred to in the Bible as a method of healing. We therefore have good grounds for using _t, as I have done several times, and I know well that often it has been my own lack of faith that has held me back from using it. I have used it on rare occasions when a real atmosphere of fellowship existed between me and the patient, and when I was convinced that God required me to dare to perform the act. Each time, however, I have reminded myself that God is not at our beck and call, but remains sovereign in sickness as well as in healing. The act has never been in vain.

In spiritual matters the important thing is always the disposition of the heart. I think it would always be profoundly dishonest to perform a solemn act banking on its suggestive effect. This would be possible for a charlatan, who might fill it out with all sorts of proceedings culled from his knowledge of individual and collective psychology. It is impossible for a Christian doctor. In any case these cures by crude suggestion, so to speak, even if practiced under hypnosis, with the help of impressive electric currents or a public display, rarely give lasting results. They tend to take advantage of the morbid suggestibility of the subject, rather than curing him of it. They suppress a symptom without bringing about any real transformation of the personality.

On the other hand, it is perfectly legitimate in Christian psychotherapy to ally the technique of suggestion with religious soul-healing, taking care, of course, not to make any false distinction between them. Take the case where an asthenia, an obsession, a false idea in the religious or moral field, or a somatic functional disorder, has been established and crystallized by the suggestive force of a mistaken idea, assisted by the emotion arising from a complex. To disentangle the complex by means of analytical psychology, and to substitute for the pathogenic idea the proper scientifically based idea of a cure, while at the same time leading the patient to a religious experience capable of bringing about a radical transformation of his outlook, is indeed a longer, more laborious, and more hazardous course than that of thaumaturgy, but it is much more effective.

Once again (and this forearms us against any formalism) the dogmatic label of the doctor matters less than the qualities he tries to introduce into his relationship with his patient. Let us leave doctrinal instruction to the theologians. But let us also recognize that all radical spiritual action is in conformity with the true doctrine, even if it is performed by a doctor who does not profess orthodox Christian beliefs. Love, honesty, understanding, patience, humility and unshakable confidence in his patient's healing are the things that bring his technical measures to good effect. His aim of course is to heal his patient, but even more it is to lead him, parallel with the cure, to the most wonderful quality of life possible on this earth: the sort of life preached by Jesus Christ, which fellowship with him and dedication to his service do more than anything else to promote. The lively practice of Christian piety is a sort of training in self-abandon. Instead of relying on futile attempts to exercise our will power, it trains us in the trusting expectation of God's mercies. In this respect it is a powerful adjunct to the technical expedient of healthy suggestion. Lastly, faith, by turning the mind toward God, and restoring it to a fruitful life, turns it away from the troubles that obsess it.

The tiny seed of faith sown in the patient's heart germinates and grows there, and gradually transforms the climate of his life. The day comes when the doctor receives a letter: "Do you know that for the first time for twenty years I am able to sleep without sedatives! I have waited for several months before writing, to make sure it lasted." Or else: "The bouts of stomach pain have disappeared, I do not know how. In the space of a fortnight they have gone. It is a gift from God." Or again: "You remember that in our conversations I never managed to feel forgiven. It has happened gradually, and I am freed from my past."

It is in the sphere of practical victories and obedience that religious faith and the technique of suggestion can most fruitfully be combined; for example, in helping a young man to face an examination that has been terrifying him, or to open his heart frankly and thoroughly to a member of his family, in confessing a sin, asking forgiveness, or repairing a wrong. To help him in this by praying with him and giving him the human confidence that comes from sympathy, is also to bring him both to an experience of God and to a healthy psychological attitude.

But, beware! The greatest religious heresies can also lay claim to the proof of experience, owing to this very law of suggestion. This is why such evidence can never be decisive unless it rests also on that of the biblical revelation. "The devil also performs all kinds of miracles," wrote one of my former patients.

Everything that men and women think, all they believe, all they feel, depends on suggestions they have received, and on the processes of thought determined by those suggestions in their unconscious. They all believe they have personal convictions and thoughts. But their convictions and thoughts would not be the same if they had read different books, had met different people, had had different parents, had gone to different schools. They readily believe that general approbation is a guarantee of authenticity. It is not so long ago that certain moral concepts such as respect for the human person irrespective of race, for marriage and the family as opposed to free love, or the concept of law as being above all human will or power, were thought of as sacrosanct. They could be violated in practice, but in principle they could not be gainsaid. It has taken recent events to show us that this apparent unanimity, far from being based on a sort of moral instinct, was due to the force of social suggestion.

Even experience is not a conclusive proof of truth, because all that is required is an absolute belief in an idea, even if it is false, for the experience it inspires to be conclusive.

This is why people generally have an instinctive distrust of the power of suggestion, so that preaching and religious demonstrations always come up against a defensive and critical attitude among the hearers. They are afraid that their suggestibility is being played upon in order to make them believe things that are not true. They have so often been disappointed after taking something up in a surge of sincere enthusiasm.

Suggestion is simply a natural law: every idea, true or false, tends to propagate itself and become a fact. No doubt suggestion played its part in the spread of Christianity, in the success of many healing acts, in the courage of the martyrs, in many answers to prayer. But suggestion can quite as easily spread some other doctrine, unite immense multitudes in false beliefs, arousing equal dedication and heroism in them.

Science studies the laws of nature. It establishes, for instance, that the orbits of the heavenly bodies, the way things fall, and the movement of the tides all obey the same law of universal gravitation. But it does not know why there is a law of gravitation. It studies the mechanics of the evolution of species, but it does not know why there is an evolution by which all things move in a given direction. Similarly it studies the law of suggestion, but it does not know why there is a law of suggestion.

Faith believes that there are laws in nature because they have been laid down by someone whom it calls God, and that it is of him and not of his creatures that we must ask the reason why.

There is a difference between the laws of the inanimate world, like that of gravitation, and the laws of the mind, like that of suggestion. In the inanimate world the will of God is fulfilled of necessity, so that everything is good, since it obeys the laws he has established.

In the world of the mind, as is shown by the existence of evil, arising from the fact that God has left man free to obey him or disobey him, one and the same mechanism, set in motion by the God-given law of suggestion, can serve either obedience or disobedience. It can help to spread either truth or error, good or evil.

Satan makes use of God's laws. He makes use of our instincts, given to us by God to guide us toward goodness and happiness, and turns them into instruments of evil and misfortune. In a profound and witty book[1] C. S. Lewis describes how Satan and his minions make use of the weapon of suggestion to achieve their ends. With the Bible, with Christ himself, I believe in the existence of Satan, that is to say an active force of evil, infinitely cunning, capable of strategic plans. I do not believe in the "amorality" of which one hears so much these days. I believe there is a battle going on in the heart of every one of us between God and Satan. Both combatants use the same psychological laws, such as the law of suggestion, for example, which science studies, and which God created for good only. Let us beware of the suggestions that come from the devil. As the old proverb says, he must have a long spoon that sups with the devil. Let us beware of the suggestions that come from our own egotistical desires, our aggressiveness, our covetousness, and all those mechanisms of the unconscious that the devil handles with such skill.

It is possible, then, to accept that an event due to faith—an answer to prayer, a healing, a conversion—so long at least as it takes place within the ambit of the natural order, obeys the laws of suggestion, without its religious value being thereby called in question. There is no reason why the eye of faith should not see it as an active intervention by God. We have here once again that double aspect of man

[1] C. S. Lewis, *The Screwtape Letters.*

that I have attempted to describe: the technical and the spiritual, his "functions" and his "values," which are not two distinct kinds of event, but one and the same fact looked at from two different standpoints. The same event is described by science, from the technical standpoint, under the name of suggestion; and from the spiritual standpoint faith considers it to be an intervention by God.

The true question therefore is not, "Is faith suggestion?" but, "This mechanism of suggestion which, by God's will, holds sway over men—does it lead them into the truth or into error?" Or again, "These ideas which spread and become actual experiences in accordance with the law of suggestion—do they come from God or the devil? And if science shows us that sometimes they come from the unconscious, do they come from what is healthy and godly in the unconscious, or from what is diabolical and pathological?"

All our behavior has its source in ideas, and all our ideas have come to us from outside. They have been suggested to us by a good or a bad counselor. They may derive from our selfishness, from our conscious or unconscious tendencies toward sensuality, pride, vanity, the exercise of power, hate, or impurity. They may also come from God—from his call to love, in humility, honesty, and self-sacrifice.

The whole drama of life arises from this perpetual concurrence of suggestions from God and those inspired by evil, the positive and the negative. This is why our hearts are always divided. Indeed, every positive idea awakens in us a negative echo. If I say: "I believe in God," the echo replies: "Are you really sure?" The two ideas go together and are propagated by the power of suggestion. The devil makes use of the resulting disorder for his own ends. He makes a person suffering from depression turn every encouraging remark we make into a negative suggestion. We say to him: "You see, you are better." He replies: "You're surprised, aren't you? You must have given up all hope for me."

But this very battle that takes place within us is a proof of the existence of God. If his voice did not sound within us, we should be altogether one-sided, and there would no longer be any battle!

One of my patients meets a friend who tells her something bad about me. She is greatly disturbed. When she tells me about it, she adds, "I think that the reason for my being so complicated is that I am suggestible but not influenceable." The expression is very apt. My patient had too much confidence in me really to be influenced and to change to another doctor. Nevertheless the criticism she had heard contained a grain of truth, as all criticism does. Inevitably it started a line of thought, and lent body to other criticisms lying dormant in her mind. The result was a conflict on my account between her positive and her negative tendencies.

The same is true in regard to our attitude to God. We cannot help meeting with plenty of people, theories, facts, mysteries, disappointments, and even—in our own hearts—proud and selfish tendencies which suggest to us all kinds of doubts about him. It is not possible for them to have no effect on us, and it is well that this should be so, because if it were not for doubt would there be any faith? If we claimed to have a trust exempt from fear or a faith exempt from doubt, should we not be hiding our fears and doubts from ourselves? Faith is a battle, the battle within imposed by these very doubts, because they do not after all succeed in silencing the voice of God.

But still, even among those who believe in God, even in ourselves when we compare one period of our lives with another, what divergences of belief there are! And all of them propagated in accordance with the law of suggestion! Once again: Where is the truth?

Thinking that an idea is true and good, or that it comes from God, does not make it so. Moment by moment, in one direction or another, suggestion and its fearful power may mislead us. Where is the truth?

Well, I believe that if we are to remain honest, we must beware of those who are certain that they possess the truth.

Compare Dr. Knock[2] with Pascal. The one is full of proud assurance; the other approaches in fear and trembling the unfathomable mysteries of life, of man, and of God. When I hear a man expounding to me his system of thought with a certitude that excludes all doubt and even all discussion, I always scent a false suggestion. He has gotten it ready-made out of some book, or naïvely concocted it for himself, in the light of some personal illuminism all his own, instead of bringing it to fruition in the combat of faith.

Conscious of the greatness of God—beyond the measure of our minds—and of the power of sin which dulls our perception, the true believer seeks his road step by step, combining faith with the most realistic self-criticism. He is always on the lookout for some sign sent

[2] In the play of the same name by Jules Romains.

from God to confirm his faith, or else to correct some error in it.

Jesus himself spent years at the workbench before assuming his mission. He himself told of his inner struggles in the desert and in Gethsemane. He went every morning to seek God's commands in prayer.

St. Paul, that giant in the faith, spent fourteen years meditating in the desert after his conversion. And in the case of so many others—St. Francis of Assisi, St. Bernard, Pascal, Luther, and our own Vinet— what struggles, what gropings in the dark, what a sense of the mysteries of God and the powerlessness of man fully to know him in this world!

We recognize the spiritual authority of these men in this very sincerity. That is why we believe them to have gotten nearer the truth than others, because it commanded their assent through myriad doubts. That is why the suggestions that come to us from them, all wonderfully consistent, seem to us more worthy of credence than those of many others who are much surer of themselves in what they hold as truth.

CHAPTER 15

Life under the
Guidance of the Spirit

Thus, faith is certainly a light, but it shines in a darkness that it never entirely dissipates in this life. It remains humble, conscious of its limitations, strict with itself. In this it forms a marked contrast with the credulity of the simple, who, won over by false suggestions, worship the idols of the day, whether it be the proud philosophic edifice of a Hegel, or the naïve assertions of an uneducated crank. Contrary to what most people tend to imagine, the greatest believers are assailed by doubts. They do not believe because they have gotten rid of all uncertainty; they believe in spite of all their hesitations, and in fear of error. The strength of their faith does not lie in its being free of unknown quantities, but in the fact that it imposes itself on their conscience despite all their doubts. "Is it not true," writes a woman who is full of ardent faith, "is it not true that I can believe that God *is,* and that I love *Him?*"

We are all constantly in need of the assurance that comes from the faith of others. I have known many church people who suffered from the solitude forced on them by their reputation as believers. Everybody looked to them as to people whom doubt could not touch. They ended up wondering whether theirs was really a living faith, or whether it was only a fossilized attitude, which they could not forsake for fear of giving a bad example to others. One such person goes to his pastor to open his heart to him, and the pastor replies: "Come, now! Why these misgivings? You are one of my best parishioners.

You are a key man in the spiritual life of our community. Don't tell me you have doubts!"

I know that I shall be disappointing more than one Christian in writing these lines. I once gave a talk on this subject. Afterwards I was told that one woman in the audience had left in a state of great agitation and indignation. What did I mean? God had transformed her life. He had granted her decisive experiences. From that day forward she had been certain that never again could she have any doubts about him. She had proclaimed the fact vigorously, and her witness had brought many souls to faith. And now someone comes along maintaining that true faith remains in fear and trembling! I asked forgiveness of that woman. As to her, so to me has God given tangible proofs of his love and his intervention in my life. It behooves me, certainly, to proclaim the fact. But sin is always on the watch within all of us. At any moment it can cloud this bright sky of assurance. At such a time one who has been proclaiming that his faith is permanently unshakable may pass through a terrible crisis. It is good for him then to discover with humility that what is unshakable is not our faith, exposed as it is to all kinds of anxiety and error, but God, who always comes to us anew, to deliver us from the grip of our anxieties and errors.

I was chatting recently with a philosopher friend of mine. "Indeed," he said, "I am not a rationalist skeptic. I think that God may sometimes speak to men, and that this may well be the most valuable thing that can happen to us in this world. But how can one be sure that any given thought, inspiration, or call really comes from God?"

In my opinion there is only one honest reply to such a question: "One is never sure." Men are mistaken hundreds, thousands, tens of thousands of times, about what is God's will for them. Hundreds, thousands, tens of thousands of times they take their own desires for the voice of God. No one is more aware of this than he who is himself trying with sincerity to follow God's will rather than his own.

When we were students we all used to read Martinet's *Diagnostic Clinique*. I remember that in his preface he maintained that most errors in diagnosis came from the doctor's exaggerated confidence in himself. Being sure of the idea in his mind, he loses his critical sense, and even sticks obstinately and conceitedly to his own opinion when a colleague puts forward a different view.

How often are we forced to recognize that something we have

thought to be God's command was only a suggestion emanating from our own unconscious or the prejudices of those about us? More important, such moments of self-revelation are often among the richest in the life of faith. Through them it is strengthened and illuminated most. Let us be frank: when faced with a choice between alternatives we are generally in a fog, incapable of seeing clearly what is God's will for us, obliged to put up with this uncertainty patiently, never ceasing to believe that God will dissipate it. Practice makes us prudent!

The practice of soul-healing, too. There are none so sure of being inspired by God as certain of the mentally sick, whose mania is so strong that they can bear no argument about the divine origin of the idea in question. I have more than once been the unhappy and helpless witness of such crises of overexcitement. A person suffering from depression, after a spiritual experience which I consider to be genuine, suddenly becomes as if intoxicated. In this state everything speaks to him—a pebble on the road, a fruit that falls; everything is symbolic; everything contains a message from God. Sometimes in these delirious ideas there are flashes of genius, but all hopelessly mixed up with projected personal complexes. It is no use trying to be severe with such patients, reminding them that inspiration may come from the devil as easily as from God, and that the best way of being sure is to submit humbly to a check of one's own views against those of one's brothers in the faith—nothing will disabuse them.

Even in so-called normal people it is not hard to distinguish in what they claim to be divine inspirations the projection of unconscious tendencies, or the return to the surface, in disguise, of repressed desires. A woman believes she has a vocation to go right away and preach the Gospel in public. But she has not had the courage to set right serious errors in her own way of life. It is obvious that she is harboring dreams of striking and distant actions in order to avoid a certain difficult act of obedience nearer home. A man who has been unable to find in faith the source of a real love for his wife, comes to me and says: "God has shown me that my marriage was not in accordance with his will. My marriage therefore has no validity in his eyes. And so it is in order to obey him that I am reckoning on getting a divorce and marrying another woman he has made me meet, and whom he is pointing out to me in my heart as the one he means me to have." Another woman is convinced that God is commanding her to go and give a piece of her mind to her mother-in-law, against whom she has for a long time had repressed feelings of aggressiveness. A man was certain that God was calling him to throw himself into an enterprise that he was quite incapable of carrying through successfully. Without taking any advice, and casting doubts on the faith of any who did not share his views, he loaded himself with debts in order to launch a business which is tottering toward ruin, and to which he clings in the conviction that God cannot fail to bring to eventual success an enterprise which He Himself has inspired.

The striking thing—and the thing that made me write that true faith remains in fear and trembling—is the unanswerable assurance of all these people.

The same thing applies to those who, after a religious experience that is more emotional than concrete, declare in their enthusiasm that their lives are quite transformed, whereas other people can see nothing new apart from this sudden burst of optimism. Scarcely have they glimpsed Christianity when they think they have understood all about it. They no longer fear any defeat. They feel that they are under the guidance, hour by hour, of the Spirit, and they no longer have any difficulty in knowing what His instructions are.

I once had a visit from a man just out of prison. He told me enthusiastically that while there he had read one of my books, and had begun to pray. He had felt sure that a new life was beginning for him. I felt increasingly uneasy as he talked. His story was too easy. He breathed satisfaction rather than humility. Even when he talked to me about the crimes that had led to his being sent to prison, there was lacking that quite particular accent that is the mark of a true conviction of sin. In a word, his conversation was too sentimental. There was no sign of concrete decisions or amends to make. I decided to be frank, and with some trepidation told him of my unease. A few days later he came back, and now his tone was quite different as he confessed to me the true story of his secret sins, which were the underlying cause of the crimes he had committed.

Faith, then, is not naïve credulity. It knows that man is wretched and blind, that it is no easy matter to see what God's will is, and that we can all be deluded by all sorts of movements in our psychic make-up. A man comes to see me, full of anxiety. He describes to me a tangled situation which he has been struggling for years to unravel. He expects me there and then to pronounce some magic word that will deliver him from all hesitation and clearly show him the divine solution. What he really wants is to escape from our human lot, from which only death will deliver us, and which means that we must struggle painfully in the dark in search of some gleam of light. Magic, as Spoerri says, is putting God to work for us, instead of putting ourselves to work for him.

Vinet[1] used to say toward the end of his life that he had only reached the first stammerings of faith.

Whether they are religious or not, men and women seem to me to have one of three different attitudes to life: a naïve and simple-minded attitude; a skeptical attitude; and an attitude that is both believing and reflective.

The simple-minded attitude is that of the sentimental person who is carried away by any suggestion. Tell him about a naturist system of dieting, a new method of self-education, or the Christian faith, and he will at once think that he has discovered the ultimate truth. He will try to get everybody else to take it up, even before he has worked out its implications in his own life. There is no more perplexity for him. This attitude can lead to terrible disillusionment. I remember one such man. He was all the more depressed because he had formerly been an exponent of Coué's method, and had asserted that it was the infallible remedy for depression. In this sense faith, whether religious or secular, is only suggestion, and succumbs to the contrary suggestions that are met with in life. Faith does not mean going forward without difficulty, but receiving the strength needed to go on despite all external and internal difficulties, and daring to look them in the face. Nothing is more dangerous from the spiritual point of view than to allow oneself to be taken in by fine words and to persuade oneself that one has found the complete answer to everything.

This attitude is far removed from the faith of the New Testament, the realism of which it is impossible to overemphasize. In its realism it is much nearer to the picture Plato gives[2] when he represents us as shut up in a cave so dark that even the most penetrating minds, such as his, cannot dissipate its mysterious gloom. We are always hoping to see the truth face to face, but all we see is shadows thrown on the wall, because the light is behind us. We see it as in a mirror as St. Paul says. Our vision is still so imperfect that we argue about what

[1] Swiss theologian and author, 1797–1847.
[2] *Republic,* VII.

we think we have seen. <u>Each thinks the reflection he has seen is the true light.</u>

Yet the astonishing, incredible fact is that the darkness is not complete. <u>There are reflections and shadows which bear witness to the fact that there is a light.</u> Despite all the darkness that persists, despite all the misapprehensions, misunderstandings, and mistakes, it is those faint gleams that count in the history of a man's life, as in the history of the world, because they come from God.[3] All those who have contributed something of value to humanity are those who have zealously sought after these gleams of light from God.

In the semiobscurity of our cave, some close their eyes, and others open them wide in an attempt to see better.

Some close their eyes—this is the skeptical attitude. "Why bother to try to see," they say, "since in any case we are never sure we are not mistaken." They would like to be sure of knowing God before coming near him, sure of knowing his will before trying to obey it. They are like the child who, when asked why he did not go to school, replied: "Because I can't read." They would like to solve on their own the eternal mystery of the universe before going to find out from him who created it. They would like to solve the problem of morality, to win by themselves a stoic victory over evil, before coming to God. But evil is the very thing that closes their eyes.

I shall never forget a certain evening I spent with an old friend. He was interested in our experiences in the search for God's inspiration in our lives. He told me frankly about his own hesitations: "I recognize that there is something in the idea that attracts me; but I am held back by intellectual objections. How can God manifest his will to a man?" I told him then about my own personal experience. What had for a long time stopped my believing in God's inspiration was not so much the intellectual objections that came into my mind, but my sins which he was asking me to give up, and the time came when I just had to recognize the fact. My friend was thoughtful and sad when he left me that evening. A week later he came back and made a confession of his sins, which he had prepared for me in many hours of meditation. Neither he nor I, of course, wanted to fall into the temptation of thinking, naïvely, that we had now been given all the answers. It was not a question of refuting the intellectual objections that are raised by the great mystery of fellowship between man in his

[3] Cecil Rose, *When Man Listens.*

insignificance and God in all his grandeur. My friend, however, was experiencing the most wonderful joy that we can know in this life. He had found faith. The real obstacles to faith are generally very simple. They are the spite, fear, covetousness, or pride that we are unwilling to confess.

The main thing for us in this world is not being sure about what God's will is, but seeking it sincerely and following what we do understand of it. Many people have expressed to me convictions, that I have considered to be erroneous, about what God wanted of them. I have refrained from arguing with them. In the first place, who am I that I should claim to know better than they what God's will is, or to judge his secret purposes, when he is leading a soul along paths that seem to me to be unexpected? And then if I argued with them I should shake their faith, and it is their faith that matters, even if they make mistakes. Their faith will bring them closer to God. And "from obedience to obedience," as Frommel said, they can be corrected by God, brought to a clearer vision of what his will is. A few years later we shall see them admitting their mistake. But it is clear that they would never have found it out if they had not first begun to obey in what they *thought* was right.

A tourist wants to set out on a journey. He asks the way, looks at the map and the signposts. Despite all his precautions, he can never be quite sure of not taking the wrong route so long as he stays cautiously where he is. If he sets out, he can always be put right as he travels and he can still arrive at his destination, even if he originally took the wrong road.

Many people would like to be sure of God's guidance before trusting to it. They are unwilling to take the risk of making a mistake. In my experience they have always waited indefinitely. "Let us seek like men who must find," writes Laberthonnière,[4] "and let us find like men who must go on seeking, for it has been said that 'he who is at the term is only just beginning' [St. Augustine]."

"We must always ask ourselves," one of my friends once said, "when we find a door closed, whether God wants to stop us, or whether he wants us to make the effort to break it down!" Sometimes we break down doors that we ought to have left alone, and stop at others that we ought to have broken open. But even our mistakes

4 Frank Abauzit, *La pensée du Père Laberthonnière*.

teach us to distinguish the Spirit's guidance more clearly, when we really want to seek it. Every event takes on a fresh significance, for we are no longer concerned only with whether it is to our advantage or not, but with what God is saying to us through it. I decide to go and see a patient. I find that she is not at home. I tell myself that doubtless the inspiration that made me come out was incorrect. But as I leave her house I meet someone who needed most urgently to see me.

Nothing is more futile than to argue endlessly about whether, on some occasion in the past, one has made a mistake or not.

I have an old friend, an excellent person, whose witness once helped me to see that the seeking of God's guidance is, despite all our mistakes, the surest rule of life. Caught up in the tragic events of the war, he found himself facing a serious decision. He prayed, he meditated with some friends. He made the choice that seemed to him to conform with God's will. But the course of events made him doubt whether he had made the right decision in his country's interest. He underwent an inner crisis. He came to spend a few days with me. Every morning we read the Bible together, before our meditation. On the last day we had read the story of Lot's wife, who was turned into a pillar of salt because she looked back (Gen. 19:26). Then my friend exclaimed "I am like Lot's wife. My life is petrified because I keep looking back. I turn that old problem over and over in my mind, uselessly, without ever discovering whether I did right or not. My life is no longer an adventure, because my faith is shaken and I am not looking for God's guidance any more. I want to start going forward again." Shortly afterward a message from a friend who had died for his country finally relit in him the flame of dedication to Christ, and his life once more bore fruit. "To will what God wills is the only science that gives us rest," wrote Malherbe.

We all find it difficult to understand God's guidance, because we lack imagination. We are the prisoners of our prejudices. A colleague once remarked to me that we are always wanting to arrange everything, order everything, reconstruct everything. If we read the Old Testament prophets we see that sometimes, on the contrary, the will of God is that everything should be destroyed, that the cup of sin be drained to the dregs, so as to make possible a resurrection. We find it hard to understand the detours along which God takes us, and it is often only afterward that we see that we had to go that way.

One of my patients was asking me for advice. With only a few days in between, she thought she had received two contradictory commands from God. Which was the true one? "Perhaps both," I said to her, "because God may wish us to go to one side on one day and to another on another day." She looked at me in surprise. Then she murmured thoughtfully: "I have always been told that God's will was 'the straight and narrow path,' so I never imagined that there could be any detours in it!" Hippocrates observed that when two men are sawing a log, one pulls while the other pushes, but both are working together toward the same result.

What I am saying here might be compared with the many essays which nature seems to have made in the course of evolution, and which are like directions taken and then abandoned. Lecomte du Noüy compares evolution with what happens to a mass of water poured out on the summit of a mountain. For one stream to reach the bottom, many more must lose themselves on the way, absorbed in permeable soil, or retained in lakes in some corrie. So, in the course of evolution, innumerable lines of our species have developed over periods of several thousands or millions of years, only to be extinguished, while one of them ceaselessly pursued its course, to arrive at man, who was to open his heart to the Spirit.

Similarly, in our lives we should doubtless never know the joy of a really fruitful inspiration if we were not ready to follow many others which do not bear the fruits we expect of them. The reader will perhaps also see that between this conception of the guidance of God and the rigid morality of principles, there is the same difference as between Einsteinian and Newtonian physics.

Thus, amid many uncertainties, we learn the patience of faith. A person's life is never changed in the way we should have imagined.

This is the answer to those who claim that faith is nothing but suggestion. What convinces us most are those divine interventions which are quite unforeseen, and which are beyond any psychological explanation.

"The divine words within," said St. Theresa, "which the mystic cannot hear, are nevertheless uttered in the soul at moments when the latter is unable to understand them, and they answer no desire to hear them."

An intellectual comes to see me. In a moment of crisis he has impulsively left his employment, to which he was well suited by his talents. His present work gives him no satisfaction, and he blames himself. We go over it all for a long time without seeing any solution. One must be honest and never pretend to have a solution, never fall victim to one's own powers of suggestion. One day, we decide to take the problem to God, confessing our inability to solve it. The next day his chief calls him into his office and asks him if he is happy in his work. After a few moments' conversation, the chief says: "For a long time I have been thinking of creating a post that would be just the thing for you. I was in fact looking for the right man for it." Then time passes; the chief seems to have forgotten about it. We are near to losing patience, and beginning to doubt. Once again we bring it all to God. Once more, on the morrow, the chief calls him. Without saying a word he has arranged everything.

Another man, also dissatisfied with his work, has made application after application, in vain. Here again I suffer with him because of the prolonged uncertainty—and the doubt it throws on my faith. Suddenly he writes to me. A most unexpected and pleasing solution has suddenly been found. But he sees that it is not mere chance. It happened, he adds, just when "I had realized that I could not do anything by myself, and had clutched at the idea that God would act for me and that all that was left for me to do was to see how he would set about it." Moreover, he himself had said in a letter to me previously: "The attitude we are able to take to our personal problems is in the end more important than their solution."

Another sign of God's intervention is to be found in acts of obedience which from the human point of view would have seemed unacceptable. A woman had left home because of the intolerable injustices to which she had been subjected. She said to me: "I want to talk to you, but on condition that you do not ask me to go back." I asked nothing of her, but a month later she went back of her own accord. God grants what he commands. His intervention is also seen in those sudden, unexpected experiences, at times of utter despair, when all at once the mind is filled with the absolute certainty of God's love, even though there has been no recent mention made of it. It is like an unexpected signpost upon an uncertain road.

If healing through faith is striking, how much more so are spiritual victories without healing. I had a friend suffering from an incurable disease. I prayed with him. I did not feel I had the right to pray for a cure, nor did he. But when he had put his life in God's hands he lived through several months of sickness in a joyous and infectious serenity which the specialist who shared his treatment with me had never seen in any other patient.

One sees people whose lives are spent in suffering, enduring failure after failure, a prey to the worst kind of social or psychological difficulties. Their faith wavers, but is never extinguished. They are a better testimony to the glory of God than many a brilliant but ephemeral success.

Suggestion may procure an unexpected liberation, but it is generally only temporary. As Baudouin himself recognizes, "Everything that suggestion has done can also be undone by suggestion." As for faith, it holds firm, even to the Cross. That is why Weatherhead writes: "True faith seems to me to have very little to do with suggestion." Rather is faith an antidote to dangerous suggestions. A woman receives one of those infamous "chain" letters which threaten you with a curse if you do not send them on to three other persons. She does not believe it; nevertheless it leaves her with a certain anxiety. She must confide it all to God in prayer in order to recover all her inner liberty.

Cases of faith healing where there can be no question of suggestion are the ones that are most striking. I often hear of astonishing instances. For example, there was a man who had a mental breakdown and had to be taken to hospital, suffering from a loss of all sense of reality. Suddenly, as if a veil had been torn apart in him, his condition changed. He came out of his dream, and went and played the piano. The doctor verified his cure, and sent him home. Only then did he learn that at the very same time as he had felt himself set free, his wife was with a believer to whom she had gone without her husband's knowledge in order to pray together for him to be healed.

In addition, I have before me the records of a number of cases of healing following upon religious conversion: a woman who had undergone for years all sorts of gynecological treatment without success; a case of chronic eczema that had gone on for years; a case of pulmonary tuberculosis; and many more. The striking thing in all these cases is that healing was in no way thought of as the aim of the religious conversion, but was on the contrary its unexpected consequence, an "added" grace (Matt. 6:33), granted to a person who when face to face with God had no other thought in his mind than his sin, his repentance, and his dedication.

CHAPTER 16

Seeking the Light

Jouffroy, a tormented nineteenth-century philosopher who had lost his faith, kept on coming back to the problem of the destiny of man. He conceded that this was the essential problem of man, on which all the others depended, but there was nothing that could throw any light on it. There is no doubt that without faith this is so. How could one find the meaning of existence, except in Him who created it? All doctors agree that one of the conditions of good health is to have an aim in life. What aim can we adopt that is not fictitious, that is more than an empty suggestion, except the fulfillment of the purpose of the creator of life?

It is quite true that we are groping our way about in the dark. But there are gleams of light, and they come from God. The only possible answer to the problem of the destiny of man is to seek without respite to fulfill God's purpose. "You fulfill your purpose in life," one of my patients once said, "on condition that you allow yourself to be guided without ever trying any tricks of your own."

The problem of our destiny preoccupies each one of us, consciously or unconsciously. That is why, contrary to what church people always say, there is no one, in my view, who is indifferent to the subject of religion. You cannot help a person if you look upon him as indifferent to religion. From his conversations with French-Swiss workers of the most varied outlook, Lalive d'Epinay comes to this conclusion: "Some assert their faith, others make a point of their skepticism, but it is rare that one meets real indifference." He expresses the view that "the indifference of the Church to social problems" is the true cause of working-class disaffection in regard to it.

I could call as witness all those who come to see me affecting indifference, and who betray in all sorts of little ways that they hope to find a strength that is lacking in their lives. They say they do not want me to talk to them about God, but they themselves keep reverting to talking about him. Or else we do not talk about him, and later on they confess how disappointed they were that our interviews were "too superficial." Or they stay away for years, and do all the things they know God does not want them to do. And then they come back in despair, because they cannot silence the voice their souls have once heard. Or else they seize the opportunity presented by some illness to come and see the Christian doctor with the idea more or less consciously in the back of their minds that there will be occasion to discuss with him the thing that is most on their minds, despite the indifference they affect. A young woman arrives with an accidental injury. While I am dressing the wound she opens her heart to me about the religious doubts that are tormenting her.

Those who pretend to be the strongest have a presentiment that the strongest thing in this life does not necessarily have to come from man. "Prayer," writes Alexis Carrel,[1] "is not only an act of adoration, it is an invisible emanation of the spirit of adoration, that is to say, the most powerful form of energy that can be brought into play. . . . Prayer is as real a force as gravitation. . . . When we pray we tap the inexhaustible motive force that makes the world go round. . . ."

So, although faith retains its humility and trepidation, it is nevertheless the source of the only enlightenment that never disappoints. Although the believer must grope his way forward, experiencing crises and turning back—wondering if he has faith or feeling himself broken by God—and setting off again, he also finds on this difficult road, despite all the apparent setbacks, realities that are notably more stable than the great systems that men invent. Philosophical and scientific theories have their day; one after another they pass into oblivion, for all their power of suggestion as a vogue. But the rock of the Christian faith remains over the centuries; and sincere seekers all come to the same experiences and the same convictions, whatever the

[1] In *Journal de Genève,* May 4, 1940.

formula or the route they adopt. "Faith," one scientist writes, "is more unshakable than knowledge." Any human suggestion may provoke moral victories and a euphoria that is very similar to the effect of faith. But they do not last. Faith knows itself to be weak and uncertain, and yet like the reed it will survive the storm better than the proud oak. It knows that in this world it can never penetrate all the unfathomable mysteries of God, and yet, however tiny the light it receives from him, this is the only light that can really show it the way. Faith alone brings true peace. "I am often astonished," a young woman writes to me in a letter after her conversion, "to discover that deep inside I am always at peace, while everything around me is in a state of hectic, nervous agitation."

If faith helps a man to find his purpose in life, this is true of nations as well. A nation is not, as is sometimes claimed, an artificial community, the arbitrary product of political treaties. It is an organism, the fruit of history—that is, of nature. It has a destiny willed by God. Like an organism, it has its instincts. By instinct it defends its life. Has not God given it this instinct of self-preservation in order that it may use its life in accordance with his will? If every nation fulfills its destiny, the world will discover God's answer to international problems. The spectacle presented by the modern world is not so attractive that we can afford to spurn the trial of a different method of guiding its affairs from that of human wisdom. Men devoted to seeking God's inspiration for their personal lives and the life of their nation will be the surest leaders. My own little country has the privilege of having had the guiding lines of its policy laid down by a man who sought them in prayer before God. The history of Nicolas of Flue (1417–1487) is a good illustration of the double character of faith, its poverty and its power.[2] Watch him as he hesitates, tormented for years by his inner call to withdraw into distant solitude. And when he sets off on his mission, he still trembles lest he is wrong. He sees in a storm a sign that God wants him to stop. He retraces his steps. But on the threshold of his house he hesitates once more. He does not go in. He spends the night secretly in the barn. And yet it is he who is to give his people commands that will have all the authority of God's commandments. In restoring peace between the Confederates, Nicolas of Flue showed Switzer-

[2] Georges Méautis, *Nicolas de Flue.*

land its destiny: that of being a modest laboratory of peace, existing with its neighbors in mutual respect and love. By his command, "Do not interfere in the quarrels of your neighbors," he gave a spiritual basis to its perpetual neutrality.

But how are we to receive God's orders, since we are never sure we are not deceiving ourselves? It has often happened that someone has come to see me, and said: "After reading your book I tried to meditate, but I received none of the inspiration you talk about. What ought I to do?" I have replied, in order to console him, that the first time I spent an hour seeking in a concrete fashion to know what God wanted me to do, I experienced the same difficulty and humiliation. I felt I had written down only my own thoughts—and what poor thoughts they were! Reminiscences of sermons or books. But as I closed my notebook an idea came into my mind, namely that I ought to go on meditating at length every day, even if I did not know very well how to do it. And at once I thought that this idea came from God. For years I had known that He was reproving me for not putting prayer and the inner life at the center of my life, making it the source of all my activity. Up to then I had, of course, been praying and reading the Bible frequently, though irregularly, with periods of spiritual drought that were particularly long. But the main thing was that this inner life was, as it were, a separate department, having no real connection with my everyday life. There was no bridge between theory and practice. The bridge I needed was meditation.

Meditation is not a psychological method. If one tries to lay down rules for it, and turn it into a method, applying it like a technique, it will no longer be living. It will have been emptied of its religious substance. I have, therefore, no recipe to suggest, unless it be to ask God day after day for his help in the organization of one's spiritual life, with the advice of the Church.

The first condition on which we shall receive God's guidance, is that we should seek it. We always think we shall not have time. We will find time if we really want to. We can take it from those useless little pastimes we find time for so readily even in the busiest lives. It increases the return we get on our time so tremendously, that we shall find we have more spare time left than we have given up to God.

A priest came to consult me one day. We talked about the organization of his life in relation to his health. He said to me: "Of course, up to ten o'clock I have my religious duties." When he had gone, I thought to myself that my need for contact with God, as a doctor, was no less than his. I could look upon my meditation as my first and most urgent appointment. Since then, as a general rule, I have not seen patients before nine o'clock. In this way I have two and a half peaceful hours available at the beginning of every day, in which I can meditate, read the Bible or some of the other spiritual treasures of world literature, examine my faults of the day before, prepare my day in God's presence, or pursue some intellectual task under his guidance. I have given up the false shame I used to feel at saying to a patient: "I cannot see you tomorrow; my whole day is booked up. I cannot encroach on the time I have promised to God." One evening during my military service, since we had to leave on horseback next day, our commanding officer said to us quite simply: "We shall not be leaving until nine o'clock, because the Catholic padre is coming with us. He has his religious duties to perform." Everybody respects that. The unfortunate thing about so many Protestant ministers, and countless sincere laymen, is that in their zeal to do their work properly, they reduce to a dangerously low level the total of time reserved for their personal devotions. When I am with a pastor, it is sometimes with less simplicity than when I am with a layman that I suggest that we should meditate together for a moment rather than entering upon a discussion.

Let each seek before God, and with the aid of the Church, his own rule—but let him have one! Would it not be true even in a business office, that if the first quarter of an hour of the working day were devoted to meditation in common, the productivity of the work, instead of going down, would increase? I thought of an illustration while sawing some wood with my circular saw. When the saw begins to get dull, it is very much to my advantage to dismount it in order to sharpen and reset it. The time I spend on this is largely made up in the speed with which it goes through the wood afterward. Similarly we get back abundantly the time we devote to sharpening and resetting our minds that have been blunted by the many difficulties and failures of life.

Countless writings underline the urgency for our modern world, with all its bustle and noise, of rediscovering the value of meditation, of silence, of prayer, of devotion. I preached it before I practiced it. If one is to help the world toward this rediscovery, one must practice it oneself. The religious life must be fed. We devote years to studying a trade or profession. Ought we to show less perseverance in acquiring the experience of God? The least player of billiards or chess knows how long he has had to spend in order to learn to play, and how many games he had to lose before winning one. The scientist, when an experiment fails, instead of abandoning it, asks himself whether there has not slipped into his arrangements or his calculations some cause of error. One of my patients had a dream. She was given the task of keeping alight the fire under the boiler. A voice kept saying to her: "Put coal on regularly. Don't let the fire go out." Recently I saw a young woman who after several years of great spiritual adventure, was swamped in overwhelming difficulties. I happened to mention to her that during the last twelve years, I could count the days on which I had neglected to write down during meditation what I thought God expected of me. A few days later she wrote to me: "I am grateful for what you said. It is a long time since I gave up the habit of written meditation. Someone told me that after a time one had made sufficient spiritual progress to be able to keep contact with God all day long, without having to reserve any special time for listening to him!"

Everything is habit in biology, and habits are created only by means of repetition. Experiments have shown how much of our behavior is determined by the mental images to which our minds are constantly returning. If we bring our minds back again and again to God, we shall by the same inevitable law be gradually giving the central place to God, not only in our inner selves, but also in our practical everyday lives.

I read in the newspaper an anecdote that goes very deep. A literary lady was holding forth in her drawingroom, deploring the fact that she had not yet been touched by God's grace. "How is one to believe that God exists?" she demanded. If he existed, would she not have gotten some answer out of him in the twenty-five years she had been addressing her requests to him? "Pardon, Madame," remarked one of her guests, "but did you ever leave him time to get a word in?"

A brief moment daily, however, is not sufficient. What is needed may be to break into one's active life with periods of real retreat. Several weeks are not too much. My whole medical career has been transformed by the weeks I spent in a retreat seven years ago with friends from the whole world over. I know, too, how fruitful are the consultations I am able to give to patients who have made a long preparation for them in some lonely mountain chalet or place of pilgrimage.

The second condition on which we shall receive God's commands is that we are ready to follow them. A patient tells me she can no longer pray. In meditation, it is not long before she is telling me that this is since a certain day when she ran away from a difficult act of obedience. Many people argue endlessly about the difficulty of knowing God's will, and yet they know that some refusal in their own lives is what is making contact with him difficult. People often come to us with some choice about which they would like to know God's will. This question remains unanswered because they have other problems that need solving—problems about which they know very well what God's will is, only they do not want to follow it, and are trying to take refuge from it in discussions.

The word "experience" which is used in connection with faith can lead people into error. I have, it is true, seen several people find faith as soon as they gave up arguing and tried simply to play the game honestly. After meditating, they put into practice the first idea that came into their minds. But I have seen others who went into an "experience" of this kind with mental reservations as to the result, so that they were treating it rather as an experiment than as an experience. They were not committing themselves to it wholeheartedly, in a spirit of submission to God. Their skepticism was the cause of their failure.

When I felt myself called to give a new direction to my medical career, I went with my family to spend a fortnight at the seaside, in order to think the idea over at leisure. I was quite disappointed at receiving so little in the way of guidance for the task I felt to be ahead of me. I felt that my spiritual life had become sterile. But afterward I saw that I had really known all along quite well what were the first steps that God was demanding of me. I had to send a letter out to all my patients, reread a book I had first read some years before, and go and ask the advice of a certain number of my teachers and colleagues. All I had to do at first was to take these initial steps, instead of looking for sensational inspiration. God would show me the way step by step. The result of performing one act of obedience is always that one is granted new light. There is a necessary connection between meditation and action. Pastor Roger Schutz stresses its importance: "Without meditation and prayer," he writes, "work is sterile because it has been torn from its source. Without work, meditation and prayer become impossible because they have become disincarnate, having no connection with daily life."

"When we talk of men of action," writes Charles Baudouin, "we tend to mean merely men who bustle about. . . . It is superficial to set the thinker over against the man of action. Action, if it is authentic, is the measure of thought."[3]

A third condition to be fulfilled if we are to receive God's commands is that we must not try to find them out on our own. It has pleased God to make human communion a condition of communion with him. We cannot alter this, so that either our problems remain insoluble in the silence of an unsociable solitude, or else we delude ourselves and treat our own thoughts as if they were those of God. The team, that is to say the community of men and women seeking together to know God's will, and working together to put it into practice, is necessary to the life guided by the Spirit, just as it is also its consequence. We do not look for advice in the community, a declaration by someone else as to what God is expecting of us, but rather an inner illumination which never comes while we remain alone, turning a problem over in our minds. A young woman wrote to tell me about a question that had become an obsession with her. She had a very pale complexion, and so had taken to using rouge. But she wondered if this practice was compatible with the honesty required by her Christian faith. Concerned to free her mind from a scruple which was holding her back when doubtless she could be occupying herself with more useful projects, I replied advising her flatly to continue using her make-up, and to leave the moral responsibility of the decision to me. The effect of my letter was unexpected. By return of post she replied that as soon as she had read what I wrote she realized that in reality she had felt for a long time that she ought not to use make-up, and her arguments had simply been a means of hiding from herself the fact that she was too concerned with the effect she produced on other people. From then on she sought to give up this concern to God. Now that she had opened her heart to someone, the worry that had been tormenting her disappeared.

The proud, self-satisfied attitude that naïvely thinks it knows all the answers is quite different from the accent of true faith. A man

[3] *La force en nous.*

comes to see me. For a long time, he says, he has felt he was being called by God. He has tried to avoid the issue, but he cannot silence the call he hears. He doubted whether it was authentic, and spoke about it to some friends, and prayed with them. They all encouraged him to obey, but he is still unsure. He comes to see me again. When we pray together he sees that he must make up his mind to follow the call, still asking God to forgive him if he is mistaken, since he is doing it sincerely. I can be sure that his decision will bear fruit! Many of our convictions remain vague, theoretical, and ineffective while we have not the courage to put them into words and communicate them to others. Sometimes those others have to be brutal with us so that we will at last make up our minds to obey! I can still hear the tone of voice of one of my patients as she recalled how a Jesuit father she had met in India had cut short all her arguments by obliging her to pray.

A fourth condition is that we must have a simple heart. Our guidance from God will suffer as soon as we oppose our thoughts to those of God, faith to reason, the supernatural to the natural, the trust that is necessary for healing to the doctor's technical treatment. As soon as we start worrying about whether we are mistaken, or whether we may be taking our own suggestions as those sent by God, or whether we are conducting our meditations "properly," trying to imitate the way other people go about them, and being afraid of the criticisms that might be made by anyone seeing our written notes—as soon as we concern ourselves with making a good impression on the person we intend to show our notes to, as soon as we are afraid we are not going to be guided, or that we do not know how to meditate correctly—then all these various preoccupations will spoil our meditation and stultify it. There is no infallible method of discovering what God's guidance for us is. I do not put my faith in a method, but in God, who is not hindered by my faults, and can correct them.

Let us hand over to God the whole of our minds, with all their thoughts, feelings, and wishes, and ask him to guide them. And then let us take seriously all we think, feel, and wish. In a book of meditations,[4] Stanley Jones clearly outlines the attitude of faith, which looks for God's instructions coming through the channel of our enlightened reason as well as through the advice of others or through some sudden extraordinary revelation.

4 Stanley Jones, *Victorious Living*.

As a matter of fact, by the next day it is generally obvious whether the inspiration has come from God or from ourselves.

I may add that dreams, as many examples in the Bible show, may often appear to be messages from God. A child remarked to his mother: "Dreams are God's movies, aren't they?" This interpretation is in complete accord with the theory of dreams put forward by Freud, who showed that they are the expression of deeply hidden desires. Such a desire may come from the devil, but it may by the same token also come from God! Here again the important thing is not to remain alone, but to check one's conclusions by getting some other person's critical interpretation of the dream.

There may be occasions where it would be more sincere not to indulge in meditation at all. I have seen several people give it up after having regularly practiced it for long periods. I have never scolded them or urged upon them that it was their duty to take it up again as a matter of discipline. Instead I have tried to understand the spiritual development taking place within them. They were giving up their meditation because they were disappointed in its quality. It had become a hollow and unprofitable habit, an effort to find fine phrases that did not come from the heart, or a mere imitation of someone else. And sometimes I have seen them come back to it with fresh life and in a quite new and personal way. One man, of an essentially artistic or mystical temperament, tries to practice a kind of meditation that might be all right for someone else, but is far too intellectual for him. God does not speak only in terms of logical ideas, but also in pictures and music. Another perceives that his preconceived ideas about God, inculcated in him by others, are restricting his inspiration to far too narrow a field.

We have to rediscover periodically the meaning of living meditation. We realize that little by little, as a friend of mine once put it, we have taken to listening to ourselves instead of to God.

Sometimes, too, we feel that we are no longer practicing meditation for love of God, but in order to be the recipients of some message from him. The emphasis has shifted, and we are slipping once more down the slope of a belief in magic. Meditation, and even the desire to be guided by God, have no longer any religious meaning once they cease to be an expression of a burning love for him.

As I write these lines, I have just had a visit from a patient for whom I have a particular concern because she is facing great difficulties, and because she longs ardently to know what God's answer to them is. Our conversation was completely sterile. I used fine-sounding but hollow exhortations to her to worry less about her difficulties. And indeed she would like nothing better than to be able to do so: she came to me, after all, to find help in doing just that, not to be preached at. I even suggested that we should meditate in prayer together. After we had done so, she had the honesty, even in the midst of the emotion she felt at the failure of our interview, to confess that she had been granted scarcely any new inspiration at all. For my part, I had written pages of notes that were so banal as to be quite useless. During my meditation on the following morning I was shocked at the realization of my failure. I rushed over to her hotel to beg her to forgive me. She had already left Geneva. I wrote to her. She replied that after a night of despair she had had the idea of going to church in the early morning to take Communion. Never had a Communion service brought her a deeper peace. God has unexpected resources on which he draws to make up the deficiencies of our ministry in his service.

In some people the very impatience and excitement aroused by their first positive experiences of meditation prevent them achieving that peace of mind necessary to a good meditation. In others self-satisfaction, arising out of their first successful attempts, becomes the cause of a lowering of the quality of their meditation.

Meditation, as Nicolas of Flue said, is alternately "a dance" and "a fight," or else it is both at once. But we continually turn to it for renewal and to find tranquillity after the rush and worry of action. I refer not only to the worry that arises from our sinful lusts, but also that which is inseparable from even the sincerest vocation of service. Helping others, if one puts one's heart into it, always involves to some extent identifying oneself with them. It is difficult to treat neurotics without letting oneself be influenced by them. It is necessary then to go into retreat in order to become oneself again. It is necessary also, as St. Francis said, to go aside to weep over our faults in order to be ready to meet with joy those who come to draw strength from us. Further, every failure leaves us fearful and stultified unless meditation puts an end to the vicious circle of negative suggestions that failure always sets up in us.

In meditation we can also learn to live the present moment, casting off the past and leaving aside the future, and all the idle, unnecessary, and trifling questions that dissipate our efforts.

One of my friends was talking to me the other day about a critical period in his life. He had taken part in politics, with some success. Then he had felt that his star was waning. Suddenly one day he had said to himself: "If it pleases God to make me a quite ordinary man who does an ordinary job day after day, I can very well accept that as well." And in fact since then he has found all kinds of new tasks to do, tasks that are much more fruitful than was his former political activity, and which he would not have been able to see if he had allowed himself to sink into bitterness. I also see many people who sympathize so intensely with the great sufferings of the world that they would like to do great things in order to deliver the nations from the scourge of war. Their modest immediate task seems colorless beside these grand ambitions. The trouble is that their ambitions are merely sentimental, and blind them to sufferings on their own doorstep. I too have sometimes felt ashamed that I was working peacefully while nations were suffering in a life-and-death struggle. But the most important thing that we can do to share in the lives of others is not to spend our time dreaming, but to fulfill our own task allotted to us by God.

Meditation is also the remedy for distraction, which is a danger into which the most gifted easily fall. It teaches us to put order into our lives, to distinguish the essential from the accessory, to discipline ourselves without false rigidity, to leave aside those things we are doing merely for the sake of respectability. For without meditation we slip either into pedantry or anarchy, or else we oscillate between them.

"Being detached," writes Spoerri, "is not a feeling, it is an event."

Meditation broadens the mental horizon. A young woman is in conflict with one of her fellow workers at the office, who torments her in all sorts of ways. The worst of it is that the conflict has become an obsession with this girl. Even outside the office she is unable to think of anything else. In meditation her mind is reawakened to other interesting subjects, and her obsession pales into insignificance in a life that is becoming richer and more diversified.

Meditation makes us independent of events, by making us dependent upon God. In this respect it is a school of leadership, for the leader is he who has the courage to assert himself alone, strengthened by his inner conviction. I remember a meeting of journalists where the question was raised as to where the authority of a journalist came from. Everyone had a go at a definition, and it occurred to me that it ought to derive from the true spiritual liberty which is forged in a rich inner life.

So, then, we must beware of attributing a magical value to God's guidance. Above all we must beware, wretched and blind as we are, of arguing with each other about it. Our basic attitude is what matters most: a sincere seeking after God's will. We must always respect that sincerity in others.

Skepticism leads many Christians into the opposite error. In order to avoid the accusation of self-righteousness, they confine themselves in matters of faith to conventional pious generalizations. They never venture upon a personal affirmation of their convictions, and they think that in this way they are being modest and avoiding setting themselves up as an example to others. They readily agree that the world ought to be more honest, and that this will never happen if no one begins, but they dare not break away from the acts of dishonesty which everyone does, for fear of being looked upon as religious enthusiasts. This is what gives the religious life of so many Christians a theoretical, sentimental, and joyless character, lacking any real effectiveness. It is what makes so many of them suspicious of religious enthusiasm—for fear of its having no lasting effect. When the zeal aroused by God's call leads to practical acts of obedience, to the practical application of a man's aspirations, when its cost can be counted in money, time, courage, initiative, and humiliation, then it is fruitful, and it is feared no longer.

A young woman wants to know whether God is calling her to celibacy or to marriage. I need hardly say that this theoretical perplexity makes her act awkwardly in front of the young men she meets. Instead of worrying about it as a theoretical problem, she would do far better simply to believe that God will surely guide her to the life He has designed for her if she seeks to obey Him step by step in every circumstance of her life. Similarly, I have seen many people putting to God some question about their vocation—often for years —and never receiving any reply. They want to be sure what God requires of them: does he want them to remain humbly in the job they have, or is he prompting them to leave it for some new task which is still vague in their minds? If they left their present post would they be running away? Or would staying in it be avoiding a challenge? Such theoretical, all-embracing questions are generally sterile. Meanwhile these people are not putting their backs into their present jobs, because they are staying in them without conviction. In this ambivalent and lackluster frame of mind one rarely receives any clear message from God. Faith consists in believing that where we now are is where God wills us to be; that He requires us to give ourselves wholeheartedly to the task that faces us now, and that He will surely lead us elsewhere if ever He wishes to do so. Having a mission means doing what we are doing in a missionary spirit. Others, who form a marked contrast with these perpetual waverers, apply this spirit of vocation to the task at hand, and seek God's guidance in every detail of the routine problems of the daily round. As a result they enrich their experience, they are appreciated and noticed, and the day comes when they are offered some other work which they may see as a divine vocation. Or it may be that in the midst of an intense and active life they are given a clear call to leave the work they are interested in and take up a new vocation.

There was one woman patient whom I interviewed whose life had been quite ruined by her habit of telling lies. She had several times already glimpsed the fact that true Christianity was the answer for her, but each time she had relapsed into her old lamentable way of life. This time she saw that she must follow out to the end the direction she had been given, namely, to pay all her debts. For some months she scrimped and saved, and worked without respite. In order to regularize her situation she had to face the humiliation of going with the truth to people to whom she had previously told lies in order to get out of difficulties. But now she tells me in a letter how happy she is. Her faith has substance at last. The painful path she has trodden has done more to transform her life than all the blanket resolutions she used to make. On several occasions patients have told me that following upon a concrete and costly act of obedience such as making amends for a wrong done, or breaking off an improper association, they have felt so happy that people have noticed it and asked if they have become engaged to be married! Sometimes God commands us to do very pleasant things, which a false and conventional puritanism has made us think were incompatible with our austere dignity.

When we realize the value of these small direct questions which oblige us to think in concrete terms, we become less interested in broad discussions and ineffective, generalized aspirations. A young man says to me: "I lack discipline." It is no doubt true, but no great change will be made in his life so long as he gets no further than this vague thought. *"In what,* for example, do you lack discipline?" "I get up late; I know that I ought to get up early in order to be able to say my prayers before the morning newscast on the radio." *"What time* must you set your alarm for?" "For six o'clock." *"What else* must you do in order to make sure you get up in time?" "First, I must be more disciplined about my bedtime. I often sit up late, wasting time on trivialities. Then I must hope that God will help me to wake up quickly, because all my good resolutions vanish when I am half awake." *"When* do you want to begin?" "Tomorrow morning." *"Is that all?"* "No, I ought to pray about it now." *"Is that all?"* "No, I ought to talk about it at home, because that will commit me still further. When I avoid talking about the resolutions I have made, it is so that people won't remind me about them when I fail to keep them." *"To whom* do you want to talk about it?" "To my younger brother." *"When* do you want to talk to him about it?" "This very evening."

An attachment to broad principles can easily lead to a stifling moralism and to the no less oppressive malaise that we feel when what we are bears no relationship to what we believe. The search for concrete guidance by God sets in motion the reversal we were considering in Chapter 12, and the passage from formal morality to true morality which is the subject of the second part of this book. Hence, it brings liberation from moralism, while leading to a much more exacting moral life.

Sometimes meditation throws particular light on medical problems. A friend of mine comes into a restaurant and jokingly remarks to me, as a sort of challenge: "I can't be right with God, old man, because I've got a frightful attack of lumbago!" We have a good laugh about it, but it is not long before he is admitting that the attack started when he was doing his gymnastic exercises. He overdid it in his pride of being still so supple and strong at his age.

Often, however, meditation reveals things that lie much deeper. Take, for instance, the patient whose thoughts ran like this: "Really, you know very well that you have cultivated your illness. You were really ill at first; but when you noticed that it brought you those marks of affection that you had awaited so long in vain from your mother, you found your illness not unwelcome. You lay down in the snow to make it worse; you rubbed the thermometer in order to make the doctor worry more; you threw your medicines away for fear of getting well; you robbed your father in making him pay for several months' stay at the sanatorium. And it was because you were afraid of life, in which you reckoned you were starved of affection; because you were afraid of standing up for your religious beliefs against persecution by the rest of the family. All that must be set in order."

This patient could have listened in her meditation to the intellectual objection: "Are you sure that it is God speaking to you? What proof is there?" But instead she listened to that other voice: "If it were God? If it were God speaking to you? Would you risk going against God?"

PART V

The Spirit
of Adventure

CHAPTER · 17

Revelation

Throughout the Bible we find that attitude which I have called both believing and thinking, and which represents a necessary, though difficult, fusion between realism and faith. It forms a contrast with the simplistic attitude on the one hand and the skeptical attitude on the other.

The Bible gives us a powerful picture of men guided by God. They are not men who make no mistakes or who claim to make no mistakes, but men who seek to listen to God and obey him. After many mistakes and acts of disobedience, humbled by disappointments and trembling before God, Moses found intimate fellowship with him, so that he was able to receive the Ten Commandments direct from God. If Abraham had not believed the order to sacrifice his son, would he have had the experience that was his at the moment when God stayed his arm from a sacrifice which so many other religions saw as the cruel will of the deity? And then there are all the prophets called by God, balking at the call they receive. "If I say, 'I will not mention him, or speak any more in his name,'" says Jeremiah, "there is in my heart as it were a burning fire shut up in my bones" (Jer. 20:9). And there is St. Peter, making his heartfelt remonstrations to Jesus when the latter announces that he is going to be put to death, and drawing upon himself the sharp reply: "Get behind me, Satan! . . . for you are not on the side of God, but of men" (Matt. 16:23). And this was at the very moment when St. Peter had just proclaimed, with the purest inspiration, his faith in the divinity of Christ. And there is the Church at Antioch receiving as it prayed the order to send Paul and Barnabas on a mission, and Paul himself "led by the Spirit" when he comes back to Jerusalem, or seeing a dream in which a Macedonian calls him as God's command to take the Gospel to Europe (Acts 16:9).

Christ himself is the incarnation of this life led in its smallest details by the Spirit. He walks peacefully, seeing in the man met on the road or the woman at the well the very soul to whom God has sent him. No rush, no concocted plan, no disorder; everything takes place in its own time, as he himself so often says. But this does not stop him from withdrawing with his disciples to seek God's guidance. He returns full of assurance, to go up to Jerusalem to face death.

All these men of the Bible accept God's precise orders—the place they must go to, the time they must go there. But they do not look for these orders as for oracles. What they seek is God. Following the *directions* they receive, they find their lives *directed* toward fellowship with God. They do not express their fellowship sentimentally, but manifest it through their faith in the concrete *directions* they are following.

Is it not because they have lost the sense of being led by the Spirit that so many church people are overworked, exhausted, and worried? Administrative regulations, projects and committees may be necessary, but they do not take the place of what is lost. Is it not for the same reason that so many of our patients tell us that what they hear in church seems theoretical and unconnected with real life?

The believing and thinking attitude is one in which we realize that we may constantly make mistakes, but also one in which we do not at the same time use this as an excuse for running away from what we believe to be God's call. It is just because we know our understanding to be so feeble that we turn toward the Bible: in order to find enlightenment that does not come from men. The knowledge of our weakness is the source of our tolerance. Our dependence on the authority of the biblical revelation, because of this weakness, is the source of our orthodoxy.

What of all those who believe that there is a God, that this God created the world and governs it in all its details; that he is at the same time omnipotent and perfectly good, despite the apparent denial of this that is implicit in the existence of evil and suffering; that he rules over the destinies of men, while still leaving them free to disobey; that, at a certain time in history, he became incarnate in the person of Jesus Christ in order to save mankind, and that Jesus Christ rose from the dead; that at one and the same time he reigns over the infinite immensity of the universe and also takes a personal interest in each individual; that he reveals himself to the individual personally, and lives in him by the Holy Spirit, showing him what is His will and giving him strength to fulfill it? Are those who believe this believing in something that is true and real, or are they victims of a grand illusion suggested to them by their imaginations, and suggested thereafter by one to another, and so passed on?

Clearly the limitations of the human mind are such that it does not have at its disposal any absolute proof that could settle the question.

Man does not know even who he is, nor where his faculty of asking himself questions comes from. And in any case he may just as easily be the victim of a false suggestion in doubting the existence of God as in believing in him. One can think what one likes; it does not alter facts. As Alfons Wagner writes, "On a sinking ship one is free to think that it is not going to sink."

Being unable to find any certain answer to our questions so long as we try to deal with them in isolation, what we need is a wider perspective which will give us an authoritative and all-embracing scale of reference. This wider perspective is that of the Bible, seen as a unified whole. It is that of the person of Jesus Christ, unique in history, and outside the norms of human psychology. Just as at the level of the phenomenon, the question "Why?" is unanswerable, whereas in the light of the evolutionary process as a whole the phenomenon falls into place as part of an over-all plan, so an individual belief is incapable of valid proof by itself, but when we view the whole wonderful, unique, and harmonious panorama formed by the person of Christ, the Bible, and the history of the Church, the evidence that God has revealed himself is overwhelming. The critic may honestly question each biblical assertion taken by itself. But when he looks at the message as a whole, as it is contained in the events and ideas presented by the Bible, he can only submit, and acknowledge that all this could not have been imagined or experienced by men without the intervention of God. The idea of a divine intervention in history is inescapable. Once this is conceded, the critic who finds difficulty in understanding or admitting any individual biblical assertion will assume that the Bible is right rather than himself.

I had an excellent old friend who did much to awaken in me an interest in spiritual things. So great, however, was his respect for the spiritual side of life and his desire not to confine it within the rigid framework of any dogmatic system that he stopped short of revelation. He accepted man's spiritual nature; he could not accept a personal God who reveals himself. He could uplift his mind to the realm of the spiritual; he could not pray to that impersonal and impossible Spirit which is outside time and space. Our fellowship was close, but it stopped there. We hardly ever discussed it, seeking as we did what united us, rather than what separated us. Years passed. He led a hard life. I met him again toward the evening of his life. I told him of my experiences over the last few years. When I had finished he said simply, but in a way that revealed all the road he had traveled since last I had seen him: "Paul, now we must pray together to thank God for what He has revealed to you, and to dedicate your work to Him." It had been granted to him to be able to reconcile total respect for the limitless liberty of the spirit with faith in a personal God who reveals Himself—a reconciliation which the intellectual always finds difficult.

A vague and composite spiritualism can never have the dynamism necessary to rebuild the world. Nor can strict dogmatism unite all our brother human beings in the task of rebuilding. What we can do is to seek for ourselves in complete submission to the biblical revelation the source of a living faith and of a life directed by Christ, without trying to impose its formulas on all those who in many different ways and along different roads, often without knowing it, are seeking the true God.

As far as we ourselves are concerned, we must submit to the Bible and to the teaching of the Christian Church, for the only way of avoiding the ever-present danger of self-deception is to have a standard of judgment outside ourselves and our suggestible minds. If the voice that speaks in our hearts in the silence of meditation is in conformity with what the Bible tells us of God, if what it suggests is humble, disinterested, honest, pure, and loving, then let us not worry; it comes from God. If not, it comes from the Tempter. But beyond the Bible and the Church, and beyond our hesitations over what they teach, stands the person of Jesus Christ. Let us seek fellowship with him with all our hearts, and we shall have the best possible guarantee available to us in this life of the authenticity of our inspirations.

As for others, however, do not let us make our theological formulas an obstacle to our fellowship with them. Let us not impede them in their search for the Spirit by telling them all the time that they are on the wrong road.

Max Huber, formerly Chairman of the International Red Cross Committee, in his book *Le bon Samaritain* puts the problem very clearly. What he says of the Red Cross is true of all charitable work, of medicine, and of social action. The Red Cross was born out of Christianity; but the very ideal of universal charity symbolized in the parable of the Good Samaritan forbids discrimination against persons, either among those who collaborate in the work or those whom it helps, on account of any differences of belief. As a result, it is in danger of losing its fundamental inspiration. It is the mission of the Christians who share in its work to draw from their own personal convictions the spirit which ought to inform the Red Cross—without, however, any intolerance toward those whose convictions are different.

The God whom we know in Jesus Christ is known to others under widely varying names and attributes. They seek him in nature; they seek him in the truth pursued by science; they seek him in the social justice and international peace they are trying to create; when they are embarrassed by their own wrongdoing and try to hide it, they show they have some inkling of his sovereign demands; behind many of the upsets in their physical or psychic life they suspect that something in them, which they cannot name, but which does not come from either their bodies or their minds, is not what it ought to be. This something is what I call "the spirit."

Many people today are thinking about the crisis through which the world is passing. Although they are of the most varying beliefs, they are arriving at the same conclusions. They realize that modern civilization has lost its soul; that technical skill divorced from faith does not suffice to bring peace and happiness; that the spirit has been relegated to the narrow confines of the Church and of private belief; that it has ceased to be a power in the real lives of men and women— in politics, economics, art, and intellectual life. They believe that this is why the world is no longer able to find any solutions to the personal, family, national, and international problems that beset it. If we try to make a particular orthodox belief the indispensable credential for anyone who wants to join in work for the spiritual reconstruction of the world, we shall turn away the majority of people of good will, whom we ought to be welcoming with open arms. Bring them our

Christian convictions, but let us hold out the hand of friendship to them. We shall be able, without denying our faith, to find a basis for common action, for they, like us, believe in the spirit.

But what do I mean by the spirit? A learned Dominican, Father Lavaud, has objected to the "trichotomist" view of man that he claimed to see in my writings, when I referred to spirit, mind, and body; whereas according to St. Thomas Aquinas we ought to have a "dichotomist" conception of man as being soul and body.

My "trichotomist" formula was actually taken from St. Paul, but I confess that I am completely incompetent to argue the point from the dogmatic angle with a theologian. I must in fact now make an admission—in a previous work I constantly used the word spirit where I ought to have been using the word mind, and *vice versa*. One of my colleagues pointed out my mistake. The mind, he said, is studied by psychology; the spirit is that which is spiritual; we do not say the Holy Mind, but the Holy Spirit. Let the dogmatists have their triumph—now it has been proved that I speak loosely of things I know nothing about, and give wrong definitions of the terms I employ. Indeed, I was embarrassed to feel so ignorant on points that were apparently so elementary. But when I talked about it to philosophers, and searched in the history of thought for what had been said on the subject by the most learned scholars, I was reassured. The fact is that the greatest confusion reigns in regard to all these notions of mind, spirit, intelligence, thought, and soul.

I am a mere practitioner, and my only wish is to help men and women. In speaking of the spirit as distinct from the mind, I have been doing no more than many doctors do when they speak of the power of the mind over the body, without intending any allusion to a spiritual or religious phenomenon. They know that the nervous system, psychological complexes, the emotions, the intelligence, the will, in short the "faculties of the mind," play a part in the material behavior of man, and in his physical maladies. I believe this too, but I believe that it is not all. I believe there is "something" more, which is neither the body nor the mind, which has to do with the relationship that exists between God and man. This "something" is connected with the religious drama of man's fall and redemption, and I think that even the most unbelieving man has some inkling of this, in spite of everything. It animates both body and mind, and expresses itself through the one as much as the other.

In his book *Die Ganzheit der Person in der ärztlichen Praxis,* Bovet also speaks of body, mind, and spirit (*Leib, Seele und Geist*).

Furthermore, my objector himself comes to my aid when he says that what I—wrongly, in his view—call the spirit, "is doubtless the superior 'part' or 'portion' of the mind, its summit, and, if you like, the summit of the summit, the *mens* of St. Augustine . . . the *Gemüt* of Tauler, the 'fine point' of St. Francis de Sales . . . and perhaps sometimes what Pascal calls the 'heart.' "

Here, fortunately, we can leave arguments over words.[1] Despite all the confusion that exists in their meaning, there is still an indefinable reality which all true seekers have tried to describe as best they could. There is the truth that man is not merely the mechanism that science has tended to represent him as, during the last few centuries. He is not merely a bundle of physical and chemical reactions, or of nervous and psychological reflexes. Beyond all this reality that is accessible to objective investigation, there lies an area of unfathomable and ineffable mystery which upsets all mechanistic calculations. This area, whether we have encountered it ourselves in those moments of truth in our lives, or have sensed it in others when we have been with them as wondering witnesses of dramatic battles of conscience, is the most important thing in a man's life—in it his destiny is worked out, by it he is made something more than an animal.

This is recognized by an ever-increasing number of doctors—whatever terms are used to express it. They see that the materialist concepts of nineteenth-century medicine will not stand up to the facts. They see how artificial in many cases is the frontier which people persist in setting up between the organic and the functional, the psychic and the spiritual. They see that all these are only different ways of looking at the unity which is man. They see that there are people who are like a machine in which all the parts are in good order, but which will not work because it has not been lubricated, or because the spring has not been rewound, and that there are conditions in which the trouble cannot be traced either to an organ or to a function.

This view of man is in conformity with that revealed by the Bible:

[1] *Translator's note:* The difficulties Dr. Tournier has been dealing with arise from the confusion existing in French between *âme* (soul, mind, spirit, feeling) and *esprit* (mind, spirit, feeling), a confusion largely absent from English. I hope I have translated in such a way as to preserve the fundamental distinctions Dr. Tournier intends.

a weak and wretched being, a prey to all kinds of fears and impulsive reactions which make his troubles worse; a being who is always doing exactly the opposite of what his heart most ardently desires to do, who has the feeling of being constantly at war with himself. And yet here is a being with something godlike in him, who is capable at any time of examining his own conscience and hearing the voice of God, which assuages his torment and brings about within him the reversal of attitude which his own sincerest efforts have been unable to accomplish.

This new man is no longer merely a body equipped with mental functions: he is what we call a person. It is that which is spiritual in man that links him personally with God, and confers upon him his inviolable dignity.

Absolute respect for the person, the human being created by God— as a spiritual being who despite all his faults and wretchedness still retains something of God—will be the basis of a better civilization, and the foundation of better health for both individual and society. I always remember a remark that someone once made to me: "In everyone I meet I try to see Jesus Christ."

Respect for the person, for the spiritual being, in oneself first: this is the key to any real liberation from feelings of inferiority, from the doubts and fears that weigh us down. To recognize oneself as created by God is to discover the road to healthy self-confidence.

Respect for the spiritual being in the child: this is the key to the educational reform which is necessary if we are to avoid the disasters of formalism in education which I have described.

Respect for the spiritual being in the patient: this is the key to a new humanization of medicine.

Respect for the spiritual being in the workman, the colleague, the citizen, and the magistrate: this is the key to any lasting solution of the grave social and political questions of the present time.

In the interesting account he gives of his numerous interviews with French-Swiss workers, Lalive d'Epinay describes their concern with material things, but he also shows that they are preoccupied with morality. He particularly points out their concern with the dignity of man, which they want to see restored. "We are treated as items in the labor market," one had said to him, "a factor in production, slaves to machines—slaves they cannot do without." And d'Epinay remarks: "This is the revolt of men who aspire to be as nearly whole as they can be, against everything that diminishes them, not only in the eyes of others, but also in their own eyes."

The value of a human life does not lie in the "rights of man," a fundamental concept of modern individualism, but in the spiritual bond that binds and subordinates him to his God and to his fellow men. It is the spirit which harmonizes the person and puts him in tune with himself. It is the spirit which also harmonizes society. This is why the problem of the "moral person" and that of society are really one and the same problem.

The concept of the "rights of man" presupposes that man is autonomous, and that he has value in his own right and not by virtue of the spirit he receives from above. It looks upon him as being capable of making a success of life through his own unaided efforts, of organizing society armed only with his intelligence and his technological skill. We see where that has led him.

We are like a child who has been given a beautiful mechanical toy as a Christmas present. His father says to him: "Come along, and I'll show you how to make it go." The child replies: "No, I want to do it myself!" He tries, gets angry and sulky, takes it to pieces, damages it, and finally admits his incompetence. Defeated, he hands it to his father saying: "There, you make it work."

We too have received a beautiful and very complicated toy: life. We try to make it work on our own. We think we are having some success; but then things begin to go wrong, and we run into personal or social disasters. The more we struggle to put things right with our own strength, the worse does the situation become, until at last we come back to God, and offering our lives to him, say: "Take over; I can't manage it on my own."

I am always struck by the extreme simplicity of this decisive inner movement. From then on a man has a new attitude. He has realized that only the Author of life can coordinate all the complicated mechanisms that go to make up life. He does not have to disown the intellect, science, or technology; he simply decides that now he will ask God how to use them. He surrenders himself; he hands over his life, his person, all his faculties, and all his possessions to God, not knowing what He will do with them.

He renounces grand personal plans. He lives each moment as it comes, step by step, eagerly seeking to know what God expects of him. I have stressed the difficulty of knowing what God's guidance is.

I must now assert that despite all the hidden reefs and all our mistakes, God's guidance is more precious and more fruitful than anything else.

Seeking after it in every circumstance of our lives is a wonderful adventure—the great adventure of life with God. It takes all those who commit themselves to it much farther than they expect. It is the source of an ever-buoyant enthusiasm.

When I have talked to people about "accepting their lives," they have often objected that it is difficult. I am as convinced of this as they are. I think now that it is preferable to speak of "loving one's life," which is a less passive term. The positive adventure resulting from the abandonment of one's life to Christ makes it possible gladly to accept everything in that life that remains painful, and in spite of it to love one's life, because even suffering becomes a source of adventure. Pascal laid stress on the boredom, the inner void, which man is constantly trying to forget. "It is unbelievable," a woman writes in a letter to me, "how life repeats itself. We change our surroundings and our jobs, but our outlook remains the same." There are many who think that, until they find that when they give their lives to God their outlook changes fundamentally overnight, and the result is that everything changes around them.

I realized once, when I was with friends who were more deeply committed than I was to this great adventure, that I still relied more on my natural gifts than on my supernatural ones. People, I realized, came to consult me chiefly because of my natural qualities, and then I felt how much more valuable, often, was the unforeseen action of a person who would not have been able to act without God's help. Under the Spirit's guidance a timid person discovers in himself a boldness unknown to the most valiant; a weakling finds an energy unknown to the strongest; an ignorant person receives flashes of intuition that are more valuable than those of the greatest scholars. One of my patients once aptly compared it to gliding, in which instead of relying on one's own engine one uses rising currents of air for support. These upward currents are what the Bible calls God's blessing. The man or woman who really tries to obey Him receives in exchange inspiration and strength which makes his life fruitful.

Anyone who takes the Gospel seriously sees that what it says is true, that if we give up everything, we receive in turn more than we had before. "The law of matter," writes Richard Wilhelm, "is that the more I pick up, the more I keep, the more I have. The law of life is that the more I give, the more I distribute, the richer I become."[2]

Taking the Gospel seriously means taking its absolute demands seriously. It means the realization that the demands of Christianity are total. It calls us to sanctity; that is, to true morality and not to the moralism of conventional respectability. Sanctity does not involve believing oneself to be perfect—quite the reverse. On the plane of true morality, it involves the recognition of everything in our secret intentions and actions that is contrary to Christ's demand for honesty, purity, selflessness, and love. It means refusing to compromise with those secret desires, and renouncing them.

We do not, as so many Christians as well as non-Christians think, seek this honest self-knowledge in order to make ourselves more virtuous—that is not at all what results. We do so in order to achieve closer fellowship with the Spirit, in an atmosphere of greater honesty. We do so in order to receive this blessing from God, which is more precious than all else because it procures in our personal lives victories which our unaided efforts have been powerless to achieve, besides increased effectiveness in our social activities. Thus our inward and our outward adventures are indissolubly bound up together.

What we can do for others and for the world at large must always begin in ourselves. Christian revolution always goes deeper than any ideological revolution because its roots are in a change of heart.

We are always wanting to change institutions, and to change other people. The Spirit always brings us back to our own inner change. A young woman came to consult me. She told me at once how her life was a tissue of lies. She was a prisoner in that most vicious of circles, that of the lie, in which one's very efforts to get out are what keeps one in. She had lied to the psychoanalyst, who had looked after her devotedly. She had lied to a Christian friend, pretending she too was a believer, in order to win his approval, so keenly did she long to have someone on whom to lean. She had lied to herself, persuading herself that she was in love with a certain man, for fear of losing his love and being left alone in the wilderness of despair into which her life of falsehoods had led her. Nevertheless her instincts told her that the only way to escape for her was in the quality of life that is to be found in Jesus Christ. She had decided to seek that life, and I had a

[2] *Der Mensch und das Sein.*

burning desire to fortify her in her resolve. I told her some of my own experiences. Among others I told her about a conversation I had recently with a certain colleague. But in my zeal, in order to make my story more effective, I "arranged" it, I gave it a twist, and attributed to my colleague a remark he did not make.

When I thought this over during my meditation next morning, I was horrified at what I had done. At the very point when I was trying to awaken in my patient the ambition to live a truthful life, I had myself been untruthful. I had a hard struggle—would I not ruin her confidence in me and undo all the good I had begun to do if I were to confesss my lie to her? Still, in the end I noted down God's command, and that gave me courage, when she came again, to make the admission I owed her. I also told her about my inner struggle and my desire to safeguard my reputation in her eyes by remaining hypocritically silent. She replied that she had in fact felt that my story did not ring true. And all at once I realized that this painful admission had done more to create real communion between us than all my fine words of the previous day.

I remember another patient who gave me great concern, because she had suffered terribly. I was convinced that she needed to be treated with extreme gentleness. But as a result of a minor misunderstanding our conversation turned into an argument. I felt it hurting her, and yet I stubbornly stuck to my point. She reacted by defying me; I lost my temper. When I had calmed down I had no difficulty in recognizing that in reality it was I who was in the wrong. I had something on my mind that day. I pretended that I had put it out of my mind, when in fact I had not. I had merely pushed it below the surface, and it was the cause of my irritability.

So the way we act toward others does not depend so much on what we say to them as on our own faithfulness to Jesus Christ, on our own fellowship with him, our own personal discipline. In short, it depends on that contact with the Holy Spirit which helps us to see His inspiration more clearly.

CHAPTER · 18

Relax!

"But," the reader may say, "is there not a danger that this life of adventure may be too much for us, this perpetually looking for our own faults, since they constantly creep back and insinuate themselves even into our most generous acts?" This would indeed be so were it not for faith. That is why people prefer to shut their eyes to their own failings and denounce those of others.

More than ten years ago I went through an extremely painful process of self-examination, when I realized how great a part pride had been playing in my religious and church life. I had fought zealously for truth and spiritual revival in the Church, I had taken the initiative in a large number of activities, and made many speeches; and the pride of being a champion of the truth, I fully realized now, had been what spurred me on, rather than the love of men's souls. That day I resolved to remain quiet, to get on with my own humble affairs. I turned down requests to take on responsibilities and to give lectures. I soon realized, however, that now I was being just as proud in refusing these things. Pride was reappearing in a new guise: that of having had a profound experience of self-examination. I felt desperate. I saw that whatever I did, whether I spoke or remained silent, the cunning enemy would always be there. I had gone down into a tunnel that led to a blank wall. In my despair I asked a young pastor, whom I hardly knew, how one could become a leader of men without sinking into the morass of pride. I must have looked particularly strained, because the pastor replied: "My dear doctor, you must first learn to smile!"

I have to admit that I found this reply excessively irritating. I felt that the pastor was laughing at me and at my worry. I felt that in the words of the Gospel I had asked for bread and had been given a stone. Furthermore, it so happened that I could not stand people who talked about their religion with complacent smiles on their faces. They were so smug and superficial. Only when I got home did I see the light. There came into my mind the simple thought that the opposite of the smiling attitude is the serious one, and I suddenly realized how seriously I had been taking myself, with my "problem" of pride, instead of simply confessing it and leaving it all to God. I saw that what was getting me down was not so much my pride as my shame at being proud, and that other utopian pride which consists in trying to solve on one's own a problem which no man can solve. I began to smile at the thought that it was just in order to relieve me of that impossible and crushing burden that Christ came and died. "Just now," writes one of my patients, "I am happy again, because I have entrusted the worst and the best of myself to God, including everything that still resists him, and also the pride that is so terrifying to me, because I am sometimes so afraid of confusing it with God. I have always been afraid of that, because with me it infiltrates itself ever so subtly into everything, and especially into my thoughts when I think I am being humble." Another writes: "See with what vanity I am writing about vanity!" St. Francis de Sales said: "There is no need for us to be surprised at finding self-love in ourselves, for it never leaves us. Sometimes, like a fox, it sleeps; and then all at once it pounces on the chickens."

A woman patient had been coming to see me for several months. She was shy, and seemed to be crushed and circumscribed by life. Our interviews seemed to be getting us nowhere. One day, after a long silence, she said quietly: "I never dare talk to you about the thing that worries me most. . . ." Silence once more, and then, hesitantly: "I am so proud!" How many people there are, pious people particularly, but also people who nurture quite secular ideals of virtue, who are crushed by their very longing to be freed from sin. They smile again only when they give up trying to do it on their own, and simply open their hearts to God's grace. After years of pain, a young woman writes: "I felt just like a tender bud opening and reaching up toward the warmth of the sun, and I imagined I could hear what it was saying: it told the sun first how it often thought, in spite of its tough covering, that it was going to freeze; it said how terrified it had been. And now it was looking up at the magnificent, warmth-giving sun. And all its movement was toward the sun, growing toward maturity. It was quite sure of itself now, because it could actually see the sun." When this happens, all life smiles upon us, despite its difficulties, and we discover all those many "small mercies" which have hitherto been unnoticed. "It is as if I had received a lovely present from a boyfriend," one girl said to me.

Two or three years after the pastor had urged me to smile, there came a certain man into my study. "I have come to thank you," he said, "for having led me to Jesus." "But I don't remember ever having seen you before!" "No doubt, but I have seen you, and all at once, when I saw you smiling all by yourself, I said to myself that the Christian life must be worth it."

I was greatly moved by that visit. It reminded me of the pastor's advice. In the past I had tried so hard to bring people to faith. And now I found that I could do better, without realizing it, simply through the joy that had come from leaving my problem to Christ. Of course, there is still the danger that I may become proud of my smile—and in fact since then I have often caught myself cultivating it! In that case it makes no impression on other people.

Thus there are three attitudes among men. There are those who shut their eyes to their sins. They are superficial, and can be happy so long as life carries them along and distracts them. But when they are tried, in trouble or sickness, they soon discover how precarious their happiness has been. Then there are those who recognize their sin and make good efforts to free themselves from it. They are often more unhappy and more ill than the first kind. They are apt to worry unduly over trifles, and carry zeal to excess. One might apply to them Talleyrand's remark: "Above all, no zeal!"

"Please leave *something* for God to do!" I once exclaimed to a man who was overcome with worries about how to avoid doing anything wrong. All this effort expended on oneself never leads to anything but fresh failure. In a talk I once heard, the lecturer called it trying to reach heaven by pulling on one's own hair. I am reminded of a child who cut his finger with a bread knife. The bread was hard, and so the child made such an effort that the knife went too far.

There is, however, a third attitude: that of recognizing our poverty, and in the knowledge that God blesses him who recognizes it, throwing ourselves on his mercy.

I have known many souls tormented even to the point of mental breakdown, who, after years of indescribable efforts that have only made them worse than before, have felt the leaden sky suddenly open above them. I shall always remember the tones in which one of my fellow doctors described such a moment, with all artificial emotion and false intoxication set aside. He felt quite literally certain that an all-powerful devil was leaving him, having been cast out by the Holy Spirit. He did not delude himself; he knew that the ills and sins that had beset him would still be lying in wait for him along the road. But from then onward his efforts would be turned toward God.

Here again we must avoid a false distinction between effort and faith. The Christian life is not complacent inactivity. When we rely on God to transform our lives we are like a man who asks the woodcutter to saw down a large chestnut tree in his garden, which he has not the strength to cut down himself. But the man will still have to busy himself with pulling out all the chestnut suckers that are left. The Christian life involves vigilant effort. The difference is that the effort is in a new direction. Instead of being dissipated in attacking all the obstacles we meet both internally and externally, it is concentrated in a thrust toward God. It is futile and depressing to expend all one's efforts against the evil within and injustices without. That is only to accord them greater importance, and increase their hold. To put all one's effort into seeking God is health-giving and fruitful.

The just inspiration of God is what enriches life and makes it a constant and fruitful adventure. What impoverishes it and brings failure is our sin, which renders us impermeable to God's inspiration. But our failures, by showing us our sin, bring us back to God. I once wrote in my notebook, after a serious failure in my spiritual ministry: "Our successes profit others, our failures profit ourselves." If we are truly inspired we can become instruments in the hand of God to bring help to others. On the other hand, if we fail, we can examine our consciences and discover the cause of the failure in some fault which we can take to God for him to free us from it.

What we should like would be to have only successes, and we think that then our witness would be more compelling. The truth is that we do not help others when we think we have arrived, but only when we fight and seek, as they do.

"Strife alone pleases us and not the victory," wrote Pascal. "We never seek things in themselves, but only the search for things."[1]

It is in the spiritual life that we recover our smile and our joy in living, when we unload from our hearts all the dead weight accumulated there by the difficulties we have met with, our disappointments, our failures, and our sin. It sometimes happens that someone over whose genuine experiences we have greatly rejoiced loses his faith. There is no lack of people who are ready to point to the fact in triumph and use it as an argument against faith. Sometimes a person whom we thought delivered suddenly commits suicide. It makes us ill ourselves, not only from disappointment, but with remorse as well. We start going over in our minds all the extra things we ought to have done for him. If we were unable to lay such burdens at Christ's feet, our whole ministry would be crushed beneath this unbearable weight.

For, though the examination of our own shortcomings is the gateway to this life of adventure, it is not its goal. Christ calls us to repentance, not so that we shall remain at this introspective stage, but so that, forgiven and set free, we can throw ourselves into action, and bring forth fruit, as he himself insists.

"When a Catholic has made his confession," writes Adrienne Kaegi-von Speyr, "and has received God's forgiveness, he considers the matter closed. He does not speak of it any more. He begins to live as a new man—which does not mean that he will not fall into the same sin again." For us Protestants, too, confession and divine forgiveness mean that the past has been liquidated, so that we can turn to the adventure of the future.

There is a necessary connection between meditation and action. Action without meditation soon becomes a disappointing scramble. Meditation that does not lead to action amounts to no more than probing about inside oneself. I have known many people whose life was in a kind of suspense because they were trying obstinately to recapture the intense emotion of a past moment of grace, through constant self-examination, because it was in self-examination that they first experienced it.

"God likes life; he invented it," one of my friends used to say. It is to the full flowering of life that he calls and leads us.

There is a need for adventure in the heart of man. I would go so

[1] *The Thoughts of Pascal,* translated by C. Kegan Paul.

far as to say that the majority of the broken lives that we see seem to be suffering from the fact that this need has been repressed and is gnawing away inside. In many people, upbringing, failures, social respectability—all the vicious circles I have described—have got the better of an adventurous nature that ought to have been able to expand, to indulge in spontaneous fantasy. It is as if their lives had been turned inside out, and we see an inverted image of their true nature. They have become timid and unadventurous, slaves to routine. Their psychic distress arises from the acute discord between their real nature and this false personality. There is a perpetual battle between the two going on inside them. Their tendency to adventure reappears in maladjusted forms: sterile reveries or sudden impulses. While their imaginations range over wide horizons of bold originality, their lives remain fossilized, as it were, in conventionally mediocre patterns. There is a sort of automatism at work in them that reminds one of insects instinctively performing inherited actions which no longer have any purpose. Or else their sudden impulses, caused by the occasional break-through of their adventurous natures, draw lively rebukes down upon them. They feel misunderstood and downtrodden. All their dynamism, instead of being directed to useful activity, seethes inside them and sets up psychic and functional disorders. A woman writes to me that her husband "told her once that he felt as if there were a completely intractable wild beast continually lurking inside him, ready to spring unexpectedly, like a panther." These people have had duty, work, and self-mastery preached at them; but they are only more undisciplined and fickle as a result, because with them work ought to have been like a game—not a duty. They refuse to conform, and sometimes react by adhering to extremist ideas. They rush into foolish marriages. They blame themselves for not being able to show their real worth in life.

Sometimes the doctor tries to liberate them by pushing them into some sentimental adventure, the mediocrity of which is incapable of satisfying their intense need for real self-expression. Besides, they have got so used to being slapped down that when the moment of happiness and fulfillment comes they feel a brake inside them, holding them back. They fight against social constraint, but have no longer the strength to free themselves from it. Even their talents—often considerable—are hidden away, and they believe themselves to be unfit for anything. In other words, it is as if "they did not permit themselves to live, to enjoy or suffer anything any more."[2]

Even Christianity seems to them nothing but a heavy instrument for exerting conformist pressure. But it is possible for them suddenly to discover its true meaning—that it is an extraordinary adventure, free from both social conventionalism and uncontrolled inner impulses. Then they rediscover the spontaneity of their true nature, together with a quite new quality of discipline: the discipline which comes from within, from fellowship with Christ, instead of from social constraint.

"Love God, and do as you please," said St. Augustine. That was his way of expressing the wonderful freedom of the Christian—the only freedom in which those who have an intense need to live can develop fully.

There are two basic tendencies in the human mind: revolution and tradition—adventure and stability, boldness and prudence. Once again, let us be careful not to set them up as incompatible opposites. Each has its own riches—power, for the first, fidelity for the second. Each also has its own dangers—pride, for the first, idleness for the second. Only in Christ do we find both in perfect harmony. He stood firm against conventional respectability and set blowing the most powerful wind of revolutionary change that humanity could ever know. He breathed life into tradition, and restrained his disciples from any violent act of revolt.

There is a rhythm of history, too. There are periods when the conventional framework of society is broken under the impact of strong personalities. Then the explosion of life is gradually crystallized, and is assimilated into society. Society eventually fossilizes into a new system of empty respectability which has once again to be broken up. God has always called in turn upon prophets to denounce the lifelessness of conventional society or a conventional Church, and upon priests to organize what without tradition would be nothing but a fleeting burst of energy.

Christianity is seen today principally in its conventional aspect. It is associated with middle-class society, of which it seems to be one of the chief props. It is also bound up with the individualism which has permeated our civilization for three centuries. The industrial masses

[2] G. Richard, in *Praxis,* April, 1936.

see it as a damper, rather than as a leaven, of social renovation. The intellectuals see in it a cramping system of thought rather than a source of renewal. I believe that our era is longing for a new outburst of life that will provide us with a way out of the present blind alley into which our bourgeois civilization has come.

This crisis of our era is symbolized by all those victims of contemporary life who are crushed beneath its weight, but long to recover their spontaneity and a sense of worthwhile adventure.

In the absence of inspired prophets, the world is looking toward the prophets of violence. The latter do not find it difficult to denounce the turpitude of respectable society, the scandal of Christians who dabble in all kinds of compromise, and the fine moral and patriotic speeches and appeals to tradition which serve to maintain unjust privileges. Even among Christians we see the conflict spreading between conservatism and revolution. There are some who look to the restoration of the explosive power of the Spirit, and others who remind them, with reason, that violence breeds violence.

Like those who rebel impulsively on the personal level, those who try to break the mold of society are impelled, even with the best intentions, to excess. They start a whirlwind. They destroy more than they create.

The prophet Elijah also (I Kings 19:9-12), in a time of spiritual drought, was seized with an access of zeal. He threw himself into a bold and sincere adventure. He stood out against the political and religious powers of his day. He spoke his mind to everybody, and worked wonders. A day came, however, when he realized the vanity of all this feverish activity, and alone in the desert he went through a terrible crisis. God spoke to him through the elements. Elijah heard the storm passing over him, and then a still, small voice, in which the prophet recognized the voice of God. Inwardly transformed, he came back to the world of men, and at once found a colleague with whom to work. He was no longer alone against the whole wicked world. He had retained his spirit of adventure, and lost the spirit of contradiction which had been making him an instrument of division rather than unification.

Jesus Christ has his own way of turning society upside down: the Cross. Instead of calling the hosts of heaven to defend him against the political and religious establishment which was harrying him, he conquered fear within himself. In the same way he leads those who give themselves to him to the inner reversal about which we have spoken, and which is the only way of resolving the dichotomy between adventure and love.

He calls us to a wonderful adventure, one that is creative and not destructive. Instead of an exhausting and fruitless crusade against the many-headed monster of external evil—of other people's sin—he calls us to an inner adventure, to a crusade against the evil in ourselves.

Instead of taking up arms against all the things around us that quite properly we find outrageous, he calls us to make war against the things we are ashamed of within ourselves. Instead of denouncing and attacking all the shortcomings of society, he calls us to recognize our own shortcomings so that we may become a healthy unit in society. The external battle fills our hearts with bitterness, criticism, and rebellion; the internal battle liberates them and brings back a smile to our faces.

Rebellion is contagious, and when men are criticized and attacked they defend themselves and launch into criticism and attack in their turn. In the same way, inner liberation and a smiling face are also infectious, and when we put right our own wrongdoing, other people begin to look to theirs.

We are all closely bound up together. Every act or word helps to propagate either good or evil. If our neighbors' faults arouse our indignation and goad us to an aggressive reply, our attitude has in its turn the same effect on them, and the resulting chain of evil cause and evil effect can play havoc in a family, a workshop, or a whole country. On the other hand, if we recognize our own faults, our neighbors will also examine their own lives. If we trust them, they will trust us. If we try to understand them, they will try to understand us. In a combat group all that is needed is one soldier animated by a spirit of bitterness for the contentment and *esprit de corps* of the whole group to be undermined; but also the example of the self-sacrifice of one man is all that is needed for them to be restored.

Christ's method of changing the world is to use the spirit that radiates from a person who has experienced a change of heart. A young woman is carrying about with her the heavy burden of her secret past. She unburdens herself to me. She is able to tell her husband all about it. She is overflowing with joy. Immediately afterward she is stopped by a neighbor on the stairs of the house.

Spontaneously, without any idea of "helping" her neighbor, my patient tells her what has just happened, and the neighbor discovers that the real cause of the depression which has been troubling her for some months lies in the secrets which separate her from her husband. A religious young man is engaged to a girl who has rejected religion. Without realizing it he is gradually influenced by her, unaware of his inner unease which comes to the surface in the form of doubts about his engagement. Suddenly he realizes the cause of his doubts, while we are talking together. His faith is strengthened once more, and he is overjoyed. His fiancée envies his happiness, and starts to pray again. A politician suddenly discovers the part that personal animosity has played in his political controversies, and comes to ask the forgiveness of his adversary. The latter is overcome, offers him the hand of friendship, and they are able to work together usefully, each respecting the opinions of the other.

Thus the external adventure of our social conduct is only the spontaneous reflection of our internal adventure. When we direct our attention toward our own inner life, it is not mere self-examination, but the result of a call by the Spirit to an inner adventure that will be the source of external action more fruitful than all the enterprises we used to conceive in the past. "Everything has a root and branches," said Confucius. "The ancient Emperors . . . in order to govern well . . . sought first to direct their families well. . . . In order to direct their families well, they began by first perfecting themselves."

When we are making plans, we look logically for those people who will welcome our ideas most. We talk about faith to religious people, and about collaboration to people who are well-disposed toward us. In the adventure of the Spirit-led life, it is often the opposite that is most efficacious. A girl could not bear the atmosphere in the office where she worked. She talked about it to those of her comrades who seemed to have the highest ideals, but without much result. During her quiet time one day when she was not at work because it was a holiday, the idea suddenly came to her of inviting to tea one of the girls in her office who did not mix with the others. Scarcely had the girl arrived when she burst into tears and said: "You were like a mother to the girls in the office, but not to me. I thought you didn't like me." And she opened her heart to her.

CHAPTER · 19

✠

Priesthood

Protestants believe in the universal priesthood, which was one of the great affirmations of the Reformation, as against the extreme clericalism of the sixteenth century. But they practice it very little. The Catholics, although they firmly set apart the ecclesiastical priesthood, nevertheless talk a great deal nowadays of the lay apostolate, an idea which has been given new life by the Catholic Action movement. Most lay people, however, both Protestant and Catholic, still often remain timid and reserved in the matter of witnessing to their faith. They prefer to look upon the exercise of a spiritual ministry as the concern of pastors and priests. The result is that the latter are too overburdened to have the time necessary for soul-healing. In the Protestant churches of my city of Geneva alone, it has been estimated that there take place every year fifteen thousand religious and parochial services, meetings, and other functions. Our Church, individualistic though it is, has lost the idea of personal religious action; it is constantly asking its pastors to sow the Word of God among large groups. The product in terms of real conversions is minimal compared with the enormous labor put into it by the pastorate. The fact is that for the seed to grow, it is not enough only to sow. The ground must be prepared for it. Though the seed may be sown broadcast, before the crowd, the ploughing of the land is done row by row when two minds meet in private. The ministry of the pastors, which is to teach "sound doctrine," as Calvin said, will be the more fruitful for being sustained by an army of laymen instructed by them with a real priestly function in view. In any case, no Christian life retains its fervor unless it is developed and constantly renewed by engaging in a

215

ministry of this kind. When I suggest it to people, they often reply: "But it would be presumption on my part to claim to be able to help others before I have solved all my personal problems. I am not ready. My faith is not sufficiently assured." This would be so if it were a matter of teaching and preaching. But that is the vocation of the pastor. For us ordinary believers, it is just when we are aware of our inadequacy, and feel that we are morally no better than those who come to us, that we can help them most.

Many people also justify on grounds of tact their reserve in regard to talking about religion to others. It is true that tact, in its positive sense, which is that of respect for the person, is all-important in the exercise of any priestly function. In this sense it is creative rather than destructive. Tact, however, has another, quite negative, sense, when it signifies more or less: "I do not meddle in your affairs because I do not want you to meddle in mine." If we are to help others, we must be ready to give ourselves to them, and open our own hearts to them.

I remember a young woman who told me of how, several years before her conversion, she had been greatly moved by a conversation with a friend who had just decided to become a missionary. The radiant joy her friend derived from her dedication to Christ and from the spirit of adventure it had awakened in her made my young woman envious. But she had thought that since she had no intention of becoming a missionary or a nurse, this question of a spiritual vocation did not concern her. Later she realized that she could serve Christ in her ordinary life, in her friendships, in her family, and in her profession as a painter.

It is simply a matter of binding oneself more closely with the members of one's family, one's friends, one's colleagues at work, taking an interest in them, and loving them enough for them to open their hearts, and of giving them whatever one has oneself received.

I have often seen people who said they had never had an experience of Christ, and yet when I have questioned them more closely it has turned out that they have had very real experiences after all. Having experiences is not everything. One also has to recognize them. What sometimes more or less unconsciously blinds us to them is our desire to avoid both the responsibilities they imply for us in our personal lives and our summons to be of service. Telling others about them is, moreover, the surest way of making spiritual progress ourselves; because having undertaken the cure of souls obliges us to come back constantly in search of strength and enlightenment from God, and to commit ourselves to being faithful to him ourselves. As I was saying just now, we meditate and recognize our shortcomings, not in order to become more virtuous, but in order to become sensitive to God's guidance. And we want to be guided by God, not because we look upon his guidance as an end, but as a means of helping others. In this way meditation avoids its chief danger, the danger of spiritual pride and self-complacency. "I have been wondering," a young woman writes in a letter to me, "if the reason why this has not happened before now is that I have wanted too much to humble myself before God—and only for my own benefit. The motive of humility ought to be love of one's neighbor. Love is not possible without humility; but humility is not possible without love. And so we must ask for both at the same time."

I have said that a priestly ministry is not principally preaching, but listening. "When a man speaks a great deal," said Confucius, "he almost always says something that he ought not to say." Asking questions of people is not the best way of getting them to open their hearts to us. It tends rather to put them on the defensive. I remember a patient with whom I was making scarcely any progress. I went to great trouble to think out what I ought to say to her. One day the idea occurred to me of having the courage to allow even an entire half-hour to go by in complete silence. Then, very gently, she began to open her heart to me on the thing that was worrying her. So long as I was talking she had always been able to avoid it.

Confession is the necessary and sufficient gateway to any spiritual action. I refer, of course, to the substance rather than the form, for many people make their confession without realizing it, through the honest attitude they take toward life. Others only appear to be confessing in talking at length about themselves, for one means of avoiding the substance is to indulge in the form. I remember one of my patients writing to me: "I really did tell you everything, but it was not a confession, because I did it too conceitedly. I lacked humility." And then sometimes too much talk about oneself can become a pretext for shirking action.

Michelet wrote: "All medical treatment is null, blind, and unintelligent if it does not begin with a complete confession." And Charles Fiessinger: "From the medical standpoint, confession must be looked upon as a wonderful agent of mental stability."

It is not only a matter of the confession of wrongs, but of the "liquidation" of all undischarged past emotions. The psychoanalysts have clearly demonstrated this process, which they have called "psychocatharsis." Vittoz has rightly insisted on the "elimination" of past impressions. It is as necessary to the mind as is the wiping of a blackboard before new writing is put upon it, otherwise indescribable confusion would ensue; or as necessary as winding the film after taking a photograph, to avoid having two images, one superimposed upon another.

A sincere account of one's life, with its shadows as well as its sunshine, its faults as well as its blessings—the sort of account one can give to a husband or wife, or to a friend, as well as to one's doctor—often brings unlooked-for relief. It also brings a quite new quality of affection, and restores one's confidence in life. "I understand him because I love him," wrote a girl after she had made a complete confession to her fiancé, "and I love him because I understand him." Many husbands and wives who when they were engaged used to have profound discussions about their ideas of life, their religious convictions, and their intimate experiences, now that they are married exchange nothing more than banal remarks about the thousand and one little annoyances of life. Sometimes all that is necessary is to remind them of the time they were engaged for a door to be opened which has been shut without their knowing how it happened.

We must know how to listen at length, never allowing ourselves to think that people are taking up our time uselessly with pointless stories about themselves. What they tell us is important in their eyes, and we condemn ourselves to failing to understand them if we do not try to understand why. I remember once I was running my eye cursorily over the comments in verse with which one of my correspondents decorated her letters, and which seemed to me to make them unduly long, when I saw that my attitude was closing my mind to a real discovery of her soul. There was another correspondent who plied me incessantly with letters full of complaints about other people. However, it was only after she had got all this at long last out of her system that she wrote me a letter that was quite different from the rest. At last she was examining her own conscience and recognizing her faults.

Long accounts that seem in themselves to be futile are sometimes necessary for the eventual creation of the atmosphere in which people can tell us what they chiefly desire to say. One of my patients wrote: "It is terribly hard to reveal to one's doctor the things that really lie at the root of one's trouble, even when one knows what they are."

Nevertheless it is always fruitful. A patient who had been undergoing treatment for months in a military sanatorium for a cardiac neurosis following upon bronchitis contracted in the service, wrote to me that one day when he was on his own he had become aware of the "problem" that was stopping him from getting better. It was his conflict with his father. He went to the medical superintendent and told him the whole story. The doctor at once wrote a closing report on the case to the insurance authorities, and returned the patient to active life, where he rapidly recovered after being reconciled with his father.

It is particularly important in real confession (i.e., of sin) not to be restricted either by time or by impatience. I remember a schoolteacher who made a long journey to see me, mainly in order to ease her conscience by making a confession to me. But she found it very difficult to talk about it, and the hour that I had set aside for her went by without her being able to finish what she had to say. So as not to hurry her I naturally suggested that she should come back during the evening; but the thread of her confession was broken, and she had to leave without being able to take it up again.

There are many other things that can prevent progress being made along this difficult road: an inopportune remark, a clumsy admonition in which a person is quick to think he sees the criticism he has been afraid of hearing. The slightest breath of criticism on our part stops a person in his progress toward liberation. If we hide it under a mask of benevolence, that is even worse than saying plainly what we think. Sometimes the confessor himself, I am sorry to say, becomes embarrassed, or wants to spare the person's feelings, and so tells him that there is no point in going into any further details. No relief comes of such half confessions. I have often seen people who have already made confessions of this kind, but to no avail, since they have made them in vague and general terms, without the minute concrete detail that costs so much, but is the genuine mark of penitence.

It is those who most need, and most desire, to make a complete confession who find it most difficult. This is particularly so when to the shame for the wrongful act is added the false shame, the "super-emotion" of which I spoke in Chapter 14, which is bound up with the social disgrace attached by convention to that particular fault.

There is no rule of thumb by which we may measure the importance of the subject matter of a confession. I was made keenly aware of this one day when, within a few hours, I heard two confessions. One, which in the world's eyes would have seemed very serious, involved a crime. The other concerned a fault which most of my readers would perhaps not even consider to be a sin at all. The second was certainly no easier to make than the first. Both were charged with specific emotion felt by the soul that faces the God against whom it has offended. A simple feeling, such, for example, as wishing the death of one's mother, may torment a person's mind after the mother's decease quite as much as some act that is condemned by public morality.

One has to be alert to the many little signs that betray the inner struggle in a person who would like to open his heart, and cannot bring himself to do so. A woman patient who has always kept on her hat, with its wide falling brim, takes it off one day with a "You don't mind?" which means "I am more confident now, and don't want to hide myself any more." Another patient forgets his appointments, which means that his unconscious is attempting to block the road along which he is trying to travel, and which he feels may lead to a painful confession. Another lights a cigarette in order to give himself an air of confidence. A woman has had a dream: in it she was coming to see me wearing a dirty apron which she had great difficulty in taking off. Another launches into long intellectual discussions about Christianity. I realized once that the reason why people are always saying they want to be "understood," is really that they want to be "guessed." They say: "You have understood me," when we have guessed what it was they wanted to say but could not bring themselves to put into words.

The classic image of the mind, in which it is represented as a lake, the lighted surface being the conscious, and the waters below, ever darker toward the depths, the unconscious, is a misleading one. It suggests that the most difficult things to bring to conscious expression in the mind are those that lie furthest from consciousness. This is not always the case. This explains why, when the barriers of censorship are lifted, the person often exclaims: "I really knew it all the time. I often thought about it, but without being fully aware of it and really facing it. I can't think why I never thought of mentioning it to you, now that I see what an important part it has been playing in my life."

In reality, everyone is looking either consciously or unconsciously for a confessor. The Curé d' Ars had coming to him "every year as many as 80,000 foreigners from all the four corners of the world." Men and women are not looking for theological or psychological science. They want love, sympathy, what in the Middle Ages was called the "gift of tears." There is not a person you meet any day in the office, in the bus, or in your own home, whom you cannot help by showing him some affection. "What man needs most is friendship," says C. F. Ramuz. Henry Brantmay, who quotes this in an address,[1] goes on to say: "The most powerful forces in his mind come to him from the Spirit, that is, from God. Faith triumphs where all else fails. Spiritual values go beyond human intelligence."

But these people who need your help are very shy. They are all afraid. Perhaps you too are afraid that conversion may go too deep, and you try to keep it in conventional channels. In order to become a confessor it is above all necessary to maintain one's own contact with God through practicing confession oneself. I was the recipient of many confidences, but I heard few confessions until I myself had started along the road of complete confession. We practice confession ourselves, not only so as to be forgiven, but also so as to be ready to hear other people's confessions without feeling uneasy. For when the confession we are hearing calls to our minds the thought of a sin we have not confessed, we start thinking about ourselves, instead of devoting our wholehearted attention to the person who is confessing. "St. Francis de Sales," writes Raymond,[2] "an incomparable spiritual director himself, says that one ought to choose one's confessor from among a thousand, and even ten thousand." If one really wants to, one can always find someone in whom one can have confidence. I have known many Roman Catholics who criticized their Church, and were lapsing from membership in it, and who have finally admitted to

[1] First International Conference on the Education of Mentally Deficient Children, Geneva, 1939.
[2] V. Raymond, O. P., *Le guide des nerveux et des scrupuleux.*

me that it was because they dared not go back to the practice of private confession demanded of them. Protestantism insists with no less force on the importance of the confession of sins; but how many Protestants are there now who really understand the meaning of their faith in this respect, expounded in fear and trembling by our Reformers? If confession is to become a living reality once again, there must be a revival in our Church of the individual cure of souls. Happily there are many today who realize this.

Discretion is an essential requirement in soul-healing. I have seen sons who no longer dared open their hearts to a mother they loved, because she passed on immediately everything they had confided in her to a father whom they feared. Discretion is a fundamental condition for the exercise of a ministry of soul-healing. It is bound up with respect for the human person. I have seen plenty of people who have turned timorously in upon themselves because someone in whom they had confided had divulged their secret.

I have also seen husbands who felt they could not reveal their secrets to their wives because they thought their wives too high-minded to be capable of understanding them.

Clergy, doctors, and laymen capable of exercising a priestly vocation are often held back from committing themselves to the searching task of soul-healing by the perhaps unconscious fear of the attachment which is known to psychoanalysts as transference. I have, unfortunately, come across several instances of pastors, doctors, and laymen having serious difficulties with a person, often sick, pursuing them with his emotional demands. Indeed, I cannot say that I myself have altogether escaped. This fear inhibits our patients as well, preventing them from being natural and sincere—the very thing they need to be. One of my patients once told me that she made a practice of going over in her mind all kinds of criticisms of me, in order to avoid becoming attached to me.

Here again, in fact, fear tends to create what it fears. The only solution is that proposed by Christianity—that we should have the courage and the honesty to admit to each other before God fears of this sort, or an exaggerated attachment, whether it be a guilty passion or affection that is too dependent, together with all its consequences. This liberates our spiritual communion from the thing that has been vitiating it.

A certain woman had suffered for years from terrible functional disorders, which had wrecked her career. She told me of her experience. One day when she was quite alone in the little church of a village through which she was passing, she received a sudden and unexpected enlightenment. She realized that the veneration, gratitude, and affection she felt for the doctor who had devotedly cared for her had, without her realizing it, taken on in her heart the complexion of love. At once the thought came to her that she ought to go and confess the fact to him and repent of it, for he was married. When she had finished her confession, her doctor talked to her about the Cross, which blots out all our sin. From then on she was able to maintain her affection for him, but now it was sanctified and liberated. Some months later the functional disorders from which she had suffered so long disappeared as if by magic.

Another patient told me of how he had been devotedly cared for over a long period by a psychoanalyst who had himself suffered from a neurosis. Their mutual attachment took on the character of a real infatuation. They could not go a single day without seeing each other. They both shared the same nonconformist outlook on life, but the patient's conscience was not easy about the moral influence that his analyst had on him. He found himself absolutely powerless to detach himself from him. He had come to a point of utter despair, when suddenly and quite unexpectedly God laid hold upon him and he became converted. He was free.

Nevertheless confession, important though it is, is not the whole of the ministry of soul-healing. A young woman comes to see me. She confesses before me that she is involved in an illicit love affair. She is penitent, but does not feel herself capable of breaking it off. What am I to do? Obedience cannot be forced. Really, the confession of a sin is at the same time a confession of the desire to give it up. No one would confess a sin unless he already believed, timidly, that he could be delivered from it by God's grace. His confession is a kind of appeal, not for admonition on our part, but for fellowship—an appeal to our prayer and our faith. One often has the impression that it is only the merest trifle that separates a person from the liberation he longs for—a paper partition. But nothing less than the grace of God will suffice to break it down. The spirit acts in liberty and in faith. Soul-healing is a sort of paradoxical harmony between spiritual sanction and spiritual self-determination; not a compromise between them, but a synthesis. A person must feel that "God is not mocked," that when the time comes when He solemnly calls, there is no escaping Him, and yet that the decision to respond is made absolutely freely and responsibly. A person must feel how much we long for him to say "Yes," and yet be certain that he will not lose our confidence and friendship if he says "No."

Each of us must look honestly at himself and adjust his own natural tendency in order to achieve a just balance between energy and gentleness in his ministry. Energy without gentleness is authoritarianism; gentleness without energy is sentimentality; energy combined with gentleness is soul-healing, whose approach is neither constraint nor moral neutrality. Hence once again everything depends on the spirit in which one acts. A patient realizes that he ought to make a heroic decision. I lead him to the foot of the wall; but he lacks the necessary courage. I am dying to speak sharply to him, but I let him go, sad and downcast. The following day he phones me: "I've done it!" The tone of voice shows how fruitful has been the painful struggle that went on in his mind after his departure.

In the field of technical action we can lead our patients along the way we want them to go, prescribing medicines and diets, and giving them the benefit of our advice. But along the road of grace we cannot lead them, but only follow. If we try to show them the light by walking in front of them, we cast a shadow over them, as Alexander did to Diogenes. Even if we lead them in this way to a spiritual experience, they will only see the light through us, and will remain dependent upon us, and less than adult. In order to attain to an autonomous spiritual life the patient has to walk on his own, in the direction in which the Spirit calls him personally, and not following a human guide along ready-made tracks. Admonition and advice will never remove the ever-recurring doubts of those who lack self-confidence. Even if we succeed, their doubts will return as soon as our support is removed. But if they have once really felt the love of God, they will have the courage to go forward without support along the path of life, despite doubts and fears.

That is why soul-healing boils down always to just one thing: taking a person into the presence of Christ—not by exhorting him, but by going with him as a brother, following him step by step along the road, praying behind him so that he will not slip back.

Our spiritual ministry is always inseparable from our own spiritual life. If we try to obey Christ ourselves, we shall see those who are entrusted to our care approaching him, without our saying anything to them. But if we flatter ourselves that we have reached a certain spiritual maturity, and presume to call others to join us in it, we shall merely be Pharisees.

The Church and the theologians have taught me the truth, but ordinary faithful men and women, through their obedience, have set on fire my ambition to live that truth. Without the Church's teaching I could not have known Christ or the Gospel, or else I should have formed mistaken ideas about them. But among lay people, those who have helped me have been those in whom I have felt such love for Christ that they have been ready to give up everything for him. The Church's teaching and the witness of the faithful are one. They help us believe that despite all our uncertainties God can speak to us, and that despite all our resistance the power of Christ can transform us. When one believes that, life becomes an adventure of personal liberation and a priestly ministry.

I have always sympathized with the theologians' fears in regard to lay witness, which can so easily degenerate into spiritual pride, especially when it is impregnated with that self-assurance which, as we have seen, is so far removed from true faith. It is the mission of the theologians to instruct and guide us laymen. But may they lead us, despite all our mistakes, to make our witness, and not to remain silent.

A schoolmistress writes me a long letter in which she sets out all the proper arguments that can be adduced against lay witness. But at the end of her letter she tells me of a memory that weighs on her mind. In her teens she had a friend who was sad and depressed. One day the friend suddenly asked her what was the secret of her faith. Taken by surprise, and fearful of giving a wrong reply, she said nothing. A few days later the friend killed herself. Since then she has been haunted by a feeling of remorse. Might her witness, perhaps, have supplied the answer which that tormented soul needed?

I myself came to that real conviction of sin which is the only road to conversion on hearing my friends talking to me about the sins that they had been forced to recognize in themselves in the presence of God. In order to remove from this assertion any conventional and exclusively Christian sense, let me once more quote Confucius: "As for me, I cannot perfectly follow a single one of the four obligations of the Sage. I have not yet fulfilled toward my father the duties of respect and submission I would prescribe for a son, nor toward the sovereign the duties I would demand of a subject, nor toward my elder brother those things that a younger brother ought to do; what I would require of a friend, I have not first done toward my friends."

Certainly we can do harm through our witness. We can sermonize others and crush them instead of helping them. We are especially prone to overdo our witness, emphasizing the light we have seen, and not mentioning the shadows that still remain, emphasizing our positive experiences and not our defeats. We are apt to paint a fine picture that does not correspond with the reality of our lives. God often points out these faults to us in the course of our meditation. But he also shows us that we betray and deny him when we do not bear witness to the mercies we have received at his hands; and that we are also betraying the trust of others when we are silent in the face of their basic questions, in missing the chance, when it is offered, of assuring them that they too, if they turn toward Christ, can experience his liberating power.

Those who argue most against us are generally the ones who are most at war within themselves. They throw their objections at us as a sort of challenge, because they would like to be freed from them, and believe in spite of them. They want to see if we can withstand their assault, in order to be encouraged to stand firm themselves. When these contradictors think they have defeated us, they are more disappointed than we are, because they know very well that what they are doing is to kill the only hope there is, that of a power that is stronger than evil. And when they take the first step along the road of obedience, their inner conflict very often redoubles its violence. A life that is seeking a way out of its prison is like one of those flying beetles that crash into all sorts of obstacles before they find their way out of the window. It often happens that those whom we try to help fall into all kinds of more serious, and sometimes absurd, acts of disobedience.

"I have noticed," a friend writes in a letter to me, "that every time I tell you something that really comes from my heart I get instant relief at the time, but afterwards it comes back and hits me worse than ever for several days before it finally disappears." So let us also redouble our love and our vigilance. We must not let go of our charges, for their disappointment would be worse than ever. Let us learn how to give one man all the time he needs in order to come to real self-dedication, for he in his turn, through his priestly ministry, will pass on to others the strength he has received.

There is one reservation that must be made here. It concerns cases of serious neurosis, and especially of mental illness. It cannot be over-emphasized, both to clergy and to laymen, that they should not persist in the attempt at soul-healing in such cases. Let these people bear their witness; surround them with love, and intercede for them in the knowledge that God is closer to the sick than to those who need no physician. But let them be sent to the doctor. The doctor finds it difficult enough to distinguish true guilt from a pathological state. I myself, not being a psychiatrist, must avoid treating them without the assistance of a specialist colleague. His technical intervention in the form of shock treatment or psychoanalysis may be more effective than all attempts at spiritual action. We can see in them, it is true, in grossly exaggerated form, all the complexes, secret mechanisms, and blockages which in normal persons or ordinary nervous cases can be resolved by a religious experience. All their acts, the whole of their behavior, everything in them that seems absurd or incomprehensible, has a meaning. But how powerless we are to perceive it, because their fixed attitudes prevent even any stirring of religious conscience in them! If we do manage to uncover the hidden meaning of their behavior, it is such a complex world, such a vast ocean, that we are more likely to drown in it ourselves than to bring them to land. We ought to thank God•for having led doctors to the discovery of shock treatment to complement our feeble efforts. I am always mortified when I see families trying to avoid shock treatment, where it is indicated, in the fallacious hope of managing with psychotherapy or soul-healing. However, although in cases of psychosis it gives incomparable results, it seems to me to be contraindicated in cases of serious neurosis, in which it has always seemed to me to make matters worse. If it has a tranquilizing effect, it is at the cost of a numbing of the moral conscience, and this, from the point of view of the patient's ultimate destiny, is perhaps worse than the disease.

There are, then, many troublesome mysteries remaining, not only in regard to the sick, but also to the healthiest. There are never too many of us—theologians, doctors, psychologists, teachers, and simply believers—to unite our efforts in a real team spirit, and to unite our technical skills and faith in the service of mankind. As in the case of errors of diagnosis, we are especially prone to go wrong when we are too sure of ourselves and fail to surround ourselves with the help of all the others. Fellowship fortifies faith, and that is the mainspring of all priestly ministry.

To have faith in Christ's victory in a person's soul, in spite of all the resistance he puts up, is the greatest help we can afford him. Lord Baden-Powell, who thoroughly understood the young, used to say: "In the most perverted of them, there is still at least 5 per cent of good. That is what we must look at. That is what we must build upon." A friend wrote to us recently about Frank Buchman, that keen observer of men: "He does not allow himself to be impressed by what people may say, and he wants to draw out the best in each of us."

But we have so little faith, that we are almost always surprised when a life is suddenly changed, when a soul is converted.

Faith is expressed in prayer. I am always astonished at the number of convinced Christians who, through shyness or false shame, do not dare to pray with their parents, their friends, or even with those who ask for their religious help. Their ministry is like a wingless bird. A bluestocking comes to see me. Our conversation marks time and turns to argument. Fortunately she herself suggests, all at once, that we should break it up and pray together.

In the great adventure of the priestly ministry we come to all kinds of blind alleys. It is always when we turn back to God, always through prayer, that the barriers are brought down and the adventure continues.

CHAPTER 20

The Spirit of Adventure

We are called, then, to exercise around us this ministry of soul-healing, to interest ourselves in others and in their deepest preoccupations, to listen to them with love, to make our witness before them, to uphold them with our faith, and to pray. This is in itself a great adventure, bringing us into contact and into spiritual communion with our fellow human beings.

Soul-healing, however, is only one part of the lay priestly ministry, which becomes an even greater adventure when we seek to integrate our faith into our professional and social activity. In caring for men's souls we are already often tempted, as I have shown in this book, to make a false dichotomy between technology and faith, between psychological and spiritual aids. But when we come to political and economic matters, the temptation is much greater.

A businessman, for instance, may exercise a spiritual ministry alongside his daily work. He may even bring it into his contacts with his fellow workers, when they come to him as men, and not as colleagues, to talk to him about their religious and moral problems. But as far as the problems of his business are concerned, he looks at them from the technological point of view. Economic laws are in complete control. He is not at liberty to obey his heart and flout these laws. He must study and work to acquire technical competence. Faith seems to him to be irrelevant to this activity. Whether one is a Christian or not does not alter the technical solution to an economic problem. Indeed, if one tries to avoid the technical study of professional problems on the grounds that one has some other source of inspiration, one only brings about disasters which discredit religion.

Similarly in politics, in social organization, in teaching, there are historical necessities, sociological or intellectual laws, which must be studied and which impose norms independent of the personal religious convictions of the individual worker. One cannot make up for one's technical incompetence with spiritual speculations.

The great adventure to which I believe the men and women of today to be called is, in every field of activity, the reconciliation of technology and faith. It is an immense task, simply because they have for so long been kept apart. In face of all the problems which our civilization has raised, but has not been able to solve, people are beginning to realize that the scientific study of political, economic, and social problems is not of itself sufficient. There is no question of side-stepping scientific study, but of giving it a new inspiration.

In religion, a person who is technically competent may find ideas that will lead to the solution of the difficulties of the world of today, although the cleverest experts have failed so long as they have confined themselves to a technological approach. The solutions to current problems will always be found to conform both to economic and social laws, and to moral and spiritual laws.

The adventure becomes bolder, however, at the point where it is no longer concerned only with formulating answers, but with attempting to put them into practice in professional life. This necessarily involves risks. Only those who are prepared to take these risks because of their faith, will make any real contribution to the building of a new civilization.

Having faith always means taking the risk implied by Pascal's famous wager: first, the risk of being unfaithful, and of being exposed to the criticisms of those under whose eyes we live, who can put their finger on our disobedience of God's requirements. Then there is the risk of failing, of being beaten in the battle of life, when we try to remain honest and disinterested; the risk of being let down if we try to love, to forgive, and to trust; the risk of losing the affection of a wife or husband, or a friend, who is not prepared to follow us; the risk of being laughed at as a perfectionist; the risk of losing our independence, our claim not to be answerable to anyone for our actions, even to God; the risk of finding ourselves on the side of many other Christians who are properly open to criticism. There is the further risk—indeed, the certainty—that our faith will be used as a formidable weapon against us, to blackmail us into giving way in the personal conflicts in which we shall be involved; the risk of being led from one act of obedience to another, farther than we would have wished, of seeing God eventually requiring of us a sacrifice of which we are incapable; the risk of mistaking the divine call, of mistaking God's guidance, in short, of being disappointed of that blessing which he promises to all who try to follow him.

The men of the Bible who show us the road of faith are those who took just such risks as these. They obeyed without being able to be sure that they were not mistaken. So today, those who exercise a real apostolate are those who have taken not only moral, but also material risks. For a businessman this often means the prospect—humanly speaking—of failure. Those whose witness affects us most are not always the clergy, whose material security is guaranteed by the Church, but men who live by faith and who demonstrate practically that God does not desert those who serve him, even if they are called upon to give up all material wealth and a regular income. Yet, let us be careful not to make a false distinction between those who are guided to give up material security and the others. We must not confuse faith with optimism or the vanity of a sensational gesture. God calls each of us in secret to make certain sacrifices which always involve a risk, even though it may differ from person to person. God speaks to the crowd, but his call comes to individuals, and through their personal obedience he acts. He does not promise them nothing but success, or even final victory in this life. The goal of the adventure to which he commits them is in heaven. God does not promise that he will protect them from trials, from material cares, from sickness, from physical or moral suffering. He promises only that he will be with them in all these trials, and that he will sustain them if they remain faithful to him. The trials will then become the occasion for the renewal of the adventure, instead of for bitterness and rebellion. Here is what a young Swedish woman wrote:

Some time ago the firm in which I worked was checked for tuberculosis, and the only positive result was the discovery that I had a patch on each of my lungs. You can imagine my surprise. I had had no suspicion of the fact. I discovered then how real God's strength is in such circumstances, and I was at once quite certain that God had a purpose for my life, wherever he sent me. I accepted everything, certain in my own mind that God was going to use my separation from the world to teach me many things. But at the same time I discovered how hard it is to leave everything—

work, friends, way of life. It really meant a sort of dying. Now I have nothing but thanks for having been granted the experience. It gives you a little better understanding of the central truths of Christianity, in which there is always suffering. Before leaving the town I went to Communion with a dozen of my friends, at a service specially arranged in church. There I felt more strongly than ever that all my sins had been forgiven me. I prayed that my new life might be all for the glory of God, and I thanked Christ, because I felt him nearer, and more real. . . ."

The disease may, however, be one of those from which there is no certainty that the patient will recover. I am reminded of an old friend, a woman of boundless energy and optimism. One might have wondered if her faith, when she was in good health and engaged in a full and useful life of spiritual service, was only the reflection of her simple and confident nature. I saw her later, immobilized on her bed of pain. In answer to her direct question, her doctor had informed her of the inevitable diagnosis he must make of her condition. She was preparing herself joyfully for death. She was more radiant than ever. Visitors flocked to see her, and found in her a testimony that was more striking than any she had given in active life and health.

I have received a visit from an elderly colleague. After a long career at the head of a hospital, he had been brusquely dismissed by the governing body, which had a young protégé to put in his place. I thought of the bitterness into which he might have sunk, of the solitude and inaction into which it would have led him, if he had not found in his faith the strength to forgive, and the confidence which lit up his face with a magnificent smile. He had at once asked himself into what new adventure God was now going to lead him; and it was not long before he was called to be superintendent of a more important hospital than the one he had left. In his new post his Christian message to those suffering from nervous diseases would be capable of bearing still more fruit than before.

We all want to stand on our own feet. I have shown in this book the tragedy of many people's lives, people who allow themselves to be trampled upon by society, or who in trying to defend themselves do so negatively and awkwardly, and so call down upon themselves a reply that is more crushing still. It is so hard to maintain our own convictions courageously in face of all our opponents and all our failures! The courage we require to make a positive affirmation of the personality will be given us if our convictions are hammered out face to face with God. Our thought and actions, instead of being a perpetual imitation, or a perpetual response to the thoughts and actions of others (two ways of being dependent on others), become real personal initiative. It is always wonderful to see someone, at the very instant when he says "Yes" to God with all his heart, discovering within himself personal tastes and high ambitions that he has always repressed for fear of being misunderstood or thwarted. People are apt to think that because Christianity demands self-sacrifice it must stifle the personality. Quite the contrary. We need only look at men to see how inconsistent their personality is when they have no living faith; how they are at the mercy of every wind that blows. Many people confuse lack of personal self-assertion with the support of Christianity. Dedication to Christ does indeed involve giving up the right to hit back aggressively, but it also means being set free from the domination of others. A girl who has never dared to stand up to the possessive authority of her mother and sister, on whom she has become more and more dependent, all at once feels herself able, after her conversion, calmly to maintain in front of them her convictions and her personal likes and dislikes. I do not want to press the point too far. I have seen plenty of people who switched over to dependence upon the person who has been the instrument of their conversion, looking upon him as an infallible oracle, and seeking his guidance rather than that of God. In such cases their families are jealous of the new attachment, and the individuals themselves are torn between the old influence and the new. This crisis itself, however, may lead them to real spiritual adulthood, to that exclusive dependence upon God which sometimes compels us to stand up even to those who have led us to him. Without this moral equality there can be no brotherly fellowship.

Another thing that strikes us when we observe men and women is how few see the truth about themselves. They complain about the things that curb their independence, and yet they have no clear idea of what they would do with their independence if they had it. A young man is obsessed with the idea of leaving his parents' home. He feels that their domination of him is the cause of his troubles, of his lack of enthusiasm, and of his failure to stick at his work. I advise his father to allow him to experience the independence he wants. It is not long before the son comes along to me saying he feels lost, and admitting that the problem is in himself. Most people think that the reason why their lives are not a bold adventure lies in their having come up against all kinds of external obstacles. But before God they recognize that it is rather because of their lack of any strong conviction. They waver between the negative and the positive answers to the fundamental questions about human existence. They touch upon them sometimes, only to fly off after some new distraction, without having taken a definite stand. As soon as they have taken a step toward a firm position, they are overcome again by hesitation and give way to the first opposing voice they hear. When asked what it was that prompted them to make the choice they did in marriage, for example, they often admit that they do not know. A chance acquaintanceship continued—rather as a result of habit and a failure to come to an honest mutual understanding, than through love and the certainty of being called to establish a home together. The day came when they had not the courage to admit their private doubts. So they bought some furniture, and drowned their unease in discussions about where to live. Occasionally it is worse still; they have let themselves be led into marriage by their parents.

In the choice of a career we see the same uncertainty. Often, for lack of any firm ideas of his own, a young man has taken up an apprenticeship because a friend of his father wanted an apprentice, another has gone into a job in which he has been told he will soon be earning enough money to live on. A third has gone to the university because his father could afford to pay—he has avoided those subjects requiring too much in the way of work. Yet another has taken some job because his father wanted him to follow him in his own business, and in order to avoid this he had to make some other choice.

Doubtless there is always some element of uncertainty remaining in any guidance received from God. But those who constantly seek his will find themselves taking a firmer and firmer stand in life. Their "Yes" and "No" become more definite, and, facing the consequences of their decisions, they learn to recognize their mistakes when they make them. Skeptics, as well, cannot be certain of avoiding mistakes: they are guided by fear, spite, and passion; they are the prisoners of the prejudices of their environment, of their daily routine, and of the habits of their family life. They have started out in life with high ideals and looking forward to a great adventure. And gradually their enthusiasm has waned, and they have become disillusioned. "The whole world," writes Georges Duhamel, "is but a funereal and discordant concert of destinies that have been missed, rejected, and yet undergone."

I once came upon an old college friend. We talked together about the aspirations we had at the age of eighteen, our enthusiastic determination to serve God and our country. Whereas his life had apparently followed a straight line, I had gone through several inner revolutions in which I had felt that my life was taking an entirely new course. And yet it was he who had turned aside, without realizing it, from his first direction. He said to me: "Life sees to it that the ardors of adolescence are cooled down." In my case, I was back once more on the line of our first ideal, and my friend soon found himself on it as well, for I had the joy of seeing him come in his turn to a decisive turning point.

This falling away in life is largely due to mental laziness. We try to do as everyone else does, and to reduce our work to a routine. The more uneasy one grows, the more does one avoid any stocktaking of one's life. When a spiritual experience supervenes, everything is called in question, and one can see how far one has insensibly fallen short. A man can then find the courage he needs to give up a job he has never performed with conviction, and in a spirit of adventure to commit himself, amidst difficulties and insecurity, to new paths which have hitherto been only glimpsed in a constant and unsubstantial dream. Or else he begins to impart the spirit of adventure, initiative, and vocation to his habitual work, and it is transfigured. He rediscovers a creative attitude. "Joy is the mark of creative activity," writes Charles Werner,[1] in his book setting out a philosophical interpretation of the Christian doctrine of the Fall. "Desire," characteristic of life and of creative activity, is in God harmoniously united with intelligence. In the creature, on the other hand, by the very fact that we are here concerned with "finite, limited beings, . . . desire is separate from intelligence." That is the cause of evil in nature and in man. When he turns back to God, man rediscovers the way to that harmony, so that his desire becomes creative once more, instead of destructive.

Our intellectual disciplines—medicine, law, letters—our political, economic, and social institutions—our work, our schools, the press, the factory—all are a part of this contemporary civilization which has lost sight of its foundations. The attempt to renew its intellectual

[1] *Le problème du mal dans la pensée humaine.*

bases in the light of a living Christian faith is a great adventure that might well catch the imagination of people who are deserting the Church. All are discontented with society as it is. Could God inspire them in their own field of action with new and constructive ideas? God is not interested only in religion and religious psychology. He is interested in art, in cooking, in agriculture, and in political economy. In meditation the imagination expands. It breaks free from the mental habits that have hemmed it in so that it could only escape in compensatory fantasies having no relevance to the mediocrity of real life. It is the individual who invests and experiments, who breaks new ground and carries the crowd with him. Every man who sincerely meditates begins to become detached from the herd, leaves the beaten track. The wind of adventure begins to blow again through his personal life, as well as through his professional or political activity, and to make its presence felt in the atmosphere of his family. His attempts to break with convention and to obey God more boldly raise new and difficult problems which oblige him to meditate more because he has left behind the well-marked highway of the crowd, and now must use his compass.

He is not yet used to it, and he makes mistakes, comes up against obstacles, has to retrace his steps, but he enjoys experiences and sights that not everyone sees. When he is tired he comes back to his God and questions him again. He opens his Bible, and receives enlightenment from it. It comes alive for him, and becomes directly relevant to his daily life. He feels himself to be in communion with the men whose story he reads there. The tang of adventure is always with him, his ardor is revived, and from one experience after another he learns that perseverance which becomes part of his nature. He tells others about his discoveries. He does not ask them to follow him, but they set out on their own paths, and their experiences encourage him. He meditates with them. He asks their advice; but much more than advice, he needs that brotherly fellowship in which one comes near to God, in which one can best make out the way one must go.

He evolves, and perceives that everything is evolving around him.

Whether they wish it or not, doctors have a tremendous influence upon the philosophical outlook of the general public. It is in vain that they claim to be neutral in metaphysical matters. It is in vain that they try to keep within what they call the limitations of medicine. It is in vain that they share in the fear of philosophy denounced by

Lecomte du Noüy in the scientists of yesterday—their patients (that is to say, everybody) undergo the suggestion, even if it is unexpressed, of their conceptions of the world, of man, and of society. If doctors are materialist, they sow the seed of materialism, even if they say nothing. If their home life is collapsing, they sow the seed of divorce, even if they say nothing. If they have a living faith, they propagate the faith, even if they say nothing.

On all hands voices are making themselves heard today—the voices of doctors and scientists—calling for a spiritual renascence in medicine. "It would appear that the suggestions of science have never been as favorable to religious conclusions as they are today," writes Jean Friedel.

To want a spiritual renascence in science is not to deny technical skill, nor to deny all that science has taught us about the technological aspect of man. It is to add the vision of man's other side, his spiritual side, without which our view of him is incomplete. Above all, it is to know ourselves, as doctors, that reversal about which we were thinking in Chapter 12. We defined it as a new attitude, in which one considers the other man from the technical, scientific point of view, as determined by outside factors and not responsible for his behavior, while considering oneself from the spiritual point of view, as a free being, responsible for one's faults. The spiritual renascence of medicine will not come from more zeal on the part of the doctor. He will continue to use all that technical science teaches him in order to care for his patients as well as possible; but he will also care for his own soul with everything that faith teaches him. Faith, far from making the doctor lazy in his scientific work, impels him, on the contrary, to unremitting work, because it makes him feel more keenly the difficulties of his task and his responsibilities. It leads him both to keep on improving his technical knowledge, and also to recognize that his scientific knowledge cannot do all that his vocation demands. Henri Flournoy writes:

Medicine cannot be put upon the same footing as the sciences. It is both less and more. Certainly we speak of *medical science*. . . . Nevertheless it must be recognized that these completely scientific medical studies do not correspond to the full extent and the extreme complexity of medical practice, which is equally an art. We speak quite rightly of *the art of medicine*. In addition, we still appeal to the authority of the famous Hippocratic oath—that is to say, to a still valid corpus of traditions and moral precepts, which go a good deal further than the simple scientific probity necessary to the cultivation of any discipline.[2]

Spiritual medicine does not set out to give moral uplift to the sick instead of treating them. It is the most scientific medicine possible, applied by doctors who are strict with themselves, and who rely on the grace of God. The doctor who has experienced in his own life the effect of grace knows that, without excluding medicines, advice, and psychological analyses, grace is more precious than all these. He looks upon all these means of treatment as given to him by the grace of God. But he knows that more important than all these gifts is the gift of grace itself—the awareness of fellowship with the Person of Jesus Christ, who suddenly, often at the moment when he is least expected, breaks into a person's life and transforms it, even if it remains bowed under the weight of suffering.

So, similarly, in every walk of life today, in commerce and industry, in politics and education, in the arts and intellectual life, there are arising men and women who, without rejecting anything of the treasures of technology and science, are trying personally to seek God's guidance, so that His grace may come to bear on their work and lead them to use those treasures in accordance with His purpose. They are united in a common aim, to whatever country or church they belong. They constitute a team, a working fellowship. They have confidence in each other, despite all their failures. They are brothers in arms. They are united by their common devotion to Christ, and they desire to help each other to remain faithful to him. They are engaged together in a life of adventure. That life is offered to all who feel themselves called to it by the Spirit.

[2] In *Archives des sciences physiques et naturelles,* May–June, 1944, p. 67.

Index

239

248 • INDEX